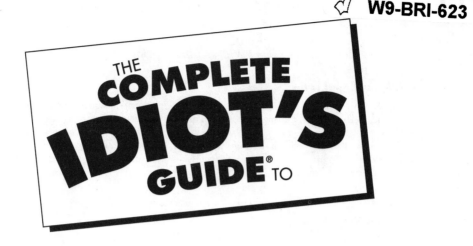

THE **COMPLETE IDIOT'S GUIDE** ® TO

Your Civil Liberties

by Michael Levin

ALPHA

For Chynna, Will, and Isaac Levin

International Standard Book Number: 0-02-864473-5
Library of Congress Catalog Card Number: 2002117440

05   04   03   8   7   6   5   4   3   2   1

Interpretation of the printing code: The rightmost number of the first series of numbers is the year of the book's printing; the rightmost number of the second series of numbers is the number of the book's printing. For example, a printing code of 03-1 shows that the first printing occurred in 2003.

Printed in the United States of America

Note: This publication contains the opinions and ideas of its author. It is intended to provide helpful and informative material on the subject matter covered. It is sold with the understanding that the author and publisher are not engaged in rendering professional services in the book. If the reader requires personal assistance or advice, a competent professional should be consulted.

The author and publisher specifically disclaim any responsibility for any liability, loss, or risk, personal or otherwise, which is incurred as a consequence, directly or indirectly, of the use and application of any of the contents of this book.

Publisher: *Marie Butler-Knight*
Product Manager: *Phil Kitchel*
Senior Managing Editor: *Jennifer Chisholm*
Acquisitions Editor: *Gary Goldstein*
Development Editor: *Suzanne LeVert*
Production Editor: *Billy Fields*
Copy Editor: *Jeff Rose*
Illustrator: *Chris Eliopoulos*
Cover/Book Designer: *Trina Wurst*
Indexer: *Angie Bess*
Layout/Proofreading: *Mary Hunt, Ayanna Lacey*

Contents at a Glance

Appendixes

Contents

Introduction

To what extent are your civil liberties—your personal rights as an American—threatened by the war against terror? What rights do you have in the first place? Where do they come from, how do they change, and how has the Internet dramatically curtailed the amount of privacy we enjoy?

The Complete Idiot's Guide to Your Civil Liberties will show you what your rights are, what the Constitution and Bill of Rights mean today, and how to learn more—and take action—when you sense that your rights are diminishing. And they are! The country—and the courts—have grown more conservative over the last 20 years. The business world has no regard for your privacy. The Internet was never even designed to keep data private … and it doesn't!

At the same time, the electorate (you and me, babe) has never felt so alienated from the political process and from the government. We just pay our taxes and shrug our shoulders at what goes on in Washington and our state capitols. The news media is a joke. They don't inform us in part because we're too lazy to be informed. We've stopped caring.

Well, rights are like muscles. Don't use them and they'll atrophy. And that's what's happening today. The major story in civil liberties is that they're on the decline, in large part because we've stopped fighting to keep them.

How to Use this Book

Rights are precious. As we'll see in **Part 1, "Introduction to Civil Liberties,"** there's nothing automatic about having freedom. It doesn't descend from the sky. It's earned, frequently with the blood and toil of the people. How did we get the broad panoply of rights we enjoy today? That's Part 1.

Then we'll examine privacy in the Information Age in **Part 2, "Privacy in the Information Age."** We'll see how everything from sex to medical records has been radically affected by changes in society and in information technology.

Next comes **Part 3, "Lawmakers and Law Breakers."** What can the police really do when they enter your home, with or without a warrant? What's legal when they pull you over? That and much more.

Then, in **Part 4, "Liberties at Home, Work, and School,"** we'll see what rights you have in the housing market, on the job, in the car, and even online.

Finally, in **Part 5, "Statutes of Liberties: The Laws That Affect Your Life,"** we'll look at some laws, some famous and some little-known, that have profound effects on your freedoms. And we'll see where civil liberties are headed in the future!

That's the plan. So let's jump right in. Freedom is precious, and protecting it isn't just a right. You're your responsibility.

And the Extras

The sidebars are a chance to provide intriguing bits of information, relevant quotations, and other supporting material.

Statutes of Liberties

The laws that govern civil liberties, either protecting or restricting your rights. As the first chapter indicates, everything from the moment your alarm clock goes off until you hit the pillow at night is governed by some law or statute—or should be. Learn the laws here.

Looking for Liberty

Individuals and organizations committed to protecting the rights of the individual. Everyone's heard of the ACLU, and it figures prominently in this book. But what other people and institutions are involved in the development and protection of your civil liberties? Find out in these sidebars.

The Law of the Land

What the Constitution, the United States Supreme Court, and other high-level authorities have to say about civil liberties. Many of our great justices were also great writers (or their clerks were!). What they have to say is often fascinating and moving.

Taking Liberties

A blend of anecdotes, information, and background material to increase your understanding of civil liberties in America. You're in for some surprises, some pleasant, others less so. But the best way to go through life is as an informed citizen. Now's your chance.

Legal Dictionary

Legal terms explained. Now you'll be able to dazzle at cocktail parties as you can explain *posse comitatus* to an eager group of *habeas corpuses*. Or something like that.

Acknowledgments

It may or may not take a village to raise a child, but it sure takes a whole crew to create an *Idiot's Guide*. My thanks as always to the following:

- Gary Goldstein, my editor at Penguin Putnam, for his continuing faith in my work.

- Jenna Robbins, who makes my work look a lot better than it does when she receives it.

- Howard Zilbert and Grace Kono-Wells, typists extraordinaire.

- Jerry Dagrella contributed Chapter 23 on tax, a specialty of his. He also performed all the research and various other tasks.

- Angela Demo, soon to be a major motion picture star and currently my fantastic assistant.

- Suzanne LeVert, at Penguin Putnam, who is very tolerant of authors like me.

- And finally to my amazing wife Suzanne and our rapidly expanding team—Chynna, Will, and Isaac—for all their love.

Special Thanks to the Technical Reviewer

The Complete Idiot's Guide to Your Civil Liberties was reviewed by an expert who double-checked the accuracy of what you'll learn here, to help us ensure that this book gives you everything you need to know about civil liberties. Special thanks are extended to Jerry Dagrella, Esq. Jerry is a newly-minted attorney with an Orange County-based law firm. He completed seven years of advanced education in five years, receiving his Juris Doctorate from University of the Pacific, McGeorge School of Law at age 22. His previous publications background and dedication to this book was a tremendous help in making it as good as it is.

Trademarks

All terms mentioned in this book that are known to be or are suspected of being trademarks or service marks have been appropriately capitalized. Alpha Books and Penguin Putnam Inc. cannot attest to the accuracy of this information. Use of a term in this book should not be regarded as affecting the validity of any trademark or service mark.

Part 1

Introduction to Civil Liberties

Without a legal system to safeguard the rights of individuals, especially members of minority groups, life would be chaos. The powerful would never cede their power to the poor and struggling; the strong would prey on the weak with impunity. How did it ever happen that individuals came to have the protection of a Bill of Rights? Why did a king of England ever find himself in so weak a position that he would have to surrender much of his power to landowners and the Church? And where do our laws come from?

In this first part of *The Complete Idiot's Guide to Your Civil Liberties*, we'll examine the roots of rights, and we'll learn just where all your freedoms were born.

You've ... Got Rights!

In This Chapter

- ◆ What are civil liberties?
- ◆ Everyday life examples
- ◆ Technology's effect on your freedom
- ◆ The post-September 11, 2001, nation

As an American, you are privileged to live not just in a free society but in the freest society history has ever known. Never before, and nowhere else, has the individual ever enjoyed so many rights—at home, at work, on the road, in every conceivable aspect of life. Granted, the system is far from perfect and many of us find our rights trampled, occasionally by others and sometimes by the government. Nonetheless, the *civil liberties*—the personal freedoms—that Americans enjoy, often taking them for granted, are truly unparalleled in the history of the world.

The Freest Society in the History of the World

The rights we enjoy were hard won, by soldiers, by demonstrators, by the revolutionaries who founded the American republic, by civil rights leaders, and by many quiet individuals who sensed that an outrage had taken place in their lives and set about to make things right. The courage of judges, legislators, presidents, and kings is reflected in the broad array of rights that we enjoy.

Legal Dictionary

Civil liberties—The rights and freedoms of individuals guaranteed by a society's laws and customs.

We are so accustomed to our freedoms that often we notice them only when they are taken away from us. Frequently the people most aware of the freedoms that Americans enjoy are those who have emigrated from other countries to enjoy those same rights and freedoms. Some are individuals who have risked their family ties, finances, careers, and sometimes lives to make the perilous crossing from distant points on the globe to American shores.

Americans have not always enjoyed the same level of freedom that we have today. There are ebbs and flows in the process of securing and maintaining civil liberties. When the country is at peace, it is natural that freedoms increase. In times of war or national emergency, as during World War II or in post-September 11, 2001, America, the liberties of individuals are often curtailed. During such times, we the people are the first ones to demand that our rights be limited, in the name of securing national security or wartime victory. One of the fascinating aspects of civil liberties is their ebb and flow, the times when civil liberties have expanded and the times when personal freedoms have been curtailed.

Looking for Liberty

Who are the "Founding Fathers?" They are the individuals credited with authoring any of the three leading documents of American freedom: The Declaration of Independence, the U.S. Constitution, and the Bill of Rights.

Think about it: You can decide where you want to live, how you want to live, with whom you want to live, what to do for a living, where and how to be educated, whether to have children, what to do with your leisure time, how to spend your money, and a wide variety of day-to-day issues without the interference of the government or your fellow citizens. It wasn't always so. In a later chapter, we will trace the evolution of civil liberties from a time when kings were all-powerful to today's world in which individuals have broad freedom to live as they please.

For now, let's take a quick look at the way civil liberties come into play in the daily life of an average American. The individual whose life we will examine is 37 years old, married but separated and in the process of getting a divorce. The mother of a 15-year-old boy, she is in a committed relationship with another man. She left her job in the field of sales about a month ago and is currently looking for a new position. She wants to move to a different neighborhood in order to enroll her son in better public schools. Therefore she wants to sell her condo and look at houses in a nicer part of town. She also is focused on finding a new job. Let's take a look at a day in the life of Laurie Order and see how the issue of civil liberties comes into play every hour of her day. We'll see the nature of Laurie Order's civil liberties as well as their limits.

6:00 A.M. Laurie Order awakens and goes to the kitchen to make coffee for herself and her live-in boyfriend, Manny Wrights, and to make breakfast for the two of them and her son Tommy. Laurie buys all of her groceries at the Super Duper Market and she belongs to the Frequent Savers Club. Like millions of other Americans, Laurie has one of those small plastic devices with a barcode on it that the supermarket check-out person swipes every time Laurie goes through the line. Laurie benefits because she gets lower prices on about a third of the items she purchases on each visit to the super-market. The supermarket benefits because it has a complete and precise record of exactly what Laurie buys and in what quantities.

Taking Liberties

The word "privacy" does not appear in the Con-stitution or the Bill of Rights, even though both docu-ments deeply defend the individual's right to privacy in countless ways.

Using that data, the supermarket is able to offer coupons on the back of Laurie's receipt for the sort of items that it thinks she might want to purchase—frequently slightly more expensive brands of the same things she normally tends to buy. The supermarket also is able to use the marketing data to determine exactly how much coffee, cereal, meat, and other items to stock, based on the shopping patterns of Laurie and their other customers. The supermarket can also turn around and sell that marketing information, with Laurie's name and address on it, to makers of coffee, doughnuts, and all the other things Laurie buys. They, in turn, target Laurie directly with mailings and coupons to entice her to purchase some of their items. Has Laurie's privacy been violated at any point in the capture and use of her personal shopping information? We'll find that out in Chapter 6.

6:08 A.M. While Laurie is waiting for the coffee to brew, she flips on her laptop com-puter at her desk in the study and checks her e-mail. A friend of Laurie's has sent an e-mail to everyone on his list complaining about the way people are now searched at airports as part of the security screening process. Because he looks as though he might come from the Middle East, this individual writes, he was pulled out of line and searched thoroughly. His bags were practically taken apart but, of course, the security officers found nothing wrong. Laurie's friend, ironically, adds that this was the first time he had ever flown on plane in his life, and he had never driven more than 400 miles from his native city of Milwaukee. Will the key words in this e-mail—airport, security, search, Middle Eastern—trigger an FBI e-mail monitoring software program called Carnivore? (I swear I'm not making up that name.) Is the FBI now empowered to monitor the e-mail of Laurie's friend? Is the FBI now empowered to monitor her e-mail? We'll find out in Chapter 6.

Her son Tommy has a friend named Sam, also 15, who seems like a nerdish, mild-mannered kid, but is in reality the internationally feared teenage Internet hacker, Cyber Freaque. Sam and Tommy are actually having a fight over whether the Pentagon or the CIA is easier to hack into. They aren't speaking. However, they are hacking into each other's e-mail accounts. Could Sam, alias Cyber Freaque, be hacking into Laurie's e-mail account? Could he be reading her e-mail, personal and work-related? Could Laurie tell? Does Laurie have a right to privacy with regard to her e-mail—i.e., does she have a reasonable expectation that no individual or government entity can read it? We'll find out in Chapter 6.

> **Taking Liberties**
>
> Alan Dershowitz, the constitutional lawyer, author, and law professor, says that "Rights come from wrongs"—when a society realizes it is trampling on the rights of an underprivileged group, it creates a right to protect that minority group.

6:11 A.M. Finished with her e-mail, Laurie now goes to the web to do some online banking, to see how she's doing on her eBay auctions, and to visit a few online retailers including gap.com and bloomingdales.com. She pays some bills at her bank site and buys a wedding present from a bridal registry list at Bloomingdale's. How secure are these transactions? Does anyone else have access to her banking information, the credit card information she used for the Bloomingdale's purchase, or even the fact that she visited these particular stores? The answers are both surprising and disturbing. We have a lot less privacy than we think, as we'll see in Chapter 6.

> **Statutes of Liberties**
>
> The Constitution never foresaw automobiles, red lights, or traffic cameras taking pictures of red light violators, but the principles contained in the Bill of Rights dictate the way we make laws about each of these things.

Her 15-year-old son Tommy has used the computer to visit porn sites. Tommy thought he had covered his tracks pretty well, by deleting the cookies and the history file, but a "dialer" program was installed during one of his downloads, and Laurie finds she cannot get rid of it. Is there any way for someone to detect that the computer has been used for this purpose? She wonders. The surprising and disturbing answer is yes. More on the Internet in Chapter 6.

6:17 A.M. Laurie and her boyfriend Paul sit down to breakfast. Laurie puts on the TV news and watches long enough to reassure herself that nothing important or dangerous is going on in the world that morning. The couple has Tivo, a television service that allows them to record their favorite TV shows and watch them without commercials. Laurie hits a few buttons and last night's *Friends* episode, sans commercials, pops into view. Does Tivo do more than record Laurie's programming preferences? You bet it does. Tivo reports all information on the household's television habits to a main computer system. Can someone else make use of this information? Has Laurie's privacy been violated?

6:31 A.M. Laurie gets dressed and reminds Paul to take out the garbage. Paul drags the garbage to the curb, where two hours from now, private investigators working for her soon-to-be-ex-husband will pick up and sift through that garbage looking for financial records that Laurie's soon-to-be-ex can use against her in court in order to reduce child support. Does Laurie have a privacy right in not having her garbage pawed through? Surprisingly, it depends in what state she lives in. On the federal level, Laurie has no right to privacy when it comes to the trash she puts on the sidewalk. Some states, however, choose to provide a higher level of privacy than does the federal government, so she may just be protected. For more information, see Chapter 11.

The Law of the Land

The Founding Fathers were deeply concerned about the power of the British governors in America to arrest individuals without warrants and hold them without bail. So these powers were denied the fledgling U.S. government. Chances are, if there's a right enumerated in the Bill of Rights, you can bet that the British denied that same right to Americans in pre-revolutionary times.

10:15 A.M. Laurie checks her messages on her cell phone as she drives to work. (Can anyone else intercept calls on her cell phone? With the right equipment, yes. Is it Constitutional? No. Can it happen anyway? Absolutely.) The third message is from Zycorp, a medical sales company calling her back for her third interview. They want to see her at 11:30. Laurie realizes that she does not have time to get home to change and pick up copies of her resumé before going in for the interview. Instead she drives to a shopping mall to find an appropriate outfit. The department store where she makes her purchase has suffered greatly from shoplifting over the past six months. They have installed cameras and same-sex security personnel to monitor the changing booths, where much of the shoplifting takes place. Are Laurie's rights violated as she unknowingly changes her outfit in the booth, under the prying eye of the secret camera? To find out, read Chapter 12.

10:50 A.M. Laurie checks her watch. She is late for the job interview. She runs a red light and, as she does so, looks in both directions to make sure that there are no police anywhere. There are in fact no police anywhere to be seen, but that doesn't

Taking Liberties

Are red light cameras protecting the safety of drivers or just making lots of money for municipalities? The answer is ... both.

mean Laurie isn't in trouble. A camera attached to the lamppost at the intersection has photographed Laurie running the red light. This date-stamped photograph, which shows Laurie's license plate in perfect detail, will result in a computer-generated ticket, fine, and points on her license. Is this a legitimate use of police power? See Chapter 13.

11:02 A.M. Laurie is on the verge of being really late for the appointment, so she steps on the gas. Unfortunately, she is exceeding the speed limit in a notorious speed trap—notorious to everyone in the community but, alas, not to her. A patrol car flashes its lights at Laurie and pulls her over. Realizing she is going to be late, she calls the people at Zycorp while the policeman is running her license. She explains that she'll be 15 or 20 minutes late, and they say it's perfectly fine. The police make a startling discovery: Two weeks earlier, Laurie's car had been involved in a bank robbery while she left it in the airport's long-term parking area while on a vacation with Paul in the Bahamas. Apparently, someone had stolen the car out of the long-term lot, used it as the getaway car for the bank robbery, and then returned it just where they'd found it—unbeknownst to Laurie and Paul. The police, in addition to writing up a speeding citation for Laurie, now want to search the entire car, from the trunk to underneath the floor panels. They also run a check on her driver's license. Can they search the car without a warrant? What information does this search reveal? Can the police use any of it in conversation with Laurie? To find out, see Chapter 13.

11:45 A.M. Laurie gets to the interview half an hour late, but Zycorp is so interested in her that they are not bothered by this in the least. Laurie meets with three different individuals for approximately 20 minutes each. The first interviewer asks about her marital status. When Laurie explains that she's separated, the interviewer asks whether she intends to remarry and have any more children. He explains that the nature of the sales job means a lot of time on the road, and that it's very tough for women to maintain that kind of lifestyle.

Looking for Liberty

Some of the most courageous individuals in the civil rights movement never became famous. They include African Americans who sought the right to vote in the American South prior to the passage of the landmark 1957 Voting Rights Act. This act was the first piece of civil rights legislation to pass the U.S. Senate since Reconstruction.

The next interviewer asks Laurie whether she is a Republican or Democrat. Most of the doctors to whom she will be selling are quite conservative and would be put off by a liberal-minded female. The interviewer also asks whether she rents or owns her home, because he believes that people who own are more stable and more likely to be better salespeople.

He also inquires about her religion because those same conservative doctors are not likely to purchase medical equipment or drugs from a sales rep not of their same religious background.

The third interviewer comments on the fact that Laurie is not wearing a wedding ring. He asks her out on a date. When she says that she is living with someone, he then asks if she would be comfortable just going out for coffee. Laurie accepts under the condition that the appointment is for business purposes. By this time, Laurie is beginning to have her doubts about this particular company. The third interviewer concludes the meeting by asking whether Laurie would be willing to take a drug test as a condition of employment. He explains that such a test is necessary because a drug company sales rep is in contact with drugs all the time, and thus the company needs some guarantee that the rep is not an addict or even a casual user.

Which of these three interviewers has violated Laurie's civil liberties? If you say all of the above, you'd be right. But why, and how? Were her rights violated? See Chapter 18 to learn more.

2:30 P.M. Laurie leaves Zycorp, a job offer in hand, but she's not sure that she wants to work at this place. The questions seemed a little bit too intrusive. She decides to keep on looking for a little while longer before she turns down Zycorp.

All this talk about drugs and medicine reminds her that she is several months overdue for a checkup with her personal physician, a kindly old man who took care of her parents as well. She calls his office to make an appointment, only to discover that he has retired from the practice of medicine. He sold his practice to a younger practitioner. The receptionist, whom Laurie has known for many years, tells her that this new doctor is a very fine young man with excellent credentials and that all of Laurie's health records, going back to childhood, are still at the same office. Does Laurie have a civil liberty interest in not having her physical medical records transferred from a doctor she knows well to a doctor she has never met? See Chapter 9.

5:00 P.M. Laurie, heading to the gym for a workout before she returns home for an early dinner, gets a call from her realtor. Her condo, which has been on the market for about five weeks, is now potentially unsaleable. An abandoned gas station across the street from Laurie's condo complex, an eyesore for many years, has

Statutes of Liberties
The legal system is often a step behind new communication and information technologies. First a technology has to come on the market and be accepted before it can be clear in what ways it can be misused. Then a legislature has to figure out how the technology is being abused, and what kind of law will really stop the bad guys from continuing to abuse it.

Taking Liberties

No one is supposed to be able to access your video store or library records, but then, no one is supposed to be able to hack into computers, either! One of the key points of this book is that we have a lot less privacy than we think, whether it's the government, our employer, or a cyber-hacker who's watching us.

been declared a toxic waste site by the Environmental Protection Agency (EPA) and targeted as a site for a Superfund toxic waste cleanup. Laurie wants to know what this means to her. The realtor explains that she will now have to disclose to any potential buyer that her condo is located across the street from a Superfund site. This is what realtors call a "cloud on the title," which means that the value of the condo will be reduced for the time—usually years—it takes before the Superfund cleanup is complete. Nobody wants to live on a Superfund site, so fair market value will be low until the issue is resolved. To learn more, see Chapter 11.

Laurie, distressed by this news, asks whether any homes have gone on the market in the particular neighborhood to which she and Paul want to move. The realtor checks his MLS, or multiple listing service, to see what's going on in that neighborhood. There are, in fact, houses available in the price range that Laurie can afford. Nevertheless, the broker tells her that there is nothing she would want to see. Have Laurie's rights been violated yet again, first by the EPA and now by the broker? Yes and yes. We'll explore this further in Chapter 11.

6:15 P.M. Laurie comes home to a series of surprising and painful developments at the condo. First her son Tommy is upset. The principal has cut his article on bomb-making websites out of the school newspaper. Her son claims that *his* rights have been violated. Have they? Laurie isn't sure.

Tommy has worse news, which takes him a little more time to divulge. The police, acting on a warrant for the next door neighbor's condo, got the wrong address due to

The Law of the Land

Improper searches and seizures were commonplace during the Colonial period, when Britain ruled America. Today, the courts and the police act in a delicate balance trying to decide what constitutes a legitimate search and/or seizure under the Fourth Amendment.

a typo on the warrant. A typist transposed the numbers. The next door neighbor not only smokes the occasional marijuana cigarette, but actually deals in fairly large quantities, much to the delight of young Tommy. The police went in to bust him, and instead came into the home of Laurie, Paul, and Tommy. They did a thorough search of the condo, but failed to turn up the large quantities of marijuana they had expected. They did, however, find a small amount of marijuana in a film canister hidden in the back of Tommy's closet, and the police want to discuss the matter with Laurie. Have her rights been violated by that search? Could that marijuana be introduced as lawful evidence in a criminal proceeding? Again, Laurie is not sure. Laurie might want to read Chapter 20 to find out what her son's rights are.

6:21 P.M. Before Laurie can digest all this news, the telephone rings. It is a credit card company asking to speak with Laurie's dog, Muffin, to offer him a 5,000-dollar credit line. Is there any way that Laurie can protect herself from the barrage of phone calls that typically come at the dinner hour? Is her privacy violated here? Is Muffin's?

7:15 P.M. After a hurried dinner, Laurie and Paul are heading out to attend a ceremony honoring the same-sex marriage of two of her gay friends. The women had been living together for three years and decided to formalize their relationship; a minister from the church that Laurie, Paul, and the two women attend will be officiating. They have asked Laurie to be a witness at the wedding. What legal rights will the two women enjoy, now that they are married? What recognition, if any, do cities, states, and the federal government afford same-sex marriages? See Chapter 5.

7:32 P.M. On their way to the church, Laurie and Paul stop at the pharmacy to pick up a prescription for a contraceptive device. Laurie thinks back to the telephone call this afternoon with her former MD and wonders who has access to her prescription records—the doctor who bought the retired doctor's medical records, the government, or anyone else? While in line at the pharmacy, Paul informs Laurie that he is disturbed by the number of break-ins that have taken place in their neighborhood. Until their condo sells, Paul has decided to buy a gun for protection. The state in which they live imposes a seven-day waiting period on such purchases. Laurie is aware that the Bill of Rights to the Constitution specifies the right to bear arms. She wonders whether a waiting period constitutes a violation of that right.

10:25 P.M. Laurie's Great Uncle Lorenzo, who has been suffering from cancer, calls distraught. He wants to end his life because he is in so much pain, and he wants Laurie's assistance. Does she have the legal right to help him? Does he have the legal right to take his own life? See Chapter 5.

11:05 P.M. After a very long day, Laurie and Paul have said good night to Tommy, who is waiting for his mother and her friend to go to bed and lock the door behind them, signaling that he will be able to start downloading more porn from the Internet without being disturbed. Any problem with that? See Chapter 6.

Once behind closed doors, Paul and Laurie begin to engage in a variety of intimate acts.

> ### Looking for Liberty
>
> Supreme Court Justice William O. Douglas was the first member of the Court to rule that the Bill of Rights contains a right to privacy. He found it in the "shadows" and "penumbras" of the various amendments that protect privacy without actually using that word.

Since this book is a "family" book, we cannot describe the nature of these acts. All we can tell you is that they are, indeed, varied. Since Laurie and Paul are not married to each other, and since Laurie is still technically married to her soon-to-be-ex-husband, would the police, if they heard Laurie and Paul engaging in these acts, have a right to enter the premises? If they did enter and see Laurie and Paul engaged in some of these acts, could they arrest the pair? Would it matter what act it is? Would it matter what state they were in? See Chapter 5.

2:47 A.M. Laurie and Paul have long since completed their activities of a private nature and are sleeping peacefully in each other's arms—until the fire alarm goes off. Their upstairs neighbor, a forgetful man in his 70s named Bo, has fallen asleep while smoking in bed. While Bo is evacuated safely, Laurie and Paul quickly throw on whatever clothing they can and rush outside.

To their surprise, they see not only firefighters and paramedics, but also a TV film crew from one of the reality shows. Does the TV show have a right to put Laurie, Paul, and Tommy on the air, as an example of a dramatic rescue from a burning building? Does Laurie have a right to privacy that would forbid the television people from showing the videotape on the air? In Chapter 12, you'll find out more.

While all these questions are going through Laurie's mind, a TV reporter approaches her and says, "I recognize you! I was going to call you in the morning! You're soon-to-be-ex-husband has just published a book detailing his sexual relationships with you and 35 other women! Would you care to comment?" Laurie, of course, would not care to comment. Laurie is not a public figure and never has been. Does she have a right to keep her private life out of a published book? Can her husband argue that he's only violating his own privacy, and not hers, or that since he's being so candid about himself that gives him the right to write so freely about other people? Laurie isn't sure. After the last 24 hours, Laurie is far too exhausted to make sense of all this. See Chapter 3. And we've touched on only a small number of the civil liberties issues this book contains.

Laurie Needs This Book

If Laurie had a copy of *The Complete Idiot's Guide to Your Civil Liberties*, she would have been able to discover the answer to each of these situations—and many others—as they arose. A shorthand way of saying "civil liberty" is "personal freedom." And freedom, especially in our information-driven society, is all about privacy. In today's world, the issue of privacy comes up repeatedly, often in ways that we do not expect.

The examples provided through Laurie Order are not theoretical, nor are they empty concepts that a professor can ponder dreamily while writing a law review article. As we have seen in this somewhat exaggerated example, the question of civil liberties touches every aspect of our lives, from our health to our sex lives to the "zone of privacy" that we are allowed to create for ourselves.

There has never been a freer society than the United States of America as it enters the twenty-first century. No place on earth offers the same degree of freedom as does the

United States, and no nation in history has ever offered its citizens this degree of privacy. And yet, the traditional formulation in common law is that "My right to swing my fist stops several inches short of your nose." In other words, each of us has a legal right to be left alone, to live our lives as we see fit, and to keep private the information that we consider no one else's business. But the fact is that there really is nothing simple about civil liberties—especially in an age of electronic communication, record-keeping, and surveillance.

> **Statutes of Liberties**
>
> Alan Dershowitz makes the point that civil liberties do not come from a divine source, as what's considered legitimate behavior in one era (like slavery) is considered illegal in another. If rights came from God, Dershowitz reasons, they would never change.

The problem is compounded because of the post-September 11, 2001, environment in which we now live. Many Americans are actually willing to trade a certain amount of their privacy, be it at the airport, online, or even in the street, for a heightened sense of security and the enhanced ability of the government to catch potential terrorists before they strike. But the question arises—how far can the government go in suspending civil liberties before it has gone too far? And who decides? And by what standards?

There has never been a more interesting time than now to consider exactly what our personal rights are, how to have them enforced, and whether or how they should be modified in order to meet the changing circumstances of the War on Terrorism. So let's journey forth together through these pages and determine exactly what Laurie Order's civil liberties are—and what your rights are, as well.

The Least You Need to Know

- A civil liberty is a right granted the individual by the state; no society has ever enjoyed the degree of freedom the United States of America has.

- There are ebbs and flows in the process of securing and maintaining civil liberties. In time of war or national security threats, civil liberties are most threatened.

- Civil liberties affect even our most mundane of daily activities.

- Modern technology makes laws surrounding civil liberties more complex than ever.

Chapter 2

A Brief History of Civil Liberties

In This Chapter

- ◆ King John the Unlucky
- ◆ America rebels
- ◆ Changes since September 11
- ◆ Why there's no john@fbi.gov

History is a funny thing. A battle lost here, some freedoms granted over there, and you and I would be drinking tea for breakfast, driving our lorries on dual-lane carriageways, and singing "God Save the Queen." In other words, we'd still be a colony of Great Britain.

Off and Running at Runnymeade

If English history had taken only a few slightly different turns, there would be no American history. It's remarkable how events that seem relatively minor at the time turn out to have consequences that ring down through the centuries.

The Law of the Land

"We the people of the United States, in order to form a more perfect union, establish justice, insure domestic tranquility, provide for the common defense, promote the general welfare, and secure the blessings of liberty to ourselves and our posterity, do ordain and establish this Constitution for the United States of America."

—Preamble to the U.S. Constitution

The first of these historical accidents to have an impact on American constitutional history came in early thirteenth-century England, when King John, who should have been called King John the Unlucky, held the throne. King John can be thought of as the Rodney Dangerfield of the English monarchy—he just couldn't get any respect. England owned land in northern France. King John went to war to protect those English land holdings in the year 1204 … and lost. Big time. He spent a fortune to win those battles, but unfortunately, it was not a king's fortune—it wasn't his money. The money belonged to the barons—the wealthy, land-owning class of Englishmen, and you can set your sundial by just how unhappy they were with their battle-losing king.

King John also lost tons of men in those conflicts in France, but unfortunately, they were not all the king's men. None of them were the king's men—once again, those soldiers lost on French battlefields had belonged to the barons. And if there's one thing a baron hates losing, it's a bunch of men who otherwise could have productively been staring at the wrong end of an ox 14 hours a day, thus enriching the baron's coffers.

It gets worse for King John. In addition to having the barons less than delighted with his lack of military prowess, the Roman Catholic Church was equally displeased with the errant king. The Church, which also suffered financially in King John's lost wars, was so upset that in the year 1207, the pope banned all church services in England. If you don't go to church, you're going to hell. This sat very poorly with both King John and the rest of the English people. John still hadn't gotten whatever message the church was trying to send, so the pope had him excommunicated in the year 1209. John recognized that he was beaten, and allowed the Church an enormous amount of power in England in exchange for removing the excommunication and resuming church services. This was in the year 1214.

Statutes of Liberties

King John was such a weak king that he ended up signing the Magna Carta, ceding much of his authority to the Church and to the barons—English landowners who held authority in the towns and countryside of England.

I'd like to tell you that in 1214, King John's luck changed, and that the new army he sent to France won back the lands he had lost. Didn't happen. King John lost yet again. This time, the barons had had enough. They took over London and demanded that King John step down. He clung to power by a thread and negotiations began. These negotiations culminated in an unprecedented grant of power from the King to the barons. The document in which these royal concessions were laid out is known as the *Magna Carta*, Latin for "Great Charter." The document was signed in the spring of 1215 in the fields of Runnymeade, just west of Heathrow Airport, which would not be built for another 750 years.

Legal Dictionary

Magna Carta—The Great Charter in which England's King John ceded royal powers to wealthy landowners and the Church.

Looking for Liberty

The founding of the British Parliament in many ways dates to the grant of power from the King to the barons in the Magna Carta.

Why is the Magna Carta remembered today? Why is it considered a turning point in legal history? At the time it was written, kings ruled by divine right. What they said was the law. This was the first time in recorded history that a king had made the electrifying concession that the people he ruled had rights and that there were limits on his individual power. This was truly unheard of, and it set in motion the entire train of civil liberties law—protection of the individual's rights, and limitations on the powers of the state—that continues to evolve to this day.

For purposes of discussing modern civil liberties, the Magna Carta provides two essential points: First this document was the first to hold that a government (even a monarchy) does not have absolute power over the individuals it governs and that individuals have rights that the government is obliged to protect. The enunciation of this principle was an astonishing breakthrough, the importance of which should not be minimized.

The second key tenet of the Magna Carta is the concept of "due process." Due process prevents the government from taking away either property or a right without prior notice that it intends to do so. The government must also conduct a hearing to determine the individual's rights if such a hearing would help prevent the individual's civil rights from being violated by the action. If the government intends to take a farm from an individual in order to build a highway, for example, the government simply can't just start doing construction. The government must first provide notice of such plans and then provide a hearing, at which the farmer could make his or her case that the land should not be taken away. Furthermore, if the government seeks to imprison or execute an individual, due process (a modern term that can be fairly applied in this case) guarantees the right to a fair criminal trial.

Due process is one of the most important legal principles in the entire realm of civil liberties law, and it is enshrined in the Bill of Rights of the U.S. Constitution in the Fifth Amendment, which states that the federal government shall not take the life, liberty, or property of an individual without a fair process first. The Fourteenth Amendment to the U.S. Constitution declares that individual states, not just the federal government, are equally bound by the due process requirement. Another important clause of the Magna Carta, number 39, decreed that "no freeman shall be captured or imprisoned … except by lawful judgment by his peers or by the law of the land." This was the first time in history that limitations were placed on the power of a king.

Taking Liberties

Much of American law is founded on the legal principles of Great Britain, which the seventeenth century settlers carried with them to the New World.

In today's world, an individual cannot be punished criminally, cannot have his or her Social Security benefits taken away, cannot be fired from a government job, and cannot even be required to open his home to the police (in most cases) without the appropriate form of due process. You can find the entire text of the Magna Carta at www.thevrwc.org/historical/magnacarta/html.

Back, Back, Back, Back, Back ...

The Magna Carta may have been the first grant of civil liberties by an absolute monarch, but it was certainly not the first legal code. That honor belongs to Urukagina's code, ordinances laid down by Mesopotamian kings around the year 2350 B.C.E. It was a stern code; according to the timetable of world history (found at www.duhaime. org/hist.htm), thieves and adulteresses were stoned to death with rocks inscribed with the name of their crime. The code also stated that the king was appointed by the gods.

Five hundred years later, we find the earliest known legal decision, a clay tablet describing the murder of a temple employee by three men. According to duhaime. org, the victim's wife knew of the murder but remained silent. When news of the crime came out, the three men and the woman were charged with murder, and nine witnesses testified against them. Two other witnesses, however, testified that the wife had been abused by her husband, that she had not been involved in the crime, and that she was even worse off now that her husband no longer lived. The men were put to death in front of the victim's house but the woman was spared.

Biblical Law and Order

The Ten Commandments were written approximately 550 years later, in the year 1300 B.C.E. It's worth mentioning that the biblical phrase "an eye for an eye, a tooth for a tooth" (which is not one of the Ten Commandments) is a mistranslation that has poisoned generations of individuals from thinking seriously about the Bible as a legal work or a religious document.

The actual translation reads, "An eye—up to the value of an eye, a tooth, up to the value of a tooth." This means that if an individual knocks out the eye or the tooth of another person by accident, that individual must pay the harmed party monetary damages up to the value of the body part that he destroyed. Biblical law does not require knocking out the eye or the tooth of such an individual—it's talking specifically—and only—about monetary *damages*.

Legal Dictionary

Damages—The amount of money a court or a law determines must be paid in order to make a victim whole and to compensate for his or her loss.

De-"coding" Legal History

There was not much plea-bargaining under Hammurabi's Code of 1700 B.C.E. Furthermore, the penalties were quite harsh: If a house collapsed, killing the owner, the builder was put to death; defamation merited a punishment of cutting out the tongue. Ditto India's Laws of Mamu, written somewhere between 1280 B.C.E. and 880 B.C.E., in which case amputation was a common penalty. Draco's Law of Greece, compiled in the year 621 B.C.E, was so severe that we still use the term "draconian" to refer to harsh measures. However, Draco's Law did institute the concept of the government punishing individuals rather than allowing individuals to pursue personal vendettas or mete out private justice. Duhaime.org comments:

> The citizens adored Draco and upon entering an auditorium one day to attend a reception in his honor, the citizens of Athens showered him with their hats and cloaks as was their customary way to show appreciation. By the time they dug him out from under the clothing, he had been smothered to death. No Athenians were charged in the crime.

China's laws were just as tough as those of western Europe. The Chinese Book of Punishments, written in 546 B.C.E., sought to limit the ways to punish those convicted of serious crimes. The acceptable punishments listed in the book included, according to duhaime.org, tattooing, cutting off the nose, castration, feet amputation, and death. We see that the rule of law in the millennia prior to the Magna Carta was based on a ruler wielding absolute power, and violent punishments for offenders of serious crimes. The Magna Carta would be the first code of law to chip away at the absolute right of governments to act as they pleased.

English Refinements

For four centuries, the Magna Carta essentially guided the relationship between rulers and the governed in England. British kings must have sought to roll back the reforms the Magna Carta instituted, because in 1628, the Petition of Right was Parliament's response to abuses of that document. In 1628, Parliament presented King Charles I with the Petition of Right, which prohibited the king from unlawful arrests and housing troops in private homes without the consent of the owners. King Charles I signed this document, because Parliament threatened that it would not raise any more taxes unless he did so. And what's a king without taxes?

Statutes of Liberties
The 1869 English Bill of Rights limited the royal family's rights. Until then, the royal family could suspend any of Parliament's laws that it did not like. It also limited the amount of money that could be raised through taxation in Parliament.

In the seventeenth century, individuals seeking religious freedom had left England and Holland to establish a free society in America. They did so at no small risk to themselves and with the knowledge that they would never see their loved ones again. One wonders how different history would be had the English government deferred itself even further, offering religious freedom to dissenters who might then not have felt compelled to leave the motherland for the New World.

At that time, England was going through great social and political upheavals; had those crises resulted in greater religious freedom and tolerance, there might not have been the need to found an American republic. The Petition of Right of 1628 gave Britons the right to petition the king and to bear arms. It also outlawed excessive bails and fines, and cruel and unusual punishment, according to freedomforum.org., William and Mary were not permitted to take the throne of England until they agreed to accept the Bill of Rights.

Rights in America

The people of the American colonies in the seventeenth century enjoyed greater freedom and civil liberties than they had enjoyed in England. In 1636, Rhode Island became the first American colony to recognize freedom of conscience, the right to worship as one chose. Five years later, Massachusetts enacted the Massachusetts Body of Liberties, which freedomforum.org describes as "the first detailed protection of rights in America." Maryland and then Virginia passed legislation detailing religious freedom.

The American Revolution, of course, began in 1776 and the U.S. Constitution was not written until 1789. What bound the colonies together during the period of the Revolutionary War? The answer is the Articles of Confederation, which many historians view as the precursor to the U.S. Constitution. The authors of the Articles of Confederation shared a mistrust of a strong central government. They therefore created a document which called for a "firm league of friendship" among the 13 states, and a weak federal government, to make sure that power resided with the states. The Articles focused on the conduct of Congress and the prosecution of the war with England and provided only limited rights—the right to travel and do business, primarily—for American citizens.

> **Looking for Liberty**
>
> "Restriction of free thought and free speech is the most dangerous of all subversions."
>
> —U.S. Supreme Court Justice William O. Douglas

The Bill of Rights, the first 10 amendments to the U.S. Constitution, grants individuals freedom of the press, freedom of speech, freedom of worship, freedom of assembly, and the right to bear arms. It also guarantees the right to due process in the case of government action that could result in the taking of life, liberty, or property—the concept found first in the Magna Carta. That right to due process is one of the underpinnings of American society today, and we will see how it touches upon every aspect of our daily lives, from driving our cars to criminal prosecutions. (Not that most of the readers of this book are involved in too many criminal prosecutions, but hey, you never know.) It's essential to recognize that the grants of rights we have discussed so far did not pertain to all people. For example, in ancient Greece, only landowners could be citizens. (Renters never get any respect.) The Magna Carta benefited the wealthy, landowning classes in England, not the serfs and certainly not most women, who generally only became landowners upon the death of their husband or father. The English Bill of Rights of 1689 gave power to individual citizens in historically unique ways, but it established Protestantism as the main religion of England, to the detriment of the rights of English Catholics.

And our own U.S. Constitution and Bill of Rights, of course, did not extend its freedoms to slaves, whom it counted only as three-fifths of a human being. The American Civil Liberties Union calls slavery America's "original sin," and it is hard to argue with that appellation. Women could not vote until 1920, and Native Americans have no rights at all under the U.S. Constitution.

Why a Bill of Rights?

Most Americans have an innate distrust of government, and that distrust stems all the way back to the founding of this country by British Colonists. We all remember from school the phrase "No taxation without representation," which led to the Boston Tea Party, in which Americans dressed up as Indians and tossed the English tea into Boston Harbor, rather than pay import taxes. British customs inspectors also could conduct warrantless searches on people's homes. The colonists wanted a say in the taxes they paid without having them imposed by a monarch thousands of miles away. And they did not want that distant monarch's local authorities to come into their homes at any time.

The Law of the Land

"The Congress shall have power to lay and collect taxes, duties, imposts and excises, to pay the debts and provide for the common defense and general welfare of the United States; but all duties, imposts and excises shall be uniform throughout the United States[.]"

—U.S. Constitution, Article I, Section 8

Power and liberty, as the ACLU puts it, are natural enemies—at least that's what most Americans think. The nation's founders believed their most important job was to limit the power of government and protect the freedom of the individual. The only question remained—who would interpret the Bill of Rights? Who had final say in these matters? The answer: The U.S. Supreme Court, whose cases we will be visiting throughout this book.

If you remember your twelfth-grade American studies class, or if you have slipped into the bitter morass of law school, you may remember the case of *Marbury* v. *Madison*. This 1803 Supreme Court case established the principle that the Supreme Court had the power to nullify laws passed by Congress. In other words, the Supreme Court would act as a check on the power of Congress, and Congress, meanwhile, was acting as a check against the power of the president. The president, for his part, could appoint Supreme Court justices, but these were to be lifetime appointments, thus insulating the justices from political pressures. Each branch of the American government—legislative, executive, and judicial—therefore have powers that the other two don't. This system is known as the system of checks and balances, which governs to this day.

America has made enormous strides in the rights of the individual in the 225-plus years since its founding. There has been an ebb and flow to that progress—and we will examine how things have evolved in specific areas of the law in each of the chapters of this book. During wartime, particularly the First and Second World Wars, both citizens and the government alike were willing to trade individual liberties and privacy in exchange for a greater level of security.

> **Taking Liberties** _____
>
> We frequently hear the terms civil liberties and civil rights. Which is which? The term "civil rights" generally refers to the government's responsibility to take positive actions to make sure that citizens have equal rights and equal opportunity under the law. Civil liberties, on the other hand, refer to the specific rights that individuals enjoy under the American system of government, such as freedom of speech, press, religion, and due process of law. It's worth noting that the terms are not precisely defined in law and are sometimes used interchangeably. Throughout this book, when we use the phrase civil liberties, we are referring in fact to the special privileges that Americans enjoy as citizens in our democracy.

American social history during both World War I and World War II is, in many ways, quite unpleasant reading. It is well known that the U.S. government interred Japanese citizens who were considered security risks. It is less well known that the U.S. government did the same thing with a variety of ethnic groups during World War I, including Eastern Europeans and Jews. In times of national crisis, there is always the tendency to go too far in order to protect the nation. Which brings us to …

Changes Since September 11, 2001

On this day, Al Qaeda terrorists destroyed New York's World Trade Center and damaged the Pentagon in Washington, D.C. Immediately after that, congressional leaders created and passed the U.S.A. Patriot Act, a law that sought to make it difficult or impossible for terrorists to continue their activities against the United States. The U.S.A. Patriot Act is actually an acronym. It stands for "Uniting and Strengthening America by Providing Appropriate Tools Required to Intercept and Obstruct Terrorism."

The law affords new powers to intelligence and police communities, both domestic and foreign, in order to thwart potential terrorists. The law permits the monitoring and interception of e-mail to a much greater degree than ever before. It also permits government agents to conduct warrantless searches if it thinks time is of the essence. There are also expanded opportunities for law enforcement authorities to locate money-laundering operations that may be aiding terrorist forces. Suspected terrorists

> **Statutes of Liberties**
>
> The U.S.A. Patriot Act, an immediate response to the attacks of September 11, 2001, limits the civil liberties of Americans in order to protect the country in a time of crisis. Some believe it suspends far too many rights and is a "laundry list" of long-desired tools for the FBI and other intelligence-gathering organizations.

who are not U.S. citizens can be held for longer periods. The law also permits increased surveillance, and allows the secretary of state to name any foreign group a terrorist organization, deport suspected terrorists, and conduct phone and Internet taps with lower levels of judicial insight.

Another change since September 11 is the introduction of military trials, where the government considers it appropriate, for individuals suspected of terrorism. Military tribunals have a much lower standard of evidence than do normal criminal proceedings and were originally to be conducted in secret—at least that was the desire of the Bush administration until public pressure forced the proceedings to be made public.

One of the problems that the U.S.A. Patriot Act (also known as the antiterrorist act) seeks to address is the fact that the FBI and other intelligence-gathering operations were limited in what kind of intelligence they could gather and how they could share information. For example, investigators who sensed that something unusual and potentially dangerous was taking place at a flight school in Arizona were not able to share records or theories with FBI agents who suspected a particular individual was planning a terrorist act. That individual's computers could not be searched or seized, due to the legal protections that benefited him as an individual on American soil. It is the hope of the U.S. government that the law will facilitate a faster and freer exchange of information among the various members of the U.S. intelligence community—the CIA, the FBI, the National Security Agency, and other intelligence groups.

> ### Looking for Liberty
>
> "We must remember that any oppression, any injustice, any hatred, is a wedge designed to attack our civilization."
>
> —President Franklin Delano Roosevelt

Many individuals and groups in the United States fear that the antiterrorist act and related measures passed by the Bush administration go too far, that we are sacrificing civil liberties on the altar of national security. They fear that the FBI's long-term "wish list" was the basis for the additional powers granted, such as the ability to observe in a surreptitious fashion individuals in a mosque or other religious setting, rather than items that were truly dictated by the needs of post-September 11 security.

In other words, according to those skeptical of the bill, the FBI simply used the terrorist attacks to obtain powers that it had been seeking for a long time. Some feel that the FBI may now be able to create databases of information that could be used to track the movements of all Americans—those who are legitimate targets of terrorist investigations, those who simply have Middle Eastern backgrounds, and other individuals who are simply swept up in the net. Critics of the antiterrorist act liken the disruption to the privacy rights of the McCarthy era of the 1950s, when Senator

Joseph McCarthy of Wisconsin led a witch-hunt against suspected communists in the U.S. government.

Those who support the intelligence community's new authority point out that all the rights and freedoms in the world don't matter if you are at the bottom of a smoking crater, as one official suggested. The irony is that the FBI has been suffering for years from outmoded communications and information-gathering tools. New cases are literally recorded by hand and the bureau currently does not have an e-mail system, as hard as that is to believe. According to a *Wall Street Journal* article on Tuesday, July 9, 2002, ("How Outdated Files Hamper FBI Effort to Fight Terrorism"), the FBI has dozens of different computer systems—none of which can speak to each other, because they are incompatible. The computer-lingo term for this is "stovepiped"— there is simply no communication among the different forms of information retrieval systems. When September 11 happened, the FBI needed to send out photos of other suspected terrorists to its bureaus. According to the *Journal*, it had to do so by *overnight mail* because the FBI—you may want to sit down for this—does not have the ability to scan photos and e-mail them to its officers.

It's almost unbelievable to think that in an era when preschoolers own their own computers and teenagers spend all day (and all night) sending instant messages to each other, the FBI cannot do so. This is because the FBI and Congress have been locked in battles for years. Congress is furious at the FBI for the way the FBI spends (or, in Congress' opinion, wastes, money). Congress is particularly peeved at the FBI's failure to come up with comprehensive plans for successful computer systems, its tendency to spend large amounts of money before getting approval from Congress, and the utter failure of FBI computer systems in the last 5 to 10 years. The FBI is only now getting around to giving its agents Microsoft Windows packages, which renders the idea that we have little to fear from an intelligence community that has to go to Kinko's to send an e-mail.

The Least You Need to Know

- The Magna Carta marked the first time in history that a king had limits imposed on his power.

- The Bill of Rights is the part of American law that protects individual liberties.

- September 11, 2001, drastically altered Americans' civil liberties.

- The FBI still does not have the capability to monitor citizens as much as the law permits them.

Chapter 3

The Right to Be Left Alone: How Privacy Rights Developed

In This Chapter

◆ Private citizens and public figures

◆ The right to be left alone

◆ Trashing your privacy

◆ The privilege of privacy

There's a great jazz song from the early twentieth century that goes "Mind your own business! And you won't be minding mine!" When you stop and think about it, the right to privacy is one of the most cherished of all human rights. We simply don't want other people to know the things about us that we would rather keep private. If we're smart, we don't tell total strangers our ATM code, information about our past relationships, how much we make for a living, whether we believe in God, or a million other facts about ourselves, personal, embarrassing, or just plain irrelevant.

None of Your Business?

Think about all the things that you may choose to keep to yourself. Perhaps you don't want people to know where you live. Or you don't want them to know your phone number, for reasons of privacy or personal safety. You may not want people to know your social security number, to avoid being a victim of identity theft. You may not want people to know how much money you carry on your person at any one time. You may not want them to know what videos you rent at the video store or what books you take out of the library. Or even what websites you visit when you surf the Internet. In short, there are a million facts about ourselves that we wish, to varying degrees, to keep private.

The tension in the law, therefore, comes when your desire to keep personal matters and information out of the hands of others bumps up against the desire of other people to know about you. What becomes important at that point is who wants to know about you, what is it they want to know, and why do they want to know it.

If you've earned any money, the IRS is certainly interested. As much as you may not want them to know, that's how much they believe they have a right to know—right down to the penny. Turn 18 lately? The government wants to know, because if you are 18 and male, you are required to register with the military. If you've recently had a baby, the government wants to know. Additionally, many people would like to be privy to that fact, so that they can sell you the wide assortment of baby gear and supplies that every family needs. Buy a new house? A *lot* of people would be interested to learn that. First of all, all the realtors, home buyers, and potential home sellers want to know exactly how much you paid for your house. That helps them better understand how much to buy or sell other houses for. Not only that, everyone from gardeners to home designers to finance companies would like to know about your new home purchase. They have a host of goods and services to sell you. You may not want the world to know what you paid for you house, or even that you bought a house. But the world considers that information a public matter. So we don't always have as much privacy as we wish.

The Law of the Land

"The right of the people to be secure in their persons, houses, papers, and effects, against unreasonable searches and seizures, shall not be violated[.]"

—Fourth Amendment, U.S. Constitution

Statutes of Liberties

Collecting income taxes, and all the personal information that goes with that process, began during the Civil War. In 1862, President Lincoln and Congress created the Commissioner of Internal Revenue and enacted an income tax to pay war expenses.

Getting Borked

In 1987, President George H. W. Bush nominated Judge Robert Bork to become the newest justice of the U.S. Supreme Court. Judge Bork's political record upset many individuals, who mounted an unprecedented campaign to keep the Senate from confirming him for the Supreme Court vacancy. To reduce Bork's chances of serving, the individuals who opposed Bork tried to find every single piece of information they could that might possibly reflect badly on him. Certainly there had been unpopular presidential choices for the Supreme Court, but the Bork nomination was the first time that a full-scale, national campaign was mounted to defeat a prospective Supreme Court justice.

One of the tactics that Bork's opponents used was visiting the local video store in Bork's Washington, D.C., neighborhood and obtaining a copy of the records of Bork's video rentals. Perhaps they paid off a minimum-wage earning clerk, or perhaps the clerk had his own reasons for not wanting Bork to make it to the Supreme Court. Bork's video rental record thus entered the debate in the U.S. Senate over whether he was qualified to serve. It turned out that Bork's taste was innocuous—there were no naughty videos, nothing x-rated, nothing embarrassing. But there was a sense, even among the people who ended up succeeding in keeping Bork from the Supreme Court, that these methods went too far. As a result, Congress passed a law making it illegal for a third party to retrieve your record at Blockbuster or other local video store. The Bork story is illustrative of the tension in privacy law. You've got your reasons for keeping information private, and other people, who may or may not like (or even know) you, have their reasons for wanting to get their hands on that information. The other fascinating aspect of the Bork situation is that it illustrates how advances in technology—in this case, the ability to rent videos and the trail of rented video titles that's created—sometimes gets a step or two ahead of the law. Let's examine the primary source for the right of privacy in today's legal climate, the landmark 1965 Supreme Court case of *Griswold* v. *Connecticut*.

> ## Looking for Liberty
>
> Robert Bork was an accomplished jurist and author by the time he was nominated for a seat on the Supreme Court. Ironically, the fact that he had published so much created a "paper trail" that afforded his political enemies ample opportunity to criticize him. Justices like David Souter, who published little prior to being nominated to the highest court, are far more likely to get through the Senate today for confirmation, because their records are less clear.

Outta My Bedroom

In Griswold, a Connecticut man challenged that state's law forbidding the use of contraceptives. (Yes, folks, back in the early 1960s, states actually made contraception illegal!) The U.S. Supreme Court declared that the Connecticut statute was unconstitutional. However, the question remained: on what grounds? What specific right did the Justices invoke to declare the Connecticut statute incompatible with the U.S. Constitution?

The Court wrote that the overall theme of the Bill of Rights was personal freedom. The government had no right to interfere in the personal decisions of its citizenry. In many ways, that's why the American Revolution was fought in the first place: to remove unwanted government interference, in that case, interference of the British government in the lives of Americans.

Justice William O. Douglas, writing for the Supreme Court, declared that the right to privacy was actually older than the U.S. Constitution, that it was part of the "natural rights" of the individual. Although he could not locate any specific language in the Bill of Rights that specifically supported a right to privacy, he said that such a right did in fact exist in the "shadows" and "penumbras" (another word for shadows) of the Bill of Rights.

How important would these shadows and penumbras be? A host of privacy rights decisions followed the Griswold case, culminating in the landmark 1973 U.S. Supreme Court decision legalizing the women's right to abortion, *Roe* v *Wade*. We'll examine issues of privacy as it relates to sex, marriage, and abortion in more depth in Chapters 5 and 7.

The right to privacy, therefore, is relatively new. There's nothing in the Magna Carta, which we discussed in Chapter 2, providing individuals with the right to privacy from those who would seek information about them. In fact, the "right to privacy," as spelled out in those precise words, only dates back to the year 1890, when Samuel Warren and Louis Brandeis published the seminal article "The Right to Privacy" in the *Harvard Law Review*.

> **Statutes of Liberties**
>
> The Griswold decision was the first time that the Supreme Court actually linked the concept of a right to privacy to the Bill of Rights.

> **Legal Dictionary**
>
> **Landmark decision**—A major U.S. Supreme Court decision often overturning a broad principle of law. Just because the Supreme Court announces a landmark decision doesn't mean the states all follow it. For example, after *Brown* v. *Board of Education* outlawed school discrimination, many states continued their practice of separate (and highly unequal) schools for children of different races.

Warren and Brandeis were highly respected individuals and the Harvard Law School, of course, is a highly respected institution. Therefore, when their article appeared advocating a right to privacy, the American legal system sat up and took notice. As Warren and Brandeis wrote, individuals have a right "to be let alone."

But what exactly does it mean to be "let alone"? What, if anything, should the government have a right to know about you? If a person is bankrupt, a felon, a sex offender, a drunk driver, or has engaged in other sorts of behavior that would affect the community, that's something that the government ought to know. But should the government have the right to know about a person's health, political affiliations, or sexual preferences? Most people would say no.

Legal Dictionary

Law schools across the country publish **law reviews,** which are journals containing articles by law professors and occasionally law students. These articles discuss the state of law in a given field and offer the authors' suggestions as to how to improve the situation in a given state or the United States with regard to that aspect of the law. Judges and legislators take law review articles quite seriously, especially if the author or school itself is prestigious.

Privacy has its limits in the business world as well. If privacy were an absolute right, an employer could not check references on a prospective employee. Colleges and universities would have no right to examine the transcripts of high school students applying for admission. Judges would have no right to know about the criminal history of a defendant. And on and on. Because of such circumstances, practically no one advocates an absolute right of privacy. Neither government nor society could function if everyone could keep every single detail about themselves private. No bank would grant a house loan, no auto dealer would give an auto loan, no stocks could be sold—the economy would grind to a halt if no one could know anything about other people or other businesses.

The questions we'll be exploring in this section are these:

♦ When are you entitled to privacy?

♦ When does someone else have a right to know information you consider private?

♦ How does technology affect our right to privacy?

As the Bork case so clearly indicates, changes in technology trigger new issues in privacy law all the time. This is especially true in the "Age of Information" in which we live. Information sloshes back and forth over the Internet every day. And it's not just the Internet.

Taking Liberties

The race is on between the makers and users of technology that violate the privacy of individuals and the ability of the government to pass judgment on and possibly make illegal the possession and use of that technology.

Take the almost ubiquitous "mini-cams" that many families have installed in their homes. Many of these cameras are for watching nannies as they take care of children. Parents can set up a mini-cam in their home, tie it into the Internet, and then watch over the Internet at work to see whether their nannies are taking appropriate care of their children. These "nanny-cams" become more ubiquitous every day in an era when both parents in most families work. Some people even have cameras on in their homes so they can watch to see what their dogs do while they're not home!

However, technology exists that would allow any person with it—including you!—to pick up the "broadcasts" from those mini-cams just by driving along the street and using that technology correctly. Imagine the information you would have—information that the homeowners would not want you to have. You would know in what room the nanny and the children are. You also can see whether a back door might be open and what valuables the house contains—information quite helpful to burglars. That's not exactly the kind of information that the average citizen would want other individuals to have.

Until Congress or state legislatures become aware of such technology, pass laws to make its possession or use illegal, and then have those laws stand up to constitutional scrutiny in the courts, it's perfectly legal (so far) for bad guys to violate your privacy in a brand new way. Congress is always a few steps behind technology, and those who would abuse technology to violate the privacy of others.

We live in an era when our privacy rights have never been so vigorously threatened, and we live in an era where Congress and the courts are finding it increasingly tougher to keep up with the changes that new technology brings.

Nothing New Under the Sun?

The early history of privacy law recognized three types of actions as violations of privacy: eavesdropping, in which one person illicitly listens into conversations that were otherwise meant to be private; assault, in which one person physically harms another person, thus depriving that person of a right to physical privacy; and trespassing, which means going where one is not invited, such as a burglar entering one's home. Interestingly, almost all of the twenty-first century technological threats to privacy fall into one or more of these very same categories. Eavesdropping today can be as low-tech as the traditional ear to the door or as technologically advanced as tooling into mini-cams. Telephone wiretaps and electronic surveillance via the Internet (reading your e-mail, watching as you surf the net) are modern methods of eavesdropping.

In this Information Age, "who we are" includes vital information about us, such as might be found in medical records, both physical (located at our doctor's office) and information stored electronically (such as at your neighborhood pharmacy). Having personal information about you in such diverse places means that trespassing not only includes breaking into your house but also breaking into files that contain information about you. Assault has traditionally been defined in the law as causing physical harm. But aren't telemarketers—who know your name, your spending habits, whether or not you own a house, the names of your children and even those of your pets—just as assaultive in nature? Who among us wouldn't consider a telemarketer's call, especially at the dinner hour or late at night, a violation of our privacy?

The Law of the Land

"The enumeration in the Constitution, of certain rights, shall not be construed to deny or disparage others retained by the people."

—Ninth Amendment, U.S. Constitution.

In other words, just because a right isn't mentioned in the Constitution or the Bill of Rights doesn't mean that you don't have that right!

Fundamentally, then, the right to privacy itself, has not changed all that much but, because of technological advances, the means by which people can invade it has evolved greatly. We want to be free from eavesdropping—we don't want people to know things about us that we would like to keep private. We don't want to be assaulted, either by a man with a gun or by a telemarketer with a computer-dialing program. And we don't want anyone trespassing on our property, whether we're talking about physical property such as our house or car, or information property such as our medical records, our credit reports, our social security number, our tax filings, or any other myriad sources of data that reveal so much about us.

Truth in Advertising

After the article arguing for a legally-mandated right to privacy was published by Warren and Brandeis, one of the first major tests over that right arose. It concerned advertising and an area of the law called the right of publicity. Specifically, companies in the early twentieth century began to advertise products with what we today call celebrity endorsements. The only problem was that the advertisers never bothered to get the celebrities permission to use their likenesses or to compensate them. The legal question thus arose: Do you have a right to privacy with regard to your physical appearance?

The courts in the early part of the twentieth century held that individuals do in fact have such a right. It was illegal for advertisers to take Babe Ruth's face and slap it on a box of Wheaties without telling him, and without paying him for the "privilege." Nor could you quote John Q. Public as saying that a particular headache remedy was effective if Mr. John Q. had never made any such statement. The issue of commercial likenesses—the right of publicity—is where the first important application of the right to privacy came in.

likeness

Statutes of Liberties

Until states began to enact privacy statues in early twentieth-century America, there was no law to protect a celebrity or a private person from having his or her identity used in an advertisement.

Looking for Liberty

"Television, whether you like it or not, is the most powerful educational force known to man and we're frittering it away and I find that unacceptable. When are we going to scream, 'That's enough!'"

—Fred Friendly, former president of CBS News

Legal Dictionary

"New York Times libel"—A reference to the libel standard promulgated by the U.S. Supreme Court in its landmark decision, *New York Times v. Sullivan*. According to that decision, a public figure can only be considered libeled if the statement in question was published with knowing falsity or a reckless disregard for the truth.

You might say, "What does this have to do with me?" Well, if you have the misfortune to be arrested, there may well be a film crew from *Cops* standing outside with a film crew. The question then becomes whether your right to privacy outweighs the media's interest in doing news stories. The real question is whether there is anything newsworthy in someone being arrested. Unless the arrest is especially newsworthy, there really is no news value, of course. But that's what the producers of these reality shows argue when they fight for their right to show you at a moment of great personal crisis. Of course, these shows must get your permission before they can show your face, which is why many of the miscreants captured on camera have their faces blacked out. Of course, they may still be recognizable to a select few by their body art or tattoos.

Supermarket Tabloids and Hollywood Stars

When it comes to privacy, there are actually two sets of laws in this country: one for private citizens and a second for public figures. You could go to law school and spend a month studying the topic, but allow me to sum things up for you in a single sentence: Public figures have virtually no rights. You heard me. If you're famous, you have pretty much surrendered the right to privacy that ordinary citizens have.

Let's say that the *National Examiner* prints a story, complete with pictures, about how a certain famous movie star was arrested for drunk driving and has trotted obediently off to rehab. Can that celebrity turn around and sue the tabloid for running that story? Well, in America, he can always sue. But he won't win. Anyone in the public eye is pretty much fair game for the media, and no matter what is said, it's practically impossible to enforce any kind of privacy rights.

Now, let's say that Joe Averageguy was on his way to see the aforementioned celebrity's new movie. On the way to the theater, Joe was arrested for drunk driving, and *he* trotted off obediently to rehab. Can the *National Enquirer* or other publication publish that information and thus violate Mr. Averageguy's right to privacy? The answer is absolutely not.

Mr. Averageguy has a right not to have his personal life bandied about in the public prints. He has a right to privacy with regard to embarrassing facts. Since he's not a celebrity, there's nothing newsworthy about the events that happen to him. It's embarrassing to be arrested for drunk driving, and the fact that he is in rehab could hinder his ability to keep his current job or get a new one. When Congress and the courts tote up his right to take care of his business privately versus the media's right to make an unreasonable spectacle of a private citizen, his right to privacy outweighs—by a substantial degree—the media's interest in telling his story.

What's the Test?

In legal terms, if a fact about a private citizen is published in the newspaper or broadcast in the media, and that fact is not true, this individual's privacy has been violated. Even if it is true, without compelling reason to put it in the paper, his rights have still been violated.

On the other hand, public figures have a much more difficult time asserting their rights. In a landmark U.S. Supreme Court Case called *New York Times* v. *Sullivan*, the Supreme Court held that a public figure only has privacy rights if something was published or broadcast with "actual malice" or "reckless disregard of the facts." This means that the public figure must prove two things in a court of law: First, that the story was untrue, and second that the publisher or newscaster printed or broadcast the story maliciously, meaning that he or she knew that the story was untrue.

Taking Liberties

The typical attitude of newscasters today is that truth isn't nearly as important as ratings; it's rare for a TV news broadcast ever to admit that it was wrong.

The Law of the Land

"The First Amendment has a goal of 'producing an informed public capable of conducting its own affairs.'"

—U.S. Supreme Court, *Red Lion Broadcasting Co.* v. *Federal Communications Commission* (1969)

But What Does This Have to Do with Me?

The right to privacy for individuals who are not public figures—in other words, private citizens like you and me—are your safeguard against information about you coming out in the media. You might wonder who would want to make you the center of a media scandal, but it could happen! Take the case of Elmer Gertz, a Chicago lawyer who found himself the target of a despicable article in a local newspaper. Gertz's legal and political activities on behalf of some unpopular clients had triggered a local newspaper to make unpleasant statements about him. Their defense: Gertz was a public figure, and therefore he was fair game for any sort of criticism that a newspaper would care to offer.

Gertz's response: "I am not a public figure. In fact, no one has ever heard of me!" Gertz actually went to the trouble of conducting surveys in a series of Chicago neighborhoods to determine whether people did, in fact, know who he was. The overwhelming majority of the people thus surveyed had never heard of Elmer Gertz. He was thus able to prove that he was a private citizen as far as the laws of libel were concerned, and so he was able to prevail against the newspaper in court.

Statutes of Liberties
A rock star whose band was criticized by a rival band found his home phone number distributed on a website. His family received threatening calls while on the road. He would certainly qualify as a public figure, although he would be able to sue his tormentors in nuisance for the upset they caused his family.

Even if you think you're an unassuming bystander, you could end up the target of a media expose. Even the littlest acts could make you a potential target. If it ever happens that someone with a newspaper, radio station, or even website doesn't like you or some principle you stand for, you will be awfully glad that the legal system in this country protects a private citizen's right to privacy.

Let's say that you are the victim of a crime, whether it be a carjacking, home break-in, or even a common mugging. What if some Hollywood producer decided that your story was so compelling that they wanted to make a movie or TV show about it? This may sound far-fetched, but the problem actually goes back half a century.

In the early 1950s, in the United States, break-ins or home invasions were far less frequent than they are today. It was so rare for burglars to come into a home and hold a family hostage that it would actually make national news. Back then, one such home invasion did occur, and a family was held hostage by gunmen for a period of hours. This experience was so intriguing to producers that a Broadway play and movie, *The Desperate Hours*, were made about the incident. The family of victims sued on the ground that its right to privacy had been violated by both works. They prevailed in court, as the Supreme Court recognized that a depiction of events so far after the fact was no longer newsworthy and the privacy of the family was therefore protected by law. This case was an important step forward in the defining of privacy rights in the era of mass communications.

Freedom of the Press

When our nation was founded, freedom of the press was a vital safeguard to allow American citizens to criticize their government without fear of government reprisal. In one famous seventeenth-century case, New York publisher John Peter Zenger criticized the British government. He was arrested and tried in secret (in a "Star Chamber" or secret court) by the British government. Freedom of the press to report on and criticize affairs of government was one of the principles for which the American Revolution was fought.

Today, however, most Americans hold the media in very low regard, believing that the media is far more interested in getting ratings by sensationalizing stories than in informing us. As a result, it's quite possible that as a society, we are far less interested in maintaining freedom of the press than we might have been several centuries ago. Members of the media no longer enjoy the support they had even a generation ago. The basic rule is that journalists can write about anything they please, as long as they do not violate the libel standards for private persons and public figures that we discussed earlier.

> **Looking for Liberty**
>
> "Freedom of the press is guaranteed only to those who own one."
>
> —Journalist and author A.J. Liebling

In his article, "Privacy Law in the U.S.A.," Ronald B. Standler cites a fascinating case that is emblematic of the freedom of the media to discuss whomever they choose, however they choose. In 1910, a certain child prodigy named William Sidis was a public figure, very much in the news. Twenty-seven years later, *New Yorker* magazine wrote an article in the sort of "where are they now?" tradition. Sidis sued the publication on the grounds that he might have been a public figure in the past, but 27 years later, he was a private citizen with the right to be left alone.

The Court of Appeals, the federal court just below the U.S. Supreme Court in importance, held that the *New Yorker* had a right to print an article about him, simply because he had been a public figure at some point in his life and was therefore still of interest to the average reader. Courts generally do not want to get involved in the question of deciding what is or isn't appropriate. As many child stars of the past have learned the hard way, once a public figure, always a public figure.

Does this mean newspapers and broadcasters have free reign to say whatever they want? Not entirely. Standler cites an Alabama case in which a newspaper published a photograph of a woman whose skirt was blown up by a wind machine at a county fair. The court ruled in her favor, stating that there was no news value in this photograph and that the photo violated her privacy. The line between the media's right to inform and the individual's right to privacy is not clearly drawn. Unfortunately, the individual's rights are going to be violated by the media long before they can be adjudicated by a court.

Journalists have certain rights that most Americans would agree are vital for the workings of a free press. The primary right to privacy enjoyed by journalists is that the government cannot compel a journalist to turn over his or her notes or work product to the police or the courts. The government, in other words, cannot expect reporters to "do their work for them." If a reporter develops information that might be useful to the government, it would be all too natural a tendency for the government to decide to force that reporter to turn over the information to the proper authority. But the proper authorities are simply out of luck—reporters are free to maintain the privacy of their work product, because otherwise, there would be a "chilling effect" on the work of all journalists.

Privacy Has Its Privileges

In the law, a *privilege* refers to the rights and obligations that arise when communication occurs within certain relationships. In relationships with privileges, one person can speak with another without fear of the second person revealing the information imparted. There are two sides to the privilege. When party A tells party B a secret, and that conversation is "privileged," which means that party B has a legal responsibility not to share that information with anyone else. And equally important, or perhaps even more important, the government cannot force party B to reveal that information.

What sorts of relationships are privileged? The classic is the attorney-client privilege. After a client has engaged an attorney to represent her in a matter, she can tell that attorney any piece of information and the attorney can neither reveal that information to others nor can she be forced to reveal that information. The privilege actually extends to the lawyers *work product*—the research and thinking process that a lawyer goes through when working on a case. The lawyer has a right—and a responsibility—to maintain your privacy.

Another type of privilege is that which exists between husband and wife. What spouses tell each other during their marriage is privileged information. A husband cannot be made to testify against a wife in court, or vice versa.

In this case, it is the policy of the United States of the America to encourage marriage and to protect the institution of marriage by not requiring spouses to testify against each other or to testify as to secrets that one has told the other. Yes, pillow talk is protected by the U.S. legal system!

Two other vital forms of privilege include doctor-patient and priest-penitent privilege. Doctor-patient privilege means that whatever you tell your doctor, or whatever information is contained in your medical record, is a matter of your privacy, which is protected in this area. As we suggested in Chapter 1, medical records are not as sacrosanct as they should be. It's all too easy for people who have no business snooping through your medical records to find out about your medical background or history. An important legal question today is whether a doctor may sell his practice to another doctor, and whether your medical records can come with that practice. After all, you did not authorize your old doctor to turn that material over to a doctor you have never met. Yet, doctors sell their records all the time.

Legal Dictionary

Privilege—The rights and obligations that arise concerning the communication between people in certain relationships. In an attorney-client relationship, for instance, the attorney is obligated to keep private what the client tells him, and the client has the right to expect that the attorney will do so.

The Law of the Land

A thorny issue in Constitutional law is "executive privilege," under which a President claims the right to prevent disclosure of certain documents, tape-recordings, or other information concerning his administration. The question of whether the Supreme Court has a right to compel a President to disclose such documents is rarely easy to decide.

Or let's take another important case. Let's say that an individual goes in for a blood test and turns out to be HIV-positive. Is the doctor obligated to share this information with the government? If a person is, say, a food handler or chef in a restaurant, is there a public interest in having this information brought to light? We'll get more deeply into the issue of medical records in Chapter 9. In theory, however, any information you provide a doctor should be confidential, but unfortunately, this is not always the case.

The priest-penitent privilege means that anything you tell your religious leader in private is protected information. A religious leader—a priest, rabbi, imam, or minister—has an obligation not to disclose information that he or she learns in the confessional or any private setting. But what if a person tells his priest, or his therapist or lawyer for that matter, that he is very angry with someone and plans on committing murder?

Just such a case came up in California in the 1960s. An individual told his therapist that he was going to kill a particular woman. The therapist made a note of this threat in the patient's medical records, but did not pass along this information to the police. The patient committed the murder, and the family of the victim sued the employer of the therapist, in this case the State of California Board of Regents, for failing to disclose the information. So we see that there is no absolute right of privacy when it comes to making statements that indicate that we intend to put others in peril. Short of situations like this, an individual in American society has a legal right to assume that anything he or she tells an attorney, religious leader, medical personnel, or a therapist or a psychiatrist will be kept secret. The family of the victim won.

The Law of the Land

"If you don't read the newspaper, you are uninformed; if you do read the newspaper, you are misinformed."

—Mark Twain, *Innocents Abroad*

There is one important person we've left off this list. That person is … your accountant! At this time, there exists no accountant-client privilege, which means that if you tell your accountant that you intend to declare only a quarter of your earnings, and you ask him to fill out your tax return to reflect that fact, you could be in a lot of trouble down the road! The IRS can actually compel your accountant to testify against you. While we at the *Complete Idiot's Guides* certainly do not advocate tax evasion, if you're really planning on such behavior, for heaven's sake, don't tell your accountant!

When Businesses Say "None of Your Business!"

The right of privacy is the privilege of individuals, not businesses. A business cannot claim to have its right of privacy violated, because it has no such right. Businesses do have the right to protect trademarks, slogans, intellectual property, "trade dress" (the design on a label or a box), and, if a business is privately held, it need not disclose to anyone (except the IRS) how much money it makes. If you were to work for XYZ Corp. and then write a book about how XYZ rips off consumers, you would be perfectly within your rights—as long as you were telling the truth. If, however, you were to sneak into the offices of a competitor late at night and photocopy their client list, you will have violated a different form of a right to privacy—you will have violated laws that prohibit corporate espionage. Nor do you have the right to write a book about your employer's business practices, under the laws regarding trade secrets.

Home Schooling

Today, millions of American parents choose to educate their children at home rather than in public school. Countless more families send their children to private, often religious, schools instead of public ones. While it seems obvious that parents should have the right to home school their children or send them to private school, this was not always the case.

Two important Supreme Court cases decided in the 1920s—*Meyer* v. *Nebraska* and *Pierce* v. *Society of Sisters*—established the fact that parents have a right to privacy when it comes to raising their own children. The Meyer case involved a Nebraska law that forbade the teaching of children in any language other than English prior to ninth grade. The state of Nebraska wanted children to learn the English language and American ideals before they were subjected to "foreign tongues and ideals," which Nebraska obviously considered inferior. The Supreme Court held that any such restriction violated the right of parents to raise children as they see fit—which in essence is a privacy right. In the Pierce case, the Supreme Court made clear for the first time that parents had the right to send their children to a private rather than public school.

Taking Liberties

Should English be the "official language" of the United States? Many, including those at www.us-english.org, believe so. Go to that website and your computer will offer a stirring rendition of the Battle Hymn of the Republic!

We spoke earlier of policy grounds for making legal decisions. While many people today debate the question of whether private versus public school education is superior, the Supreme Court was not seeking to handle that difficult question. Rather they wanted to affirm on a policy basis the fact that the United States was in favor of letting parents do what they considered right for their children. In other words, there is a legal presumption that parents know best, and the Supreme Court sought to enshrine that presumption in law by making clear that parents had the right to send their kids to private school. Today, almost 80 years later, these Supreme Court decisions provide the foundation for the rights of parents to educate their children as they see fit. Both cases are seen as the foundation for later decisions that uphold the right to privacy with regard to marriage, sex, abortion, and other vital rights, all of which we will discuss later in this book.

Now that you've seen how privacy rights have evolved from the simple case of whether a person's likeness can be used in advertising without his permission all the way to twenty-first century issues of electronic privacy and privacy of the area of personal choice, let's go more deeply into these issues—and we'll start with the most cutting-edge issue of all: cyber-privacy, or privacy in the age of the Internet.

The Least You Need to Know

- ◆ Public figures and private citizens enjoy different privacy laws.

- ◆ The subject of the right to privacy goes back only as far as 1890 and has only been a firm part of American law since the 1960s.

- ◆ Privacy law can be broken down into the areas of trespassing, eavesdropping, and assault.

- ◆ A privilege is a relationship where a second party will not divulge information from a first party.

Chapter 4

Where Do Laws Come From?

In This Chapter

- ◆ Sources of law
- ◆ Our English heritage
- ◆ Attending class actions
- ◆ Fitting the Bill (of Rights)

Laws come from many sources in our society: federal and state legislatures, the courts, and the common law, which we inherited from our English forefathers. They also come from federal and state constitutions (produced by the legislatures), treaties, executive orders (written by the president), statutes (written by Congress and the state legislatures), and administrative regulations (rules decreed by administrative agencies such as the Federal Communications Commission or the Federal Drug Administration).

The federal and state legislatures are the primary source of laws. On the federal level, Congress passes bills all the time, creating new rights, limiting others, changing the tax code, criminalizing certain behavior—whatever is considered necessary for the success of the nation.

Federalism: The American Way

Before there were 50 states, there were 13 colonies. Before the 13 colonies would agree to come together and form a single nation, they demanded—and received—guarantees that their rights in many important areas would not be abridged by the federal government. For example, the federal government can regulate interstate commerce—business affairs conducted across state lines; however, anything that occurs within a particular state is, for the most part, none of the federal government's business (unless it is conduct that violates Constitutional freedoms, as we discuss throughout this book).

In our federal system, states have a great deal of power to regulate the lives and businesses of their citizens. State legislatures pass laws on subjects ranging from the environment and motor vehicles to abortion and advertising. By and large, local matters are solely for the state to decide, and the federal government cannot tell the states how to operate. The question of what is properly the authority of a state and properly the authority of the federal government is not always easy to answer; such issues are decided in the court system, to which we will turn next.

Taking Liberties

When you are in law school, the first thing you learn is to reach for the statute book when you are seeking to inform a client whether something is legal or not. The bound volumes of laws of the states and the federal government contain the answers to many, if not most, of these questions.

Legal Dictionary

Stare decisis—The principle of law stating that judges are bound to follow precedents, or previous decisions on the same issue, when deciding cases.

The second great source of laws in our society is the court system. As we will discuss, judges follow a philosophy called *stare decisis*, which means that they consider themselves bound by previous decisions in similar cases. The higher the court, the freer it is to ignore previous decisions, but the courts generally extend great deference to prior decisions. If a case is important enough, judges will write lengthy opinions explaining their rationale for deciding the case as they do. When the highest court in the land, the U.S. Supreme Court, makes a decision, legal scholars, judges, lawyers, the police, and regular citizens study those opinions carefully, trying to determine exactly what new rules of law have been created and how those rules are to be used.

Sometimes the U.S. Supreme Court will create a new "test" by which similar laws are to be judged constitutional or unconstitutional by lower courts. Those tests can sometimes be very difficult to understand or implement, and courts around the country sometimes guess at how best to apply those tests. Sometimes courts are not even sure *which* Supreme Court test is applicable in a given case. (We'll see some examples of that later on in this book.) When that happens, it's very likely that the Supreme Court will end up hearing the issue again, in order to provide a higher degree of certainty for everyone.

We have two different sets of courts in the United States. (We have many more than that, but there are two basic categories to examine.) The first are the state courts, and the second are the federal courts. The state courts decide matters involving local citizens—lawsuits, divorces, wills and estates, and business issues. If a federal law is involved, a federal court would decide that case. When our nation was established, there was great concern that a litigant from Massachusetts, say, who had to sue a person in Georgia would not get a fair hearing in the southern state. Presumably, the judge and the jury in Georgia would provide too much of a "home court advantage" for the defendant. Similarly, if the Massachusetts litigant were to sue in Boston, the Georgian defendant wouldn't have a chance. For that reason, Congress created the federal court system, which allows individuals from different states to sue with a much greater certainty that both sides would get a fair hearing.

Taking Liberties

Federal court judges have special constitutional protections; they cannot be removed for making unpopular decisions, nor can their salaries be lowered as punishment. Sometimes, when they haven't gotten a raise in a long time, they claim that inflation constitutes an unconstitutional "lowering" of their salaries!

There are certain requirements for filing in the federal court system. There must be complete diversity between the parties—meaning that if you are from Massachusetts, you cannot be suing anyone else from Massachusetts (with some exceptions, of course). The amount in question in the lawsuit must be substantial, to merit the time and bother of the federal courts. Generally, federal court judges are paid better and work in nicer courthouses, with better access to law libraries and clerks (research and writing assistants for judges).

A decision made in a state trial court generally goes through one level of appeals before it reaches the supreme or highest court in that state. Decisions from state supreme courts in which questions of federal law are involved can then be appealed to the U.S. Supreme Court.

Trial courts in the federal court system are called U.S. District Courts. Decisions of those courts can be appealed to the U.S. Appellate Courts. Appellate court decisions can be appealed to the U.S. Supreme Court. While the Supreme Court is under no obligation to take on any particular case (although it does examine all death penalty appeals), we see that cases from both state courts and federal courts can make their way up the ladder to the U.S. Supreme Court, should the litigants so choose.

Who's In Charge Here?

A decision by the U.S. Supreme Court is binding on all other courts in the country—everyone has to do what the Supreme Court says. Of course, if Congress does not like a Supreme Court decision, it can either pass a law, overturning that decision, or it can start to float a constitutional amendment, which would change the provision in the Constitution that the Supreme Court is interpreting.

Decisions of state supreme courts are only binding on courts in that state. If the Florida Supreme Court were to reach a decision tomorrow, that decision would not be binding anywhere but in Florida. For the most part, the states uphold each other's legal decisions. For example, if you get divorced in Virginia, your divorce will be recognized in all 50 states. This is not always the case, however. A gay couple that enters into a domestic partnership agreement in Vermont may find that that agreement is not acknowledged in some of the other states. As long as a state does not have a policy against a particular kind of rule from another state, it will enforce that other state's rules. This is known as *comity*, the means by which all states get along.

Sometimes states themselves have conflicts. In that case, two states at odds with each other over a given question would go directly to the U.S. Supreme Court for resolution of that dispute.

Legislatures can make law; the courts interpret those laws. The other important source of law in the American system is the "common law," which is the body of law that the settlers brought with them in the seventeenth century when they left England. The common law refers to settled principles of law that had been determined over the centuries by Parliament and the English courts. The basics of modern landlord-tenant law, employer-employee law, marriage and divorce law, real estate law, business law, maritime law, and many other aspects of modern American life are governed by principles from the English common law.

Taking Liberties

Federal appellate court decisions, which are one rung down the ladder from the U.S. Supreme Court, are the rule of law for the states for the region in which that court is located. The United States is divided up into 11 judicial districts, and each region of the country may have its own interpretation of certain laws, based on the decisions of the various federal appellate courts.

Legal Dictionary

Comity—The idea that courts in one state accept the legal decisions, such as divorces or marriages, of other states. Without comity, you'd have to get married 50 different times!

Another way of understanding the common law is to think of it as the accumulation of English and, later, American legal thought over the centuries from the Magna Carta (which we discussed in Chapter 2) to the present day.

How does the common law apply today? If the courts have not spoken on a given subject, and if Congress or the appropriate state legislature has not passed a law in that area, lawyers and judges will look to the common law for guidance as to how best to understand the question. So, it can be safely said that the legal system in the United States, based on federal and state laws and the common law of England and America, truly stretches back over a period of almost a thousand years.

Another source of law is the president of the United States himself. (Or herself, I might add, so as not to run afoul of equal protection doctrine.) The president may issue Executive Orders, which have the force of law and can literally change a major aspect of American law or society overnight. For example, President Harry S. Truman, after the close of World War II, signed an Executive Order which integrated the U.S. Armed Forces, which had been, for the most part, segregated, even through World War II. Executive Orders have frequently been used in the area of civil rights, in cases where the president deems that Congress is either unwilling or unable to act quickly to remedy a wrong.

Class Actions

While class actions are not sources of law, they are often sources of rights for millions of Americans who otherwise would not have access to the legal system. A class action is a situation where a court determines that a large number of individuals could potentially bring the same case, over the same set of facts, against the same defendant or defendants. Examples would be products liability issues, such as breast implants, contraceptive devices, or poorly built cars or trucks. A court will certify a case as a class action in order to streamline the litigation process. This way, one set of lawyers handles the case for everyone in America who may have been harmed by a particular defendant.

A class action allows a case to go forward in which all potentially injured individuals can have their rights addressed.

The good points about a class action are that few individuals have the time, money, or resources to structure a case against a major

Looking for Liberty

In the Erin Brockovich story, many individuals in a town knew that they had health problems, but none of them individually had the resources to bring a case against the utility that was alleged to have caused the harm.

corporation, like a tobacco or drug company. Also a potential defendant in such a case may not realize that he or she has been harmed by a defendant. A class action suit often serves to inform potential defendants of their rights.

Class action cases are also helpful to the defendants (the people or companies being sued) themselves. It's a lot easier to defend one case in one courtroom at one time than to defend the same kind of case hundreds or even thousands of separate times in courtrooms scattered across the country. Class actions give defendants a chance to marshal their own legal resources and make their own best case.

Who really wins in class action suits? Often, it's the lawyers. The plaintiff's lawyers negotiate an agreement that barely offers any benefit to the defendants. For example, about 10 years ago, an airline frequent flyer program, of which I was a member, was determined to have violated the rights of its frequent flyers. A class action ensued. As a member of that class, as part of that settlement, I received "script" or coupons for future flights on that same airline—I didn't actually see any real money. The coupons themselves offered discounts of approximately 11 dollars on coast-to-coast flights, and even then the airline did not make it easy to use that script. The rules that they created were so complex and arcane that one almost had the feeling that they were seeking to have people just give up entirely on trying to collect on those 11-dollar discounts. (Would an airline actually do such a thing? Oh, never!)

Taking Liberties

Class actions may be brought in federal or in state court. The plaintiffs (the people bringing the suit) must convince a judge that a case should be deemed a class action. Only when a judge agrees will he or she "certify" the case as a class action.

The lawyers, on the other hand, got a lot more than worthless 11-dollar coupons. As is often the case in class action suits, the lawyers walked away with millions of dollars—that's dollars in real money, not airline script. The justification for paying lawyers handsomely in class action cases is that these cases often cost hundreds of thousands or even millions of dollars to mount, with no guarantee of success. If a class action suit fails, the lawyers who "fronted" the money to make the suit happen end up with nothing. They are taking a risk, and the American class action system seeks to reward that risk—and those rewards are often quite handsome.

The First Freedom

It is probably no coincidence that the first freedom enumerated in the First Amendment to the U.S. Constitution is freedom of religion. The First Amendment reads, in relevant part, "Congress shall make no law respecting an establishment of religion, or prohibiting the free exercise thereof[.]" Why did the authors of the Bill of Rights place freedom of religion at the top of the list? Perhaps because the United States was originally settled and founded by individuals who left the Old World in search of religious freedom. As we learned in grade school, the Puritans settled New England because they were dissatisfied with the nature of the Anglican faith in England. Religious leaders such as William Penn, a Quaker; and Roger Williams, a Puritan; founded colonies on the American continent not because they sought political or economic freedom but because they wanted to live their religious lives as they chose. It's true that there was an economic element in the British decision to create a colony in Virginia, but the impetus for many if not most of the original settlers of the American nation was to practice religion as they saw fit.

The "Founding Fathers" of the United States—those individuals who were involved with the creation of the Declaration of Independence, the U.S. Constitution, or the Bill of Rights—also saw an important need for the protection of religious freedom. These individuals were often quite suspicious of organized religion. Many of them were deists, people who believed in God yet did not subscribe to Christianity or any other religion.

Taking Liberties

The Founding Fathers believed that it was dangerous to concentrate too much power in the hands of a government. This belief was based on European history, which showed the dangers inherent in allowing the church and state to be too closely allied.

The U.S. federal government, at its founding, was much less powerful than it is today. Back then, there was great fear about placing too much power in the hands of the federal government, relative to the states. In many ways, the founders deliberately weakened the federal government so that the states initially would not lose too much power. Indeed the Tenth Amendment to the U.S. Constitution specifies that any power not specifically mentioned in the U.S. Constitution be retained by the states.

Full Faith and Credit

The U.S. Constitution was written at a time when the country consisted of 13 states, each of which had its own set of laws. Now that the fledgling nation was to govern itself, a way had to be found to give some of the power to the new federal government and yet allow each of the states to retain some of their own powers. The federal-state relationship thus created is a thing of beauty that has lasted more than 225 years. Under the Constitution's *full faith and credit* clause, each state may pass its own laws, so long as they do not violate the U.S. Constitution, but each of the other

} states is required to uphold the laws of those other states. The phrase "full faith and credit" is an eighteenth-century way of saying that if State A passes a law, State B has to respect that law, unless the law violates the public policy.

Legal Dictionary

Full faith and credit— The clause in the U.S. Constitution requiring states to honor each others' rules and decisions unless the law violates the public policy of another state.

Statutes of Liberties

The phrase—"Congress shall make no law respecting an establishment of religion"—simply means that no particular religion shall be established as the "state religion" or official religion of the United States. It also means that the government cannot favor one religion over another.

Looking for Liberty

America's separation of church and state came about not because the founders were atheists (most were not) but because they mistrusted religious leaders.

If the Founding Fathers did not want the federal government to be all-powerful, it was essential for them not just to leave a great deal of power in the hands of the states but also to keep religious power separate from governmental power. This is why the First Amendment addresses what is called the "establishment" of religion. Today, we live in an era when some religious figures are under suspicion for failure to live up to the nobility of their calling. The late eighteenth century was no different, and the Founding Fathers wanted to make sure that the power of the church would never be commingled with the power of the government.

The second aspect of religious freedom guaranteed by the First Amendment tells us that Congress shall make no law "prohibiting the free exercise" of religion. This means that, provided that it is not against law or the accepted codes of conduct, every individual in America is free to practice the religion or faith to which he or she subscribes—or not to practice any religion at all—without any government interference.

Intriguingly, the same Congress that passed the First Amendment also called on President Washington to declare a day of national thanksgiving to God. The United States was never meant by its founders to be a nation devoid of religious or spiritual content. Many of the Founding Fathers, although they believed in God, did not accept the Divinity of Jesus, did not consider themselves Christians, and thought very little of religious leaders.

According to Steven Morris, writing in *Free Inquiry* in Fall 1985, George Washington never called himself a Christian, although he was a supporter of freedom from religious intolerance. John Adams, the second president of the United States, criticized the "pretended sanctity of some absolute dunces" among the clergy. He was clearly no fan of religious leaders. Adams wrote, "Twenty times in the course of my late reading, have I been upon the point of breaking out, this would be the best of all possible worlds, if there were no religion in it."

Thomas Payne, the fiery author of *The Age of Reason* and *Common Sense*, two documents that spurred the American public to seek independence from Britain, wrote that he did not believe in the creed professed by any church at all. Payne wrote, "Each of these churches accuse the other of unbelief; and for my part, I disbelieve them all." Thomas Jefferson, the third U.S. president and the author of the Declaration of Independence, wrote that early Christian leaders deliberately over complicated the teachings of Christ to create "profit, power, and pre-eminence" for themselves. James Madison, America's fourth president and "Father of the Constitution," wrote that Christianity's legacy was, for the most part, "pride and indolence in the Clergy, ignorance and servility in the laity, in both, superstition, bigotry, and persecution."

In short, the same leaders who gave us the phrases, "In God We Trust" did not trust religious leaders, did not consider themselves "Christians," and did not want Christianity to be America's state religion.

Today, the focus of the debate over the First Amendment has to do primarily with schools. Should the government subsidize religious education? Should the government be involved with faith-based programs that provide social services? If so, to what extent should the government monitor or limit the religious teachings of those faith-based organizations? Should students have the right to a moment of prayer or even a moment of silence in public schools? Is it permissible to post the Ten Commandments on the walls of public schools?

By and large, the answers to these questions boil down to two simple answers: money, yes; religious teachings, no. In other words, the Supreme Court found that it is constitutional for state and federal government to support religious education, either through grants, financial assistance for bussing, or, more recently, a voucher system enabling parents to opt out of public school systems and place their children in private schools with some financial assistance from the state. On the other hand, when it comes to any sort of religious teaching or behavior in schools, the courts are almost entirely uniformly opposed. It is unconstitutional for a school to post the Ten Commandments, allow a moment of prayer during the school day, or allow prayers to be spoken at assemblies.

Taking Liberties

Voucher systems are opposed by most public school teachers' unions, who are worried about their own jobs. Society is beginning to recognize the right of lower income parents to rescue children from failing public schools (a right that wealthy parents have always enjoyed).

Another area in which freedom of religion becomes an issue is when there are public displays of religious symbols, as in crèches or depictions of the nativity on public property during the Christmas season. The Supreme Court has held that it is legitimate for cities and towns to place nativity scenes or Christmas trees on public property, on the grounds that such symbols are now aspects of secular holiday celebrations and are not considered religious symbols specific to one religion. Critics of these decisions point to the fact that the Nativity is indeed a depiction of the core belief in Christianity, the importance of the coming of Jesus Christ. According to this line of reasoning, the Supreme Court is wrong to say that the nativity is a secular tradition, because it is at the heart of Christianity. Some legal scholars see, in decisions permitting the placing of nativity scenes on public property, a tendency toward establishing Christianity as the civic religion of the United States.

The matter of freedom of religion also arises when the Supreme Court must determine what exactly constitutes a religion. This is a question that courts try to avoid as much as possible, for fear of running afoul of the First Amendment. But there are some religious practices that are forbidden by other laws, such as the use of peyote and animal sacrifice. Also, the question arises as to whether individuals in the military can wear religious symbols, such as a cross, a Star of David, a yarmulke, or dreadlocks (for Rastafarians). The courts usually come down on the side of the military, which has regulations demanding that everyone wear identical uniforms, to the exclusion of religious headgear. Once again, the question of establishing a civic religion arises when courts permit individuals to wear, for example, a cross around their neck while not permitting any orthodox Jews or Sikhs to cover their hair in accordance with their own religious law.

The Least You Need to Know

- States have a great deal of power to regulate the lives and businesses of their citizens.

- There are many levels to the U.S. court system, with the Supreme Court having the final say on a given matter.

- European history taught the Founding Fathers that it was dangerous to give the government too much power.

- The United States was founded by Europeans wishing to escape religious persecution in the Old World.

Part 2

Privacy in the Information Age

Thanks to the Internet, e-mail, and the electronic collection of data, your personal life has been reduced to a series of bits and bytes sloshing through computer networks around the globe. (Sorry to break the bad news to you.)

In this section, we'll examine the status of privacy rights in the new millennium. We'll consider whether and how the government can intrude in your private life. Topics to be discussed include such controversial issues as abortion, pornography, and same-sex marriage to the everyday issues of cyber-privacy, medical records, and your credit report. Orwell's Big Brother had nothing compared to the Internet. Find out what rights you have left in these areas.

Private Choices, Public Debates

In This Chapter

- Abortion's uncertain future
- The rights of same-sex couples
- Civil unions and marriage
- Sodomy statutes in today's world

In this chapter, we're going to examine some of the most difficult social issues we face: abortion, same-sex marriage and civil unions, the government's right to regulate sexual behavior among consenting adults, and the question of assisted suicide. The question that unites all these issues: At what point does the government have the right to regulate private conduct?

Perhaps the single most divisive social issue in the United States over the past 30 years is the question of legalized abortion. No question touches on so many different aspects of life—the personal, the political, the religious, the medical. And no question polarizes Americans the way the abortion question does.

Currently, doctors perform approximately more than 1.4 million abortions annually in the United States. Abortion has been legal since the 1973 passage of the landmark U.S. Supreme Court case *Roe* v *Wade*. The decision in *Roe* identified and defined a woman's right to an abortion (under certain circumstances) as part of the general right of privacy afforded by the Bill of Rights to the U.S. Constitution.

Abortion was legal in the United States up until the last half of the nineteenth century, when states began passing laws against it, largely at the behest of newly organized physicians. By 1910, all but one state had criminalized abortion except when necessary to save the life of the mother. However, eventually a new movement achieved legalization in three states prior to *Roe* v. *Wade*, Alaska, Hawaii, and New York.

In this chapter, we'll discuss the abortion issue along with other civil liberties issues involving the right to make choices in our private lives. Specifically, we're going to see how the development of laws granting gays and lesbians the right to enter civil unions and marriages. Not long ago, homosexuals could neither engage in sex nor enter legal unions, but we'll see how the world, and the laws, have changed to permit gays and lesbians many of the same rights and freedoms as heterosexuals.

Abortion: The Persistent Question

In a seven to two majority, the Supreme Court reached The *Roe* decision, which was written by Justice Harry Blackmun, a Nixon appointee. *Roe* v. *Wade* established a trimester framework to govern abortion regulations. Almost no regulation at all is permitted during the first trimester of pregnancy; regulations designed to protect the woman's health, but not to further the state's interest in potential life, are permitted during the second trimester; and during the third trimester, when the fetus is viable, prohibitions are permitted provided the life or health of the mother is not at stake.

Looking for Liberty
One of the greatest perks of being president of the United States is that you get to name U.S. Supreme Court justices. In theory, your political views are enshrined for decades as those justices decide cases as you would have them do so. Surprisingly, some justices end up making decisions that are radically different from the way their appointing presidents expected. Justice Blackmun's abortion decision most likely surprised and disappointed President Nixon, a conservative, who put Blackmun on the Court.

In 1992, in a case called *Planned Parenthood* v *Casey*, the Supreme Court moved away from the trimester approach to regulating a woman's legal right to have an abortion and instead took a slightly more conservative stance. Under *Casey*, a woman still had the right to seek an abortion, but states had the power to limit the conditions under which she could obtain that abortion—as long as any limitation did not place an "undue burden" on the woman seeking the abortion.

An enormous amount of litigation followed as women, doctors, and lawyers struggled to determine what an "undue burden" meant. It turned out that, under *Casey*, states could require that doctors perform abortions only in hospitals or clinics (and not their offices), and states could also insist that a woman wait 24 hours between the time she consults a physician and the time she has the abortion. Under *Casey*, a state could also require either parental or court consent for minors seeking an abortion. In short, states had much more power to regulate abortion under *Casey* than they did under *Roe v Wade*.

There is a limit to that power, however. For example, the state of Pennsylvania passed a law requiring spousal notification of an abortion, meaning that any married woman wanting to have an abortion would have to prove that she informed her husband before she underwent the procedure. The Supreme Court invalidated that law in the *Casey* decision on the grounds that it did in fact present an "undue burden" to a woman seeking an abortion.

In many ways, the abortion debate centers on the question of whether a fetus is a "person" and is therefore entitled to the same rights as enjoyed by individuals after birth. Those opposed to abortion bring scientific evidence and religious beliefs to bear, seeking to prove that both science and God view a fetus as a person who deserves equal protection under the law. Those who favor a woman's right to an abortion declare that a fetus, up until viability, is a *potential* human being, but nothing more, and therefore is not deserving of legal protection. In other words, they claim that the choice of a woman to abort a fetus prior to viability is a private matter, and one that should not be regulated by the government. In this

Taking Liberties

There are two basic approaches to constitutional interpretation. One camp, generally the conservative side, looks primarily to the intent of the Founders when it interprets the words of the Constitution. Those in the other camp, generally more liberal, believe that the Constitution is a "living" document, one that is shaped by history and current social and political imperatives.

Taking Liberties

When is a fetus a person? In California, a pregnant woman protested a ticket for driving in the carpool lane. She claimed that her unborn child constituted a second "person" in the car, thus justifying her right to use the carpool lane. (She lost.)

way, the abortion debate concerns not only the rights of the fetus but also the rights of women to choose what happens inside their bodies.

The Debate Continues

As we all know, the language surrounding the abortion debate is heated and emotional. For example, on websites of those who wish to see the elimination of legal abortions, one finds comparisons of abortion providers and Adolf Hitler.

On the websites of those who favor a woman's right to choose, you can find comparisons between a fetus prior to viability and a strand of human hair—after all, both contain the DNA that can lead to the creation of a human being, in one case, by growing in the womb, and in the other case, by cloning in a laboratory. Yet, no one would think to extend the definition of "human being" to a strand of hair containing human DNA, despite the potentiality of the DNA on that strand of hair to become a human being.

Those opposed to abortion often cite the fact that the *Roe* v. *Wade* decision passed by a seven to two majority—the exact same majority on the Supreme Court that passed the Dred Scott decision, which essentially legitimized slavery in the mid-nineteenth century. Just as Dred Scott was wrong, so *Roe* v. *Wade* is wrong, they argue, and they expect the United States to overturn Roe entirely for moral reasons.

The Future of Abortion

The *Roe* and *Casey* decisions remain lightening rods in our political and social life, particularly in presidential elections. Indeed, one of the most striking aspects of the highly unusual confirmation hearings for Justice Clarence Thomas during the administration of President George H. W. Bush was the fact that he claimed that he had never discussed *Roe* v. *Wade* with anyone. It seemed unlikely that an individual involved in the court system at such a high level as Justice Thomas would never have discussed such a subject, even with friends. That revelation touched off a firestorm of debate about Thomas's suitability for a position on the high court. In 1992, presidential candidate Bill Clinton promised that, if elected, he would only nominate to the Supreme Court individuals who were clearly pro-choice.

In any event, even if the Court reversed *Roe* v. *Wade* and denied a women's right to an abortion, the fight would not necessarily be over. The debate would no doubt shift to the role of Congress, which has the power to pass a law specifying a woman's right to choose. Congress would rather not have to deal with this most delicate and emotional of social issues, but if *Roe* and its progeny were overturned at the Supreme Court, it is almost certain that Congress and state legislatures would have to take up the abortion debate, either in terms of federal or state law or in terms of a new constitutional amendment regarding abortion and a woman's right to choose. For now, at least, abortion is a question that, in America, will not go away.

Statutes of Liberties

Today, the future of *Roe* v *Wade*—or what remains of it after *Casey*—is very much in doubt. It's very hard to predict what sort of Supreme Court justices President George W. Bush would nominate, should any vacancies arise. There is still on the court a solid four votes to overturn *Roe* v. *Wade* (Justices Rehnquist, O'Connor, Scalia, and Thomas). Should any of the other five justices step down for any reason, it remains to be seen whether President Bush would make the abortion question a litmus test for nomination to the highest court.

Same-Sex Marriage and Civil Unions

In today's American society, gays and lesbians do not enjoy many of the rights that heterosexuals take for granted. First and foremost of the fundamental civil liberties denied homosexuals is the right to marry. It seems so obvious, and yet the freedom to marry is a civil liberty that the courts have only guaranteed for less than half a century. In the 1967 case, so aptly named *Loving* v. *Virginia*, a mixed race couple challenged Virginia's antimiscegenation statute, which forbade individuals of different races to marry one another. Seventeen states still had such laws on the books when *Loving* become law in 1967. So even the right of heterosexuals to marry has not been absolute for a long period of time.

Why is marriage so important? And why should the government take such an active interest in determining who should and should not get or stay married?

The answer to the question of why marriage is considered so important has its roots in religious history. The Judeo-Christian ethic teaches that marriage between one man and one woman is the basic desire of God and the basic building block of society. (We'll discuss religiously sanctioned marriages involving multiple partners in a later section in this chapter.)

In Western society, governments have traditionally stepped in to enforce the concept of marriage because that tradition holds that marriage creates the possibility for a stable relationship between two people. Under this theory, stable relationships create stable societies. Marriage, so it goes, offers both emotional and economic support to a couple and provides them with an ideal (or, perhaps, just idealized) vehicle for bearing and raising children. We all know of so many marriages that have not lived up to this blissful state. Nevertheless, most people tend to believe that marriage is the optimal state for individuals to grow economically, spiritually, and as members of society (at least until something better comes along).

There are essentially three kinds of potential legal same-sex relationships: marriages, civil unions, and registered domestic partnerships. In the United States today, the third category—registered domestic partnerships—are the most prevalent, and many cities and states across the country permit gay and lesbian couples to register. Such registration affords same-sex couples some of the same rights that heterosexual married couples enjoy, especially with regard to freedom from housing discrimination, spousal job benefits, and other day-to-day issues. It works this way: A couple that registers for domestic partnership status cannot be turned away as potential renters or homebuyers even if the landlord, realtor, or seller does not personally approve of homosexuality.

Legal Dictionary

Civil union—A government-sanctioned relationship similar to marriage in which same-sex partners enjoy certain legal rights like government benefits and housing protection to which married couples are entitled.

The next step up in terms of rights for same-sex couples is the *civil union*. A civil union is like a marriage in many ways, in that a same-sex couple in a civil union is entitled to all the legal benefits of marriage that would be granted to a male-female couple. The biggest difference between civil unions and marriage is that a civil union is recognized only in the state in which it is created. At this point, there is no obligation for other states to recognize the legality of a civil union formed in another state.

This lack of recognition has many implications. For one thing, a couple who moves into a state that does not recognize civil unions would not retain the civil liberties that attach to that union. Second, a couple who breaks up in that state wouldn't need to get a divorce or otherwise legally terminate the first civil union.

Looking for Liberty

The New York Times in mid-2002 announced that it would begin to list civil unions in its section formerly devoted solely to weddings. When The New York Times makes that kind of change, can the rest of the country be far behind?

Another important difference between marriage and civil unions is that there is a host of federal benefits available to married couples that are unavailable to individuals who join in civil unions. For example, Social Security benefits, the right to adopt, and many other important situations are governed by federal rules. Married couples enjoy countless benefits and protections that those in civil unions are denied.

For many in our society, marriage provides a context—a religious and/or moral context—for the act of sex, and that's what makes the debate about homosexual unions complicated. To some, the primary purpose of sex, and indeed of marriage, is procreation and the maintenance of family life as we know it. In fact, marriages can be annulled (or canceled, from a legal point of view) if one of the two parties fails to consummate the marriage, either because of choice or physical limitation.

On the other hand, courts have generally held that marriages involving members of the same sex, whether male or female, are invalid because the possibility for heterosexual sex—and therefore of procreation—does not exist within such a relationship. Courts have also shied away from recognizing the validity of marriages involving transsexuals, declaring that "man-made" sexual apparati do not meet the requirement of the potential for traditional male-female sex and having children.

> **Looking for Liberty**
>
> Quentin Crisp, the author of *The Naked Civil Servant* and other noteworthy books and a well-known speaker on gay lifestyle issues, was once asked whether gays should have equal rights. "What?" he replied, feigning shock. "And be equal to the sad people?"

Hawaii and Vermont

Currently, no state in the United States offers same-sex marriage. A *Wall Street Journal*/NBC News poll determined that two thirds of Americans expect same-sex marriage to be legalized within the next century—but we aren't there yet. There is no state in the union where two individuals of the same sex can apply for a marriage license or be married. Two states, however, have taken strides toward acknowledging the rights of same-sex relationships. They are Hawaii and Vermont.

In 1993, the Hawaii Supreme Court held that the state's ban on same-sex marriage was unconstitutional. The U.S. Constitution, the Supreme Court of Hawaii wrote, contains an "Equal Protection Clause" that states that all individuals are entitled to equal protection—that is to say, equal rights—under the law, and that no individual state can pass a law limiting or denying those equal protections or equal rights.

> **The Law of the Land**
>
> States are required to accept as legally binding the decisions of other states, unless a state's public policy would be violated by the other state's decisions. This is a critical factor in the question of national acceptance of gay marriage and civil unions.

The Hawaii Supreme Court looked to *Loving* v *Virginia*, the case we discussed at the beginning of this section. To the court, the Hawaii legislature had no more right to deny the right of two same-sex people to marry than did the Virginia court to deny that right to people of different races—and for the same reason: It would constitute a breach of the citizens' equal rights.

In 1993, the voters in Hawaii thereupon passed an amendment to the state constitution granting the legislature the right to reserve marriage only to male-female couples. Just when it appeared that Hawaii would be the first state to recognize same-sex marriage, it turned out not to be the case.

Taking Liberties

What's the law? Sometimes, it's what a court decides. If the state legislature doesn't like a court's decision, the legislature can pass a law explicitly overruling that decision. But then individuals can challenge the law, in which case the courts would decide if the law is constitutional! That's why legal experts watch the U.S. Supreme Court so closely, to see what the law *really* is!

The honor of becoming the first state in the union to offer civil union to same-sex couples belongs to Vermont. In 1999, the Vermont Supreme Court declared in *Baker* v. *State of Vermont* that the Constitution of the State of Vermont required the state to treat lesbian and gay couples the same way it treated heterosexual couples. This decision triggered a huge amount of legislative activity in Vermont, resulting in the passage of a law offering civil unions to same-sex couples. In Vermont, these new civil unions provide same-sex couples all the benefits of marriage that state law offered to married Vermont couples.

The rights now afforded same-sex couples in Vermont include the right to adopt, equal rights in housing, the right to equivalent treatment with regard to one's estate, and many more. In Vermont, a couple in a civil union must obtain a divorce in order to legally end the union. The Vermont civil union has both a legal and a ceremonial aspect to it. The legal aspect refers to the rights that Vermonters who enter into same-sex civil unions now enjoy. The ceremonial aspect means that a same-sex couple in Vermont can put on a religious or civil ceremony with the same solemnity (or lack thereof) of a heterosexual marriage.

Vermonters are not the only ones who can enjoy the ceremonial aspects of civil union in that state. Couples from other states can travel to Vermont—and many do—in order to enjoy the ceremonial aspect of Vermont's law. Of course, when they get back to their home states, they are not afforded the same rights that Vermonters living in Vermont enjoy, because no other state has officially recognized the concept of the same-sex civil union. In fact, if a couple from New Jersey were to travel to Vermont and engage in a civil union, upon their return to New Jersey, their relationship could be deemed never to have existed, and they could enter into either marriage with a heterosexual partner or registration with a same-sex partner, without dissolving the Vermont civil union.

Other states do not accept Vermont's civil union simply because they don't have to, and because, at this time, they don't want to. This takes us back to our discussion of "full faith and credit" in the previous chapter.

Under the terms of the Full Faith and Credit Clause, if a couple is declared legally married in one state, then that couple must be considered legally married by all the other 49 states. If a couple is considered divorced by one state, members of that couple can enter into marriages in any of the other 49 states without fear of prosecution for bigamy. That new marriage is considered legally binding in each of the 50 states. (Full faith and credit applies to many more provisions than the questions of marriage and divorce, but we'll just focus on the subject at hand.)

The Future of Same Sex Marriages

After the actions in Hawaii and Vermont, but before any state has legalized same-sex marriages, many other states—35, to be exact—were concerned that a same-sex marriage entered into in one state would have to be considered valid throughout the rest of the country. Between the period of 1995 and the present, these 35 states all passed laws preventing recognition of out-of-state, same-sex marriage licenses. However, some states abstained from passing such legislation. This inaction doesn't mean that these states accept same-sex marriages, but that they simply have not passed laws that declare they will refuse to recognize same-sex marriages performed in other states. Is it valid for states to pass laws preventing the recognition of out-of-state, same-sex marriage licenses? Until an actual same-sex marriage license is issued somewhere in the United States by a state government, the couple moves to another state and challenges the second state's law, and then brings that case before the Supreme Court, which decides to hear it, we cannot say for sure. As discussed in Chapter 4, no court, not even the U.S. Supreme Court, can declare a law unconstitutional ad hoc. There has to be an actual court case with actual litigants who have an actual stake in the outcome in order for the U.S. Supreme Court to declare the constitutionality or unconstitutionality of a given law.

Recently, the U.S. Congress passed a "Defense of Marriage Act." In theory, this law gives states the power to declare same-sex marriages from other states illegal. In point of fact, the Defense of Marriage Act is most likely unconstitutional; Congress does not have the authority to pass a law overriding the Full Faith and Credit Act. Congress can only change the Constitution by passing an amendment, which would then have to be ratified by the states. Congress cannot simply take one part of the

Constitution that it doesn't like and declare it null and void. That's just not how the game works.

It's entirely possible that congressional leaders knew, even as they were drafting and passing the law, that it would never be considered constitutional. It may have been passed simply as a means of placating conservative voters and campaign contributors. Since there are no same-sex marriage licenses issued in this country at this time, and thus no opportunity for a legal challenge to the federal Defense of Marriage Act to develop, the law stays on the books. On January 1, 2002, California became the second state (after Vermont) in the United States to offer same-sex registration or civil unions. Outside the United States, only the Netherlands, a traditionally liberal society, offers equal marriage rights to gays and lesbians. Denmark, France, Iceland, Norway, and Sweden offer equivalents of civil unions. Some cities in France and Spain offer partnership registration, but there is no semblance of marriage or even civil union rights as a result of those registration options.

Statutes of Liberties

Bigamy is the state of being married to more than one person. Polygamy is the state of having multiple marriage partners at the same time. In the comedy classic *A Night at the Opera*, Groucho Marx asks a woman if she would marry him. She explains that she couldn't because she is already married, and it would be bigamy. "It's big o' me, too," Groucho tells her with a leer. It may be big of you, but bigamy is against the law in these United States. Alaska, California, Florida, Georgia, Indiana, Kansas, Minnesota, Missouri, New York, Texas, Utah, Washington, and Wyoming all make bigamy a criminal offense.

In sum, is same-sex marriage a civil liberty? Not at this time. As society recognizes the fact that there are an estimated 20 million lesbians and gays in the United States, and that six to 14 million children are living in gay or lesbian households, social attitudes towards same-sex marriage may change. There may come a time when states issue same-sex marriage licenses and afford gays and lesbians the same rights that heterosexual couples already enjoy. For the time being, the reality is that same-sex marriage still appears to be a long way off.

Dubious Liaisons

More and more states have taken their *sodomy* laws off the books after their state Supreme Courts have found them to be unconstitutional invasions of privacy. These laws, generally passed in the nineteenth century, prohibited "unnatural" sex, specifically oral and anal sex, as well as bestiality. In general, the government no longer feels a sense of responsibility to monitor the sexual practices of their citizens or even to determine which sexual practices are acceptable. There are certain exceptions, of course; children are a protected class, and sex with a minor is a crime in every state of the union.

The move to overturn sodomy statutes began in Illinois in 1962. Since then, 27 other states have followed suit and have decriminalized many sexual practices, except those involving minors or those involving prostitution. The state Supreme Courts of four states—Georgia, Kentucky, Montana, and Tennessee—have declared their state sodomy laws unconstitutional, and courts in seven other states—Arkansas, Louisiana, Maryland, Massachusetts, Michigan, Minnesota, and Texas—have recently seen judicial decisions either striking down particular sodomy laws or calling for an end to their enforcement.

Legal Dictionary

Sodomy—The term "sodomy" comes from the biblical story of the cities of the plain, Sodom and Gomorrah. According to biblical commentators, the men of the city of Sodom practiced homosexuality, and for that behavior, the city was destroyed. The term has since acquired a broader connotation, including anal intercourse, bestiality, and oral sex.

In 18 states, sodomy laws still remain on the books, although whether they are enforced is a matter of speculation. Penalties for violating sodomy statutes, held misdemeanors in some states and felonies in others, range from 60 days in prison and a 500-dollar fine in Florida, to life in prison in Idaho. Make your travel plans accordingly.

Your Right to Die

The question of assisted suicide is deeply profound and troubling, and like abortion, it will not go away quickly. Also, like abortion, it is the subject of an important U.S. Supreme Court decision which has essentially set the tone for legislation regarding the topic. In a 1997 case, the Supreme Court unanimously upheld decisions in two states—New York and Washington—that criminalized assisted suicide. In other words, in those two states, the state legislatures passed laws making it a criminal offense for a doctor (or anyone else) to assist someone with his or her suicide. The constitutionality of those statutes was called into question by those who favor the controversial practice. The Supreme Court ruled that individual states do have the right to pass laws making it a criminal offense to assist someone with his or her suicide.

Today, dozens of states have followed the actions of New York and Washington states and have passed legislation making assisted suicide illegal. Only one state in the

United States permits physician-assisted suicide. That is Oregon. The Oregon law says that a doctor may prescribe—but not administer—a lethal dose of medication to a patient with less than six months to live. In addition, two doctors must agree that the patient is mentally competent (able to understand the consequences of this momentous decision) and is acting voluntarily.

Taking Liberties

The most famous individual associated with assisted suicide is, of course, Dr. Jack Kevorkian, who was convicted in Michigan on charges related to assisted suicide.

It is worth noting that suicide itself is not against the law, although it is deeply abhorrent to most thinkers in the Western tradition. Some suicide help-lines go by the philosophy that every attempted suicide is actually a cry for help. As the philosopher Milton Dicus once put it, "The reason people scream when they jump off bridges and buildings is because they have changed their minds." If suicide itself is a legal, if controversial, practice—one condemned by many—why is it illegal in all but one state to assist someone with the ending of his or her own life?

For the answer, we can look to that 1997 Supreme Court decision. Chief Justice William Rehnquist wrote:

> The state has an interest in protecting the poor, the elderly, and the disabled persons. The lives of disabled and elderly must be no less valuable than the lives of the young and the healthy .... The difficulty in defining terminal illness and the risk that a dying patient's request for assistance in ending his or her life might not be truly voluntary justifies the prohibitions on assisted suicide we uphold here.

In other words, the Supreme Court was concerned that the weak and the ill could be coerced into ending their lives, and therefore it is the public policy of the United States to prevent such scenarios from happening. The American Medical Association filed a "friend of the court" brief in this same case, along with 51 other medical groups. The doctors wrote that there is a critical distinction between refusing life-sustaining treatment, which is permissible, and taking active steps to end life. In sum, in all states except Oregon, the individual does have the right to take his or her own life, and an individual has the right to refuse life-sustaining treatment. But "mercy killing," no matter how merciful it may appear to the dying person or his or her loved ones, is still considered killing in the eyes of the law.

The Least You Need to Know

- The future of abortion in America remains uncertain and hinges on new additions in the U.S. Supreme Court.

- The courts in a few states are beginning to accept the concept of civil unions for gays and lesbians.

- While sex with a minor is a crime in every state of the union, states have removed many laws that today are considered to violate the privacy of the individual.

- Only Oregon permits assisted suicide; it is illegal in all other states.

Cyber-Privacy:
Who's Watching You?

In This Chapter

◆ Internet privacy

◆ Narrow-casting = narrow minds?

◆ How far will it go?

◆ Protecting your children

James Bond was an amateur.

If you attended the January 2001 Super Bowl in Tampa, Florida, I hope you were smiling as you entered the stadium. That's because, unbeknownst to you and everybody else coming to see the game, all attendees were surreptitiously photographed by law enforcement authorities. Those photographs were immediately scanned by computer and compared to the faces of known terrorists and other unsavory types. The government was thus able to figure out who, if anyone, might threaten the safety of the spectators and participants at the Super Bowl. Keep in mind that this event took place *eight months* prior to the September 11 attacks!

In this chapter, we'll discuss the impact that computer technology has upon our civil liberties.

Smile—You're on Cyber Camera!

Technology, particularly computer technology, has gotten pretty sophisticated. As we'll see, the government, police, hackers, employees of Internet service providers, and anybody with a credit card can hire a snoop to trace virtually every move you make on the Internet. They can read your e-mail, see what websites you frequent, check what newsgroups you belong to or post to, and even see where and when you shop. Sure, you might be logging on in the privacy of your own home, but if you think you've got any privacy once you send or read e-mail or surf the net, we've got a virtual bridge we'd like to sell you.

The new FBI e-mail surveillance program, Carnivore, which allows the FBI to monitor all of the e-mail sent by you and everyone else in the country—and probably the world. And what Carnivore doesn't capture, Echelon will. This program, reportedly developed by the National Security Agency—the official code maker and code breaker for the U.S. intelligence community—can monitor Internet traffic all over the globe.

Taking Liberties

Keep in mind that the Internet wasn't created with privacy as a goal. Its original purpose was to allow the military, and then scientists, to share information, not to keep their identities private.

In theory, the government—whether we're talking the about FBI, the CIA, the NSA, or your local constabulary—needs a warrant in order to monitor your e-mail or search through e-mail you've sent or received. But, in fact, privacy concerns have not completely caught up with the government's ability to watch you as you voyage through cyberspace. Do I sound paranoid? Well, as former Secretary of State Henry Kissinger so aptly put it, "Even a paranoid has real enemies."

How exactly do Carnivore and Echelon work? This information is not entirely in the public domain, but we'll give it our best shot. The FBI's Carnivore software requires a court order for its use. If the court agrees with the FBI that a particular individual may be committing crimes, agents will install special equipment on computers of the suspect's Internet service provider, such as America Online and EarthLink. Carnivore software intercepts all the Internet activity of the person the agency is investigating, including e-mail, website visits, chats, everything. Carnivore then has ways of determining which of the messages or website visits relate to potential criminal activity. That's all we know. Unlike Carnivore, the National Security Agency's system,

Echelon, reportedly does search for key words in e-mail letters that may indicate terrorism or criminal intent.

The September 11, 2001, attacks on America instantaneously changed the way many Americans feel about Internet privacy. On September 10, 2001, most people had probably never given the concept much thought. To the extent that people did worry about such things, their concerns centered on the safety of giving out credit card information over the web and, perhaps, whether or not anyone could tell that they were visiting porn sites.

A day later, everything changed. In the post-September-11 environment, most Americans would be happy to know that the government has a means of tracing e-mail among potential terrorists. In times of national security crises, we are frequently willing to trade off a great deal of privacy for a measure of security. But how much privacy do we really have on the Internet, and how quick should we be to relinquish it?

> ### Looking for Liberty
>
> "Freedom of thought and the right of private judgment in matters of conscience, driven from every corner of the earth, direct their course to this happy country."
> —Samuel Adams

Even before September 11, 2001, many Americans were concerned about the amount of supposedly private information the Internet contains. According to attorney Anthony Rollo, speaking at a Practicing Law Institute conference on consumer privacy in spring 2002:

> The Internet is the most effective, systematic gatherer of personal information ever known. As a consumer casually browses the Internet, every electronic move leaves a footprint that may be tracked and recorded on multiple databases for all eternity.

What sort of information does the Internet track and trace? How about this: first and last name. Past and present addresses. E-mail addresses. Telephone number. Social Security Number. Gender. Birth date. Household income. Financial and credit account data. Medical information. Purchasing history. Rollo adds that when computers are capable of creating and generating electronic signatures, analogous to the way we sign checks and legal documents, Internet commerce will explode.

How bad is it? Really bad. The total lack of privacy that consumers have on the Internet seems so unreal that when you learn about it, you think you're watching a bad science fiction/horror film, except it's all true. Here are some examples from Anthony Rollo of just how bad it is out there:

◆ On one occasion in the late 1990s, the Social Security Administration accidentally posted all of America's Social Security information online. Abuse of the Social Security system soared.

◆ A hacker, or individual adept at breaking into computer systems, got inside the client list of CD Universe, a music seller on the web. The hacker stole the names, addresses, and credit card information for 300,000 online customers, and demanded a 100,000 dollar ransom in exchange for not posting that credit card information on the web. The company wouldn't pay, and the hacker, true to his word, posted the credit card information and personal data of all 300,000 people. The FBI quickly shut down his website, but it was up there for a while.

◆ In February 2000, a programming bug on the H&R Block website made private tax information of its customers available to other customers. In other words, if you had filed your taxes electronically through H&R Block, other H&R Block customers could see how much you made, how much you received in alimony or child support, how much you gave to charity, and how much you paid in taxes. They fixed it, of course.

Legal Dictionary

Identity theft—A crime in which an individual steals your personal data in order to get credit cards, Social Security benefits, or a host of other things in your name.

◆ In 2001, there were 300,000 cases of *identity thefts*.

The Fascinating You

What makes you so fascinating to businesses? In a word, money. The Internet, as we have seen, is the world's easiest consumer information-gathering tool ever. For business owners, the most frustrating thing about advertising is that it's been impossible to target the specific consumers who are most likely to buy. Sure, Honda can send out postcards to its former customers, but how could they possibly know whether any given customer wants to buy a new car at this time, can afford to buy a new car at this time, or even still lives at the same address? That's why companies are so excited about using the Internet to learn everything about what you like to buy, when you like to buy it, and how you like to buy it, so they can *"narrow-cast,"* or narrowly targeting, their marketing efforts directly at you.

Legal Dictionary

Narrow-casting—Advertising to the smallest market segment likely to purchase a product.

Most consumers actually don't mind that sort of selling, a fact that plays into the hands of businesses.

Ever go to Amazon.com? If you pick out a particular book to buy, Amazon will recommend books that have been purchased by individuals who bought the same book you did. That's an example of narrow-casting a marketing message. Similarly, if you have ever shopped on e-Bay, you will be invited to visit the other auctions conducted by the same seller from whom you are seeking to buy. The theory is that if you like the game-worn Mets baseball cap, you'll also be interested in a game-worn Phillies jersey the same seller is offering. Many consumers like the idea of getting information so neatly tailored to their own interests. The problem is that the cost of such e-tailing, or Internet commerce, is your privacy.

Privacy for Sale

There are two ways to approach the entire issue of privacy. In Europe, the overriding approach is to consider privacy an absolute, fundamental human right. It therefore becomes the responsibility of the government to protect the right of online privacy of individuals and consumers. The other approach, the one predominantly followed in the United States, is to treat privacy as a commodity, something that the consumer can barter away for an item he or she considers valuable.

Here's an example of how to understand the concept of privacy as a commodity. Have you ever gone to a store and bought something, and at the end of the transaction, the salesperson said, "Would you like to receive news of future sales events via e-mail?" In that situation, which is fairly common, you're being offered the right to trade, or barter away, your Internet privacy in exchange for something you consider valuable. If the idea of e-mail notification about future sales sounds like a good idea to you, you can provide your e-mail address. If you don't want to be contacted via e-mail, you can say no. In other words, your privacy is a commodity, and it's up to you whether to keep it or sell it.

What happens once the store has captured your e-mail address? Will they keep it in a vault, hidden away from all prying eyes? Or will they sell that list of consumers interested in a given product to anyone else in the marketplace? The fact is, once you give your e-mail address to a business, say a baby store, it becomes—like your home address and any other information the baby store can retrieve about you—a valuable commodity in the hands of this baby store. They can sell your e-mail

Taking Liberties

One key question in online privacy is whether you have to "opt out" of the practice of renting or selling your e-mail address to other marketers, or whether you should have the right to "opt in" and only let your name be sold with your express permission.

address, along with the tens of thousands of other e-mail addresses they collect, to other businesses. What kind of businesses would be interested? How about publishers of baby-related magazines? Pediatricians? Grocers (who sell baby food, and would like to sell some to you)?

Once those other companies buy your name, what's to stop them from reselling them to other companies? One business tells another business, and then another business tells another business … and before you know it, everybody in the world, including, potentially, bad guys who like to break into the houses of families where there are babies, know all about you. So the next time someone offers some "free notification via e-mail," we suggest strongly that you keep your e-mail address to yourself.

ROM, but You Can't Hide

Giving someone your e-mail address is one thing—although you may not be able to control who ends up with access to it, you've only provided a way for whoever has it to send you mail.

But other actions that occur online are far more insidious. The truth is, technology now allows businesses, the government, hackers, and other assorted folks to determine your identity while you're online, without your permission or knowledge. What technology do they use in order to breach your privacy?

> **Statutes of Liberties**
>
> Your boss has a legal right to read the e-mail you send and receive at work through your work-related e-mail account. At the same time, your boss cannot usurp your password and then log in and access your private e-mail from an anonymous internet account (like Yahoo).

Everything starts with your IP (internet protocol) address, which is a number that you probably don't know and that typically looks like this: 137.45.219.171. These numbers act as the equivalent of your telephone number or license plate on the Internet. Sure, you may be known as toughguy@leavemealone.com, but that's just an easy way for you to be quickly identified. Imagine if you had to tell everybody a random 12-digit number in order for them to send you an e-mail to your home, and another 12-digit number for your office, and yet another for your e-mail-enabled PDA. Yikes!

Most of us spend at least a little bit of time trying to figure out really cool e-mail addresses for ourselves, or we are assigned e-mail addresses that are intuitive and easy to remember, such as JoeSmith@company.com. That makes a great deal of sense. But on the Internet, you have another identity, fixed and unchangeable for as long as you keep your e-mail address, and that is your IP address. Your IP address doesn't change, and it's left behind on almost everything you touch on the Internet.

Every time you do anything online, whether it's visiting a website, sending or receiving e-mail, or visiting a chat room, your IP address is stamped on that transaction. If you read or post anything on a newsgroup, your IP address goes with you. If you visit a website that has ads (and virtually every business or entertainment website has ads today), your IP gets transmitted to those third parties who actually put the ads on those pages. If you want to see exactly how, in technical terms, your IP address can be used to trace your identity, visit http:// consumer. net/IPpaper.asp. What does an IP address tell about you? It answers the following questions: What kind of computer are you using? How big is your screen? Where are you? And most important of all, who are you?

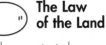

The Law of the Land

"The greatest dangers to liberty lurk in insidious encroachment by men of zeal, well-meaning but without understanding."

—Justice Louis D. Brandeis

So your IP address reveals more about you than you may realize.

Who Wants a Cookie?!

Then there's the trouble with cookies—and I don't mean the hip-widening, chocolate chip variety. There's another kind of cookie, and you don't keep it in your kitchen. This cookie lives in your computer, whether you know it or not, unless you choose to erase them.

Computer cookies are actually small strings of computer code deposited on your computer by pretty much every website you visit. Cookies help companies keep track of which sites you have visited, passwords (if necessary to navigate to that website), the kind of computer and browser you use, and even your credit card information. Ever wonder how Amazon knows it's you? It's because they deposited a cookie on your computer. Some cookies can not only tell who you are and what you're doing as you visit a particular website, but they can even read each other

You really have to wonder whether the computer that you bought is there to help you—or is there to help the many businesses in the world who want to sell *to you*. The data that these cookies collect—and can read about each other—can be sold to any marketer interested in someone like you. Then your data can be resold, and resold, and resold.

Let's say that you purchase things from an online retailer. In that case, your name, address, phone number, and credit card information is likely to be stored in one of those cookies. It's not very hard at all for a savvy cookie-reader to figure out who you are and to compose an accurate portrait of what you do on the web—with your name attached. Internet privacy? Fuggedaboudit.

Taking Liberties

Cookies can tell who you are and what you're doing as you visit a particular website, and some cookies can even read each other. So if you visit websitex. com, the site will deposit a cookie on your computer. A company called Websitex.com places a cookie on your computer that can actually read all the other cookies on your computer. Thus it can form a fairly broad—and accurate— picture of what you like to do online.

Orwell Had It Good

Your computer has many ways of telling the world who you are. Right now, let's look at two more ways the Internet deprives you of privacy. The first is web bugs and the second is log files. A web bug is an invisible bug, or string of code, placed on e-mail and websites. A web bug tells the sender of an e-mail or the owner of a website that someone operating that computer, has either read the e-mail or visited the website. Barnes & Noble and Microsoft, among others, use web bugs to determine whether you have read marketing e-mail they send you.

It gets creepier. When you visit a website, a fascinating doohickey (no, that's not the technical term) called a "log file" keeps track of who you are, what you did at the website, and when you did it. There are actually companies that produce log file readers that sort through the tons of information you unknowingly provide a website. The readers can then identify you—by name. George Orwell was good, but he could never have come up with this.

Where is all of this Internet technology heading? In a word, convergence. Convergence is a telecom industry buzzword meaning that voice communication (your telephone calls), e-mail, and web surfing will all happen via one device. There are already early forms of convergence out there, but in just a few short years, it is entirely likely that absolutely everyone will be getting their e-mail, surfing the web, and using the telephone from a single handheld device. What does this mean in terms of privacy? A lot.

> **Looking for Liberty**
>
> "We defend and we build a way of life, not for America alone, but for all mankind."
>
> —Franklin Delano Roosevelt

During the rescue efforts immediately following the September 11, 2001, attacks on the World Trade Center and the Pentagon, police and fire units used the global positioning information given off by cell phones to identify where people were in the collapsing structures. Yes, your cell phone actually emits information allowing those with the proper technology to figure out where your phone is. So as we move into a world of complete voice and data convergence, where you and everyone else are doing all your communications work (voice, data, e-mail, Internet, everything) on a single, handheld device, not only will marketers know what you're doing they'll know where you're equipment is and, therefore, where you are when you're using it. If you're really interested in privacy, move to Borneo, get rid of your e-mail provider and don't make any collect calls.

By now you might have guessed that surfing the web at work is not just a bad idea, it's a Really Bad Idea. The courts have held that you have no reasonable expectation of privacy when it comes to using the Internet or sending e-mail at work. Over one third of all businesses today monitor their employees' use of e-mail and the Internet. If you're downloading naughty pictures during your coffee break, they know.

Furthermore, businesses are often the target of anonymous negative postings, or *flames*. There are a wealth of fascinating sites on the web on which individuals can "anonymously" offer their thoughts about what it's like to work for a given company and flame away their frustrations. I put the word "anonymously" in quotes because your anonymity is far from guaranteed. If a business wants to track down who's been saying all those scurrilous things about them, they can either use some of the tools we have already discussed or go to court to find out from which computer the offending e-mail was sent.

Legal Dictionary

Flame—To criticize someone's online posting, often in vituperative terms.

Lynn Chuang Kramer, writing in the *Texas International Law Journal* in Spring 2002, writes that businesses are increasingly using courts and the legal system as detectives to determine who their anonymous critics are. The legal term is "piercing the veil of anonymity." Businesses are going to court, claiming that they are being defamed, or wrongly criticized, by these anonymous individuals. But is it defamation that they're seeking to stop, an attorney asks in a *New York Times* article ("Questions On Net Anonymity," October 17, 2000), or are businesses merely seeking to intimidate those who would criticize them?

Solutions for Cyberspace

To date, the U.S. government has largely relied on self-regulation by the private sector to protect the privacy of consumers, which is a little like the virtual fox guarding a virtual chicken coop. Yes, Congress has passed and presidents have signed into law bills that purportedly protect your online privacy, but they are often window dressing or they fail to keep up with the brilliant ways in which businesses can glean your private information. Also, keep in mind that tax dollars may run the government, but lobbyist dollars keep Congress running smoothly. Even though countless Internet privacy-protecting bills are introduced in the U.S. Senate and House of Representatives each year, many deceptively protect the ability of companies to continue getting your information.

Actually, the government is often just as interested in your online secrets as is business. First government investigators can lurk, or monitor activity in online chat rooms, without a warrant. If the government wants to see what e-mail is stored on your computer, and has probable cause for doing so, it can get a warrant. Searching through your stored (or even deleted) e-mail is no different than searching through a desk drawer—all in a day's work for investigators. If they want to intercept e-mail that you are sending and receiving, that does require a higher standard of proof that you are up to nefarious deeds. And the USA-Patriot Act, passed in the weeks following the September 11, 2001, attacks, relaxed standards for law enforcement officials seeking to monitor or intercept e-mail and other forms of communication.

Taking Liberties

A parent who sets up a computer with Internet access in a child's bedroom is begging for trouble. Porn, perverts lurking in chatrooms, and violations of your child's privacy (name, address, phone, etc.) await!

On the one hand, the government has left to business the issue of regulating privacy violations, which is a bit of a joke. On the other hand, the government itself will follow you online if it thinks you're doing things you shouldn't be doing. And everything that we've discussed so far assumes that your personal information, which others are obtaining without your knowledge or permission, is accurate!

> When every financial transaction that a consumer makes is being compiled, manipulated, analyzed, and re-analyzed, the chances for mistakes increase. What happens to the consumer who gets tagged with the wrong information and, as a result, cannot get the mortgage rate or healthcare that he wants or, even worse, is never able to correct the wrong information? What happens when the misinformation is not misinformation at all, but a case of identity theft perpetrated by hackers?
>
> —Lynn Chuang Kramer, "Private Eyes Are Watching You: Consumer Online Privacy Protection—Lessons From Home And Abroad," Comment, *Texas International Law Journal*, Spring 2002.

What Can You Do?

Short of going offline forever, there are some steps you can take in order to protect your privacy online, since the government is in no hurry to do so. I want to recommend two websites to you. The first is www.privacy.net. This outstanding site, offered by Consumer.net, offers a wide range of information about how to protect yourself online. You can find out how to "opt out" or have your personal information removed from databases and lists sold for marketing or other reasons. Every time you apply for a credit card, telephone service, or home loan; enter a contest; or even register your car or get a driver's license, your information becomes available to anyone who wants to pay for it. You can learn how to get off these lists at privacy.net. Privacy.net also offers you a fascinating—and free—tool. When you visit their site, click on "Analyze Your Connection," and you will see exactly how information about you and your computer is transmitted every time you do anything online. There is a host of other fascinating information here, and I cannot say enough good about this site.

The other site to visit is www.russkelly.com. This site offers a wide range of information about what you can do to limit what's known about you and what information you spread, often inadvertently, every time you go online. Russkelly.com provides a variety of private and government information sources about Internet privacy, most of which are free and some of which you have to pay for. It's definitely worth checking out.

Protecting Your Child

Children are especially vulnerable in cyberspace, for a number of reasons. First they often lack the experience that adults have in fending off marketing messages. (Although, when you look around at our consumer society, it would appear that adults aren't too good at that, either.) The Internet is a phenomenal marketing tool, especially for young and vulnerable cybersurfers. Collection of children's personal data is an enormous problem on the web.

Websites draw information from children in ways both overt and covert. The obvious method is to have kids register as part of fan clubs or interest groups/Federal law today prohibits businesses from collecting information from children without explicit parental consent, but the sophisticated, Internet-savvy child can easily defeat those safeguards. (Or they can find a more Internet-savvy friend to show them how.) Although it is illegal, as we have seen, businesses that market to children sometimes imbed technology in their websites that draw personal identification information from the child's computer to the company without knowledge of the child or the parent.

Looking for Liberty

Yes, your federal government is a leader of liberty. In 2002, the Federal Trade Commission forced Eli Lilly, a drug manufacturer, to cease releasing over the Internet the names and e-mail addresses of more than 600 users of Prozac. (Just one more thing for them to worry about!)

The Internet provides everyone, even children, with access to inappropriate material, such as pornographic websites. Despite the many methods implemented by well-meaning companies to protect our kids, there are still loopholes that allow them access to sites with names that would make even Larry Flynt blush.

Legal Dictionary

Blocking software—
Software programs to allow parents or others to deny access to certain types of websites, such as porn sites or hate sites. Unfortunately, kids are generally far more web-savvy than their parents—and usually can figure out how to disable such software or find sites that aren't blocked.

There exists several means of blocking your child's access to online pornography and other inappropriate material. Unfortunately, none of them is fool-proof. Sites such as Net Nanny or Cyber Sitter provide (for a fee) software that theoretically blocks your children's access to pornography. I say "theoretically" because there are far more porn sites than can be found on even up-to-date lists of antiporn *blocking software* programs. Also, an astute young cybersurfer can find ways to defeat or even uninstall porn-blocking software.

Another problem with porn-blocking software is that it can also block access to legitimate sites that share particular key words with porn sites. For example, the word "breast" on a website could trigger a violation and shutdown of the Internet browser, whether the individual using the computer is seeking to look at porn or seeking information on breast cancer. Porn-blocking software will in fact block 70 to 80 percent of the pornography available on the web, but that still leaves plenty of inappropriate material for your kids to find.

Chatrooms are by far the most popular place for kids to go online, but they also provide an environment ripe for harassment. In a chatroom, a child (or an adult) can have a discussion with two dozen (in some cases, more) individuals who share a particular affinity or interest. There are chat rooms to discuss every conceivable issue, from aviation to zoology. For adults, there are chatrooms for gays, single parents, people suffering from Parkinson's disease—you name it. At any time of the day or night, there are people online conducting a discussion about that issue or topic.

Kids just love chatrooms—no two ways about it. The problem is that just as children behave inappropriately in the real world, so they do in the online sphere. For example, children occasionally use foul, coarse, or otherwise inappropriate language with other children in their communications. They may ask children for passwords or other personal information. Worst of all, adults masquerading as children can come into chatrooms, looking to strike up conversations with children and perhaps even lure them to sexual encounters. If you discover that your child is being harassed or is the subject of inappropriate advances, report that information to your service provider. The service provider is then responsible for cutting off Internet service to the offending party.

When you take together these three problems—exposure of private information, access to inappropriate materials, and inappropriate behavior in chatrooms—the Internet is clearly an uncontrolled playground when it comes to children's safety. The only adequate form of control that a parent can have over a child's experience online is to be present whenever the child uses the computer. Experts suggest not keeping computers in children's bedrooms but instead in the family room or den. If you don't want your kids to be accessing the Internet in ways of which you might not approve, and if you do not want businesses or perverts trying to learn about your children, your best option is to password-protect your computer and keep the password secret from your kids.

When your author was growing up in the 1960s, the only real threats to children in the form of home entertainment were soap operas and *The Newlywed Game*. Today, it's a whole new ballgame. The information superhighway can actually be a sewer line into your children's playroom, unless you are willing to take the time and trouble to insure otherwise.

> **Statutes of Liberties**
>
> Worried that your cable operator might be selling information about you and your viewing preferences? The Cable TV Privacy Act of 1984 forbids such practices. But who trusts the cable TV industry?

The Least You Need to Know

- The government has ways of monitoring the Internet activities of anyone in the world.

- Technology has made it possible for businesses to "narrow-cast" their advertising.

- Every move you make on the Internet is tracked and very easily found out by other sites.

- The best way to protect your children online is to monitor their Internet access and keep the computer in the living room.

Chapter 7

Let's Talk About Sex

In This Chapter

- Prostitution
- Obscenity vs. pornography
- Privacy in the bedroom
- Internet porn

The law has had a lot to say about sex: who can have it, under what circumstances, what kind, who can watch, whether it can be paid for, and whether you're entitled to do whatever you want in the privacy of your own home. Is the right to enjoy sex a civil liberty? Not really. There are still many limits to your rights in this private area, even in an era of almost unparalleled sexual freedom. In this chapter, we'll examine the limits the law places on having sex, paying for it, and viewing it online.

As you'll see, how the law affects the sexual lives of Americans is often complicated. Prostitution is still illegal in most of the nation, for instance, although it flourishes in virtually every city. The line between obscenity and pornography is as difficult as ever to draw. Although sodomy laws remain on the books in many states, you are largely free to do whatever you want—sexually speaking—with any other consenting adult in your own bedroom, but that's been true for less than 40 years. And when you sneak a peek at online porn sites, it's laughably easy for many, many people to be watching you click away. How do they do it? Read on.

The First Profession

A debate that won't go away is the subject of whether prostitution should be decriminalized. Although it's unlikely that it'll ever be legal to be a prostitute or to hire one, the issue remains at the forefront because it touches on so many flashpoints for society—the question of choices about sex, medical issues, police issues, issues about socioeconomic level, violence … it's all here.

Spying is commonly referred to as "the second oldest profession." You can take a wild guess as to what the very *oldest* profession is. You can find references to prostitution in the book of Genesis and in the frescoes in the ruins at Pompeii. Prostitution has always been with us and it's not likely to ever disappear; the question is whether and to what extent society should regulate it. Although it's not technically a civil liberties issue because it relates to private, consensual behavior among adults, it does provide some interesting subjects of debate.

> **Statutes of Liberties**
>
> The same impetus that led to the criminalization of prostitution also led to the Pure Food and Drug Act, which required manufacturers of food to produce pure, wholesome products; it could be argued that the antitrust laws which sought to clean up big business a century ago were also an outgrowth of that same desire to clean up society.

Prostitution remains illegal in all but a few Nevada counties because it is considered a threat to family life, because of a fear of the spreading of venereal diseases and HIV, because (some believe) it victimizes women, and because on a societal level, we don't believe in the concept of paying for sex.

And yet, if you open the Yellow Pages of virtually any moderate-sized city in America, you will find advertisements for escort services—but most of these companies offer far more than a casual dinner date. "Escort" is a common euphemism for "prostitute," but for the most part, the police turn a blind eye to this thinly veiled form of organized prostitution. In addition, streetwalkers ply their trade on the streets of most cities in the United States, often with a similar tolerance from law enforcement. How much of that tolerance is due to police corruption remains an equally compelling debate.

Proponents of the decriminalization of prostitution argue that it is a "victimless crime," that no one is forced to use the services of a prostitute or to become a prostitute and that no one is hurt in the process. In addition, they argue that the cost of monitoring prostitutes is extremely high for police departments, and actually opens police officers to a source of corruption and temptation that would not exist were prostitution legal. If prostitution was legal, the government would also have better control over public health issues, such as the monitoring and testing for sexually transmitted diseases like HIV.

Those opposed to the decriminalization of prostitution say that there are indeed victims when prostitution is allowed to flourish. Women and men, sometimes as minors, may be forced into lives of prostitution simply because they have no other means of paying their bills or supporting their families. Illegal drug use and addiction are common partners to prostitution, forming a vicious cycle of abuse and crime.

Moral as well as legal issues arise. Some people feel that the availability of sex for money degrades family life and degrades the men and women who pay for sex. Communities suffer when prostitutes parade themselves at particular street corners or in certain neighborhoods where families with children live.

Taking Liberties

The problem with legalizing prostitution is that there really is no current successful model in the United States. Nevada's experience doesn't provide enough clarity for other states.

Opponents of the legalization of prostitution point to the counties in Nevada where state-chartered brothels have existed for some time. The deeper you peer into the lives of the women who work in those brothels, opponents say, the less appealing the life there appears. Because Nevada permits prostitution only in those counties, there are very few places where women can work legally. The women in these brothels have very little freedom to set their own working hours or to turn down clients who are drunk or otherwise undesirable. Also, they are required to hand over half of their fees to the brothel and must pay for towels, sheets, and other implements of the trade, often at inflated prices. While the experience in Nevada may provide a sense of temporary relief for the clientele, it does not provide a national model that would be satisfying to all society.

Obscenity and Pornography

We can talk about the derivations of the words "obscenity" and "pornography," but legal definitions are much harder to come by. Obscenity comes from the ancient Greek prefix ob-, meaning "off," and skene, meaning "stage" or "scene." In other words, if there were something that you could not portray on the stage of a theater in ancient Greece, it was considered ob-skene, or obscene. Pornography is a word derived from ancient Greek. "Puerne" is the ancient Greek word for "prostitution" and "graphine" is ancient Greek for the verb "to write." Pornography literally means writing about prostitution.

What right does an individual have to view pornography or obscene material? And where does that liberty end and the power of the government to prohibit discussion of that material begin? For centuries, the legal definition of pornography and obscenity has eluded law makers, jurists, and the public at large.

Even if we could define the terms, other issues still exist, including whether or not the government should be empowered to regulate the production, distribution, sale, possession, and use of obscene or pornographic material and, if so, to what degree. Should either obscenity or pornography be protected by the First Amendment and its right of free speech? Or should the government protect people—especially children—from obscene or pornographic materials?

The single best book, for my money, on the subject of obscenity law is Professor Edward de Grazia's *Girls Lean Back Everywhere: The Law of Obscenity and the Assault on Genius*. Professor de Grazia notes that the question of obscenity regulation often turns on the issue of protecting children. In his book, Professor de Grazia highlights one of the first modern obscenity cases, which took place in England in the late nineteenth century. The case involved the importation and translation into English of the French novel *La Terre (The Earth)* by Emile Zola. In this novel, there is a single paragraph involving a farm girl inserting a bull's penis into a cow for the purpose of insemination. The English leaders opposing the sale of the book feared that the passage would have a terribly negative affect on young women. They railed that soon English young people would become "just as debauched" as the French. (Sacré bleu!) Zola prevailed, and *La Terre* became available for sale in England.

Many famous American and British authors have been prosecuted for obscenity, and their publishers did not always support them, often knuckling under to authority rather than standing up for First Amendment rights. For example, the great English author D. H. Lawrence was so devastated by his English publisher's failure to support him in an obscenity trial that his health broke. He ended up moving to the American Southwest to recover.

In the United States, Theodore Dreiser also underwent a trial for obscenity after his novel, *An American Tragedy*, was published in Boston. Prosecutors liked to bring obscenity cases in Boston because of the city's reputation for its puritanical standards, a reputation it had earned in its long history. According to Professor de Grazia, the attorney representing Dreiser was none other than the great trial lawyer Clarence Darrow. Darrow argued to the jury that there were only 17 or 18 paragraphs involving sexual content in the entire novel. Even if a young person were to comb through the densely written 800 pages to find those few paragraphs, and even if that child were to be negatively affected by those passages, should all adults be deprived of a great work of literature?

The jury came back with a verdict: Deprive adults. We don't want to take any chances with our precious youth. Dreiser lost and was convicted of breaking obscenity laws. The book was "banned"—booksellers could not offer the book for sale legally in the commonwealth of Massachusetts.

The Law of the Land

According to the Constitution, pornography is not necessarily obscene. The problem is that it's very hard, from a legal point of view, to determine whether something is pornographic, obscene, both, or neither.

Another obscenity case involved one of the masterpieces of twentieth-century literature, James Joyce's *Ulysses*, which was originally published in France because no English or American publisher would dare take it on. The publishers of the book could not even find any Parisian typesetters to set the book because they were all offended by the language and sexual imagery of the novel. (It's hard to imagine what would make a Parisian typesetter blush, but apparently *Ulysses* did the trick.) The publishers had to go to the distant city of Rouen, made famous by Monet for his paintings of the city's cathedral, in order to find typesetters who could not speak English, and therefore, would not be upset by their work.

Once the book was published, it was made available in France and eventually in England. The U.S. courts initially judged the book obscene. If you were coming back from Europe via ocean liner in the 1920s or early 1930s, your bags were even searched at the dock in New York, and customs agents would have confiscated copies of *Ulysses* or any other novels considered obscene. Individuals would actually smuggle copies of *Ulysses*, one at a time, by rowboat between the cities of Windsor, Canada, and Detroit, Michigan.

In 1933, a more enlightened American federal court judge took the time to read *Ulysses* and came to realize that this was a work of art and not merely a book that appealed to prurient interests. (As someone who has developed a certain amount of familiarity with the works of James Joyce, let me assure you that if you want to get titillated, it takes a lot of work to have a sexual experience by reading *Ulysses*.) The novel was finally considered not obscene and could be published safely in the United States.

Other leading authors, such as Edmund Wilson, Vladimir Nabokov, and William Burroughs, author of the *Naked Lunch*, all underwent obscenity trials during the mid-twentieth century. When society generally became more open toward sexual matters in the 1960s, the U.S. Supreme Court followed suit.

In 1973, the Supreme Court defined obscenity in *Miller* v. *California* using a three-pronged test. The obscenity test asks (1) whether "the average person, applying contemporary community standards," would find that the work—taken as a whole—appeals to the *prurient* interest; *and* (2) whether the work depicts or describes, in a patently offensive way, sexual conduct specifically defined by the applicable state law; *and* (3) whether the work, taken as a whole, lacks serious literary, artistic, political, or scientific value. The first two prongs are judged under a community standard, which requires the court to determine how the material in question is viewed in the community in which it is presented; the third prong, however, is judged under a national standard, which requires the court to assess the common views of the country as a whole.

That's a long way of saying that if a regular Joe in your hometown thought that a book is primarily sexual in content, it is obscene. Because the standard is based on local, community values, it also means that the same material might not be considered obscene in another community that has different standards. This approach to defining obscenity makes it particularly to create *difficult* obscenity laws within the context of the Internet, which has no community boundaries.

Legal Dictionary

Prurient—Tending to excite lust; from a Latin word meaning "to itch or burn."

Drawing the Fine Line

The best-selling inside-the-Supreme Court book *The Brethren*, by Bob Woodward and Scott Armstrong, recounted hilarious tales of Supreme Court judges and their law clerks gathering on a weekly basis to look at pornographic films to determine whether or not they were considered legally obscene. One of the Supreme Court justices declared, "I may not be able to define obscenity, but I know it when I see it." My civil liberties professor at Northwestern Law School, Martin Redish, rephrased it this way: "I may not be able to define obscenity, but I know what I like."

The country knew what *it* liked: sexy movies, sex-filled magazines, and more of them. Standards loosened with each passing year.

Today, we live in something of an "anything goes" environment when it comes to regulation of obscenity. Not much is considered obscene anymore, unless children are involved. In an era when some of the biggest purveyors of X-rated material are the national hotel chains and telecom companies that provide in-room movies to a grateful public, it's hard to find a place where anyone still cares enough about obscenity to try to regulate it. The Internet changes everything as well, with its instant access to any kind of sexual material a person might care to view.

Today, the marketplace—not the courts—pretty much determines whether something is beyond the taste of the American public. When it comes to sex, either through prostitution or pornography, people are free to do pretty much whatever they want (once again, as long as children are not involved in any way). It's a fascinating double standard that our society permits anything of a sexual nature to be unregulated while it still cracks down on alcohol, tobacco, and gambling. I'm sure there's a message here, but it's awfully hard for me to figure out exactly what that message is. Perhaps it's nothing more than this: If standards are good, maybe double standards are twice as good!

> ### Looking for Liberty
>
> Some feminist commentators have sought to remove the First Amendment free speech protection from pornography based on the new theory that pornography does great harm to women.

The Feminist Perspective

The feminist critique of pornography focuses on studies that shows that consumption of pornography increases the amount of male-on-female sexual violence in our society. Pornography itself, they say, is a contributing factor in the high number of sexual assaults and other sex crimes committed against women. If pornography were not permitted, the rates of such sexual violence would diminish.

Feminist commentators also argue that women who appear in pornographic photos and movies do so only because they are forced into such work. They are either kidnapped, physically beaten, or otherwise obliged to appear in pornographic movies. Women have to be subjugated through violent means into appearing in pornography, and therefore it should not be deserving of First Amendment protection. Feminist experts also argue that pornography downgrades the dignity and importance of all women. They say that it is impossible for a man to look at the women who appear in pornography without having a lower opinion of all women in society. So far, the courts have not been open to this line of reasoning, and the feminist critique of pornography has not resulted in a change of the law.

Outta My Bedroom!

Perhaps the most important case involving the elusive "right to privacy" in the U.S. Supreme Court was that of *Griswold* v. *Connecticut*, decided in 1965. A Connecticut man challenged a state law that forbade the use of contraceptives. (Yes, children, back in the early 1960s, states actually made contraception illegal! I know it seems so hard to believe.) The U.S. Supreme Court declared that the Connecticut statute barring the use of contraceptives was unconstitutional. But the question remained, on what grounds? What specific right did the justices invoke to declare the State's Constitution statute incompatible with the U.S. Constitution?

Taking Liberties

It's hard to imagine that less than 40 years ago, it was illegal to purchase or use contraceptives in many states.

The Court wrote that the overall theme of the Bill of Rights was personal freedom. The government had no right to interfere in the personal decisions of its citizenry. In many ways, that's why the American Revolution was fought in the first place—to remove unwanted government interference. The Court then linked this freedom from government interference to a "right to privacy" for the first time. Justice William O. Douglas, writing for the Supreme Court, declared that the right to privacy was actually older than the U.S. Constitution, that it was part of the "natural rights" of the individual. Although he could not locate any specific language in the Bill of Rights that specifically supported a right to privacy, he said that such a right did in fact exist in the "shadows" and "penumbras" (another word for shadows) of the Bill of Rights. How important would these shadows and penumbras be? A host of privacy rights decisions followed the Griswold case, culminating in the landmark 1973 U.S. Supreme Court decision legalizing the women's right to abortion, *Roe* v. *Wade*.

The Least You Need to Know

◆ The line between obscenity and pornography shifts with society's mores.

◆ *Griswold* v. *Connecticut* was the first time that the Supreme Court linked the right to privacy to the Bill of Rights.

◆ Many of the twentieth century's greatest authors were tried for obscenity.

◆ Feminist commentators link male violence to the viewing of pornography.

Chapter 8

Do the Wrong Thing

In This Chapter

◆ Advertising sin

◆ The war against tobacco

◆ Gambling state by state

◆ Your right to "Supersize"

The late, great comedian W. C. Fields is credited with the aphorism, "Anything I like to do is either illegal, immoral, or fattening." If it fits into one of those three categories, there is a very strong chance that the federal government (and the states) wants to regulate it.

This country was founded by Puritans, individuals who were seeking the freedom to practice their religion, not the right to act in a licentious manner, and there are definitely puritanical strains in American culture that date back to the moment when the pilgrims set foot on Plymouth Rock back in 1620. If anything, American culture can be defined as the ongoing battle between those who seek pleasure and those who are intent on stamping out all forms of fun.

As the musical group the Persuasions sing "One night of praying, and six nights of fun/The odds against going to Heaven are six to one." In this chapter, we're going to examine the civil liberties issues inherent in what could be called the "freedom to sin"—whether and how the government can regulate the advertising or use of tobacco, alcohol, gambling, pornography, obscenity, and even fast food.

For Your Own Good?

To what extent can or should the government regulate the conduct of individual citizens? Should individuals be free to make private choices about behavioral issues such as the drinking of alcohol, smoking cigarettes, or the use of obscene or pornographic materials? At what point should the government step in, and why, and how? Or are these issues better left to individuals to decide for themselves? When the government regulates private behavior, civil liberties issues are raised.

> **The Law of the Land**
>
> The Eighteenth Amendment of the U.S. Constitution prohibited the sale and consumption of alcohol. This amendment was later repealed when it proved ineffective.

Perhaps the clearest way to grasp how the federal government wavers between limitations and license is to imagine a parent of an 18 year old. At times, the parent wants to give the teenager all the freedom in the world to go out, explore, and develop a sense of maturity. At other times, the parent looks at his child with horror, and says, "Oh my gosh! This child is completely unable to make intelligent decisions about all the dangers out there! I'd better make the decisions for my child!"

That's how the government views you. Over the years, the federal government has displayed a schizophrenic attitude towards its citizenry. On the one hand, citizens are capable of making intelligent, rational decisions for themselves. At other times, the government takes a paternalistic attitude toward its citizens and treats them with an attitude of "father knows best." Let's see how this attitude plays out in a variety of personal-choice issues that, now or in the past, have been branded as sinful.

If you are old enough to remember the football bowl games of January 1, 1969, then you remember the last day that television could legally carry ads for cigarette smoking. The 1960s was the era in which the U.S. Surgeon General issued his first report linking cigarettes to a variety of fatal illnesses, including lung cancer. Before that time, cigarettes were a ubiquitous part of American life and popular culture. You can see the Ricardos smoking cigarettes on reruns of *I Love Lucy*. Virtually every character, even the "good girls," smoked cigarettes in the movies. Even the medical profession was recruited into the sales force for cigarettes; during the 1950s, ads ran everywhere proclaiming that "doctors prefer Chesterfields."

By the 1960s, however, it was clear to everyone (including, evidence now shows, the manufacturers of cigarettes) that smoking was dangerous to your health. Congress stepped in and forbade the appearance on television of cigarette ads as of January 2, 1969. That January 2 date was a compromise with the tobacco industry—both football bowl games on New Year's Day represented the last gasp of televised advertising of tobacco.

Or did it? Today, as NASCAR increases in popularity beyond its traditional Southern and Midwestern base, you see news about the "Winston Cup," one of the highest honors a race car driver can achieve. Characters have gone back to smoking in the movies and on TV programs. How influential are these two forms of media in the day-to-day behavior of millions of Americans? Consider this. In the 1930s and 1940s, when the diamond industry wanted to promote the use of diamonds in engagement rings, it paid millions of dollars to the movie industry to portray female characters showing off their enormous engagement rings to admiring friends. Because of such *product placements*, millions of marrying Americans equated the size of the stone with the size of the fiancé's love for the woman he seeks to marry.

Taking Liberties

In 1999, alcohol companies placed their product in 233 motion picture movies and episodes of 181 different television series. In the 15 shows most popular amongst teens, eight had paid alcohol product placements.

Legal Dictionary

Product placement—A situation where a company or industry pays money to incorporate favorable mention of its product or service in a movie or television show.

There is no doubt that television and film are highly influential in terms of the personal decisions that people make. The question is whether government should regulate those messages.

Commercial Speech

In legal terms, advertising is commercial speech and there are special rules that the Supreme Court has developed in case law that address it. The basic idea behind commercial speech is that the company is paying money to influence the way you think, either through ads; the hiring of publicists to influence editors at newspapers, magazines, or TV shows; or through product placement.

In the past, the Supreme Court held that commercial speech was not entitled to First Amendment protection. Although the First Amendment says that Congress shall make no law abridging freedom of speech, the Court determined that advertising was not speech deserving of constitutional protection. Indeed, not everything that comes out of a person's mouth is not protected speech. You cannot yell "fire" in a crowded movie theater when there is no fire. Nor is "hate speech"—speech that is abusive or assaultive—protected by the U.S. Constitution. Likewise, commercial speech was not considered speech protected by the First Amendment for decades. What did it mean in practical terms that commercial speech was not protected by the First Amendment? Very simply, it meant that the federal government, or state governments, can regulate that speech. It means that an advertiser cannot look to the First Amendment and say to the government, "You have no right to make me back up my claims or remove my advertising." Because of this, the federal government, through the Federal Trade Commission and the Federal Communications Commission, for decades was able to regulate which commercials could go on the air.

Taking Liberties

Free speech is free to those who can effectively fight the FCC.

The Law of the Land

In *Virginia State Board of Pharmacy* v. *Virginia Citizens Consumer Council* (1976), the U.S. Supreme Court struck down a law that prohibited the advertising of prices for prescription drugs. The Court noted that pricing information was important to consumers and the First Amendment protects the "right to receive information" in addition to the right to speak it.

As is so often the case in American constitutional law, things changed. In a 1976 decision involving a Virginia law that banned licensed pharmacists from advertising the prices of prescription drugs (*Virginia State Board of Pharmacy* v. *Virginia Citizens Consumer Council*), the Supreme Court granted commercial speech First Amendment protection. The Court announced that there are three important reasons why commercial speech should be protected:

1. Just because commercial speech is trying to make money for a business does not mean that the First Amendment protection does not obtain.

2. Consumers need information in order to make informed choices. Without First Amendment protection, consumers do not have full access to information. (Keep in mind that this decision was handed down decades before the Internet, in an era when you could not simply click a few buttons and find out prices nationwide for different products or services.)

3. Denying First Amendment freedom to commercial speech was "paternalistic"— that the government was overstepping its bounds in deciding what the public should or should not know.

In other words, the pendulum had swung from the government feeling a responsibility to make decisions for individuals to a new framework in which the government believed individuals should make decisions for themselves.

Not long after the Virginia decision, the Supreme Court announced in another case (*Central Hudson Gas and Electric Corp* v. *Public Service Commission*, 1980) the rules under which commercial speech would be considered protected by the First Amendment. In *Central Hudson*, the Supreme Court issued a rather complicated test that allowed the government to return to its paternalistic approach—under certain circumstances. The test is so complicated that reasonable legal scholarly minds differ as to when the government can step in and regulate commercial speech and when it cannot.

That brings us to the question of the tobacco industry.

> **Taking Liberties**
>
> The billion dollar tobacco settlements brought by the federal government in 40 states almost faltered when Congress hesitated to approve it on the basis that the private lawyers handling the matter would receive upward of 15 billion dollars in contingency fees.

Tobacco and Free Speech

During the Clinton administration, the federal government took aim at Big Tobacco and forced a multi-billion dollar settlement with the tobacco industries, ostensibly to pay for medical costs borne by the states in treating individuals who had become ill through smoking. In other words, the cigarette companies were found to have placed a dangerous instrumentality—cigarettes—into the marketplace, and were therefore responsible for the effects that cigarettes caused. This did not happen by means of a new law; rather, it was the settlement of the government's lawsuit against the tobacco companies.

Part of the agreement between the federal government, the states, and the cigarette manufacturers was to limit severely the ways in which manufacturers marketed cigarettes to children. That's why you haven't seen Joe Camel around much lately. The friendly, big-nosed animal was believed to appeal to children and to make cigarette smoking seem attractive to minors. As part of the settlement, Joe Camel is gone, never to return (unless the law changes). Also, it is harder and harder for young people to buy cigarettes in convenience stores or anywhere else; thus the disappearance of cigarette machines in most areas of the country. In other words, the federal and state governments have stepped in to ensure that young people have a very difficult time getting started smoking. *through settlement agreement - not law*

Casinos, Cigarettes, and Kahlua

If you take the logic of the Supreme Court in regulating the kinds of cartoon figures that can hawk cigarettes, can regulation of other forms of "sin" be far behind? Not necessarily.

Another important Supreme Court case involving commercial speech made the ruling that the government of Puerto Rico could legitimately ban ads for the territory's casinos if the ads were aimed at residents. In *Posadas de Puerto Rico Associates* v. *Tourism Co. of Puerto Rico* (1986), the Court held that it's okay for Puerto Rico to advertise its casinos on the mainland or in other countries around the world, but it's not okay to advertise to the locals. This is an extreme example of paternalism; it implies that people in Puerto Rico are simply not wise enough to make rational decisions about casino-going, and they have to be protected from knowledge of the fact that casinos actually exist on the island. On the other hand, the law implies and the Supreme Court affirms, if rubes from the 50 states or around the world want to try their luck in a Puerto Rican casino, bring 'em on.

Taking Liberties

Most states ban all forms of gambling, but make an exception for their profitable lotteries.

Another act that some states consider naughty—and others nice—is the purchase of lottery tickets. You can buy Power Ball in certain states, while others conduct their own lotteries. Still others have a policy of not permitting state-run lotteries. Sometimes, lottery states are situated right next to states that forbid lotteries, as is the case with North Carolina and Virginia. In *United States* v. *Edge Broadcasting Co.*, the Supreme Court decided a case in which a company operated a radio station in northern North Carolina, just three miles south of the Virginia line. More than 90 percent of the radio station's listeners and advertising dollars hailed from Virginia. The station wanted to broadcast ads for the Virginia state lottery, but North Carolina sought to keep those ads from airing. North Carolina argued that state residents should not have to be "inundated" with ads for lotteries, which are contrary to the policy of the State of North Carolina. North Carolina went to court—and won.

The U.S. Supreme Court decided in the *Edge Broadcasting* case that states opposed to lotteries had rights, too, and that it was legitimate for a state to crack down on lottery advertising even though the lottery was taking place in a neighboring state. Once again, there is a First Amendment right, but not for people who like to sell items such as lottery tickets.

When it comes to alcohol, some states have sought to ban all advertising for all forms of alcoholic beverages. Two such states are Mississippi and Oklahoma. Intriguingly, in the Mississippi case, the U.S. Court of Appeals said that there is no link between advertising and liquor consumption and thus upheld the ban on advertising liquor. In Oklahoma, the U.S. Court of Appeals found it "hard to believe" that there was a connection between advertising and the amount of alcohol consumed. Nevertheless, the court let the ban stand. So here you have two different courts coming to two different conclusions about the efficacy of advertising, but using that same differing rationale to reach the same conclusion. Does this mean that ads for alcoholic beverages could be banned in other states in the United States? Yes, indeed. Any time you have a product that is politically dicey—alcohol, gambling, cigarettes, etc.—there is a limited First Amendment right for businesses who want to advertise those products or services.

The Law of the Land

"The states' role in our system of government is a matter of constitutional law, not of legislative grace."

—U.S. Supreme Court Justice Lewis F. Powell, Jr.

You might ask how it could be that the First Amendment could say, "Congress shall make no law abridging the freedom of speech," only to have the U.S. Supreme Court turn around and abridge all the speech that it does not like. However, there was never an intention that *all* speech would be protected by the First Amendment. Indeed only one kind of speech was considered important enough to merit First Amendment protection back in the days when the Bill of Rights was under debate.

When our country was founded, the government wanted to protect any speech that had to do with political thought. The authors of the Bill of Rights did not want any handicap on political debate, an issue that is one of the central aspects of the American way of life. As we will see in Chapter 14, it is legal to burn the American flag or advance political approaches that are contrary to the views of the mainstream and the majority because the freedom to speak dissenting views (religious or political) was an essential goal of the Founding Fathers.

The Founding Fathers created a system that would let political debate flourish in order to maximize freedom of opinion and political freedoms. There is no connection between a business seeking to sell its products and the furtherance of political debate in society. Therefore, some argue, the First Amendment protects political speech but not economic speech where the "speaker"—the advertiser in question—is simply out to make a buck. Others argue that advertising has great social value, because it alerts consumers to the products and services that will enhance their lives. Does this mean that economic speech should therefore be entitled to First Amendment protection? The jury is still out, which is to say that the U.S. Supreme Court has not made a clear decision on this point and legal scholars still debate it.

Legalizing Drugs?

Over the past 20 years, there have been calls to decriminalize some or all drugs that are currently against the law to possess, sell, or use. The American Civil Liberties Union and the former mayor of Baltimore, Kurt Schmoke, are among the most prominent individuals who call for the decriminalization of drugs.

They argue an interesting rationale. The court systems are clogged with cases of small-time drug users who would be better off in treatment than in jail. The use or possession of marijuana, for example, could be considered so trivial that it is a waste of police, court, and prison resources to go after individual users. The libertarian approach suggests that individuals should have the freedom to make personal decisions about matters such as drug use. Most importantly, if drug use were legal, the government could both monitor it and tax it, making it much safer.

Taking Liberties

This year, Uncle Sam will spend over 19.2 billion dollars of our tax money, at a rate of 609 dollars per second, on the War on Drugs.

Statutes of Liberties

Marijuana is now legal in eight states, though strictly for medicinal purposes.

Nevertheless, it is highly unlikely that America will decriminalize drugs in the near future. The bottom line is that politicians have to be elected or re-elected, and as with other issues relating to "sin," it's hard to find more than a handful, to say nothing of a majority of Congress, in favor of a fundamental change in the drug laws.

Furthermore, many state legislatures are seeking to pass drug paraphernalia laws. These laws, known as "head shop statutes," seek to forbid the sale of items, such as bongs or roach clips, used in the processing or taking of drugs. Such statutes sometimes fail to pass constitutional muster because they are "overbroad"—they sweep too many products into the mix, and potentially could punish individuals who sell items that are not drug-related at all.

Such statutes also fail for vagueness reasons. A law is considered unconstitutional if it is too vague as to what activity is criminalized. Laws are expected to give people a clear idea of what is legal conduct and what is not. If a law is too vague, then the community cannot know how to behave in a legal manner. It is considered a vital aspect of constitutional protection that we have only laws that are clear as to what conduct they are prohibiting.

States have been working hard to tailor their head shop statutes to accord with state constitutions and the U.S. Constitution. The prevalence of head shop statutes indicates that America is in no mood to legalize drugs. Smoke 'em if you've got 'em, as the expression goes, but don't let the police find out.

Supersize This!

Most people are familiar with the case in which a customer successfully sued McDonald's for selling her a cup of hot coffee that burned her when she spilled it on herself. It turns out that this was not a frivolous suit. The case revealed that McDonald's had the practice of adding scalding hot water to coffee in order to mask the fact that the coffee was weak and diluted. It was this extremely hot water that led to the plaintiff's severe burns and triggered the lawsuit.

Then there's the case of 56-year-old Caesar Barber, a five-foot-ten, 272-pound New Yorker who sued fast food chains on the grounds that their food made him fat. A New York lawyer who loved to see his name in print took this man's case and actually brought suit in New York courts against Burger King, KFC Corp., Wendy's, and McDonald's, alleging that the food these companies serve cause obesity. The lawsuit alleges that the companies are misleading in their posting of nutritional information and do not offer healthy items to go alongside the fat-and-grease-laden burgers and fries.

Why would a lawyer sue big companies? There is a certain amount of publicity value to be gained from filing such suits. This particular lawyer would not have had his name in the *New York Daily News* and other fine journalistic institutions if he had not so filed. On the other hand, it often costs big companies more money to fight suits than to simply give in and offer a small settlement in hopes of making the lawyer and client go away. Cases like these trivialize the importance of the legal system in protecting the real civil liberties of Americans.

The Least You Need to Know

- States have the right to enact laws that ban gambling and even lottery ticket sales.

- The extent of the government's paternalism tends to vary depending on current societal issues.

- The issue of commercial speech remains largely unresolved.

- Although a hot topic, the legalization of drugs is not likely to happen anytime soon.

Your Medical Records: Prescription for Privacy

In This Chapter

- ◆ A grim diagnosis
- ◆ Exposing yourself
- ◆ Medical records and the law
- ◆ The electronic insurance company

Let's start with the bad news first. The shocking truth about privacy rights with regard to your medical records is this: You don't have any!

If I'm exaggerating, it's only slightly. Thanks to the ubiquitous computer, the privacy of your medical records has never been threatened from so many directions at the same time. This is another important aspect of the way in which our privacy is threatened even without our knowledge.

The Truth About You: From the Beginning

First of all, more information is created and stored about us than ever before in human history. For example, according to the *Journal of the American Medical Association*, a typical birth certificate included only

15 items just 40 years ago. Today, there are more than 200 data fields on the average birth certificate, which means that from the moment a baby is born, a vast amount of information about his or her health and the health of that baby's parents is now being stored in a computer. As we all know, anything stored in a computer can be retrieved—by those with authority and those without.

Second, doctors have been forced to become better record keepers, in part because of the increased bureaucracy in the medical field and in part by the increase in the number of malpractice suits brought by their patients, some frivolous, some justified. In addition to being good general practice to keep track of a patient's health and treatment, keeping good medical records help doctors should it become necessary to defend themselves in a malpractice suit. Third, these days, we reveal far more information about ourselves than we may realize. Ever visit one of those informal health screenings in front of the supermarket? If you allowed them to take tests to measure your blood pressure or cholesterol and provided them with your name and address, that information has value. It has value to marketers who want to sell you weight-reduction programs, cholesterol-reducing medication, blood pressure-reducing pro-grams, and so on. That information can find its way into health record databases maintained about you by insurance companies or others interested in access to medical records. We also reveal information via the Internet. When you log onto a chatroom or discussion group or join a newsgroup about a particular illness, it may not be advisable to use your real name, date of birth, zip code, or any other identifying features about yourself unless you don't care who knows it. There is absolutely no guarantee of privacy in public forums such as these, and yet many people believe that their information is somehow being held in confidence.

Legal Dictionary

Smart card—Any kind of credit card-sized information retrieval device that contains private information. In terms of medical records, your insurance card could be programmed to contain your entire medical history, which could then be visible to any health-care provider or employer.

Fourth, the truth may be "out there" on *The X-Files*, but in real life, the data is out there and it is surprisingly easy to pull together pieces of information to form a complete picture of an individual's health record. For example, if you know the birth date, sex, and zip code of an individual, you can retrieve that person's health records with surprising ease. It may sound hard to believe, but those three little facts uniquely identify 87 percent of the U.S. population.

According to the *Journal of the American Medical Association*, a computer privacy expert took those three facts and was able to retrieve health data for William Weld, the former governor of Massachusetts. She found that only six people in Weld's hometown of Cambridge, Massachusetts, shared his birth date. Three were men and three were women. She eliminated the women and was left with three possible individuals. She then compared those individuals with Weld's zip code and found that only one of them lived there—and that was Weld.

This is not *The Complete Idiot's Guide to Breaking Through Security Firewalls and Hacking Information About Total Strangers*, so we cannot reveal exactly how this computer expert went about getting the data on Bill Weld. (Actually, I have no idea how she did it.) The fact indicates, however, just how little privacy any of us really has when it comes to our medical records (or pretty much anything else).

What's in Your Medical Records, Anyway?

A whole lot. Whether you smoke or hang glide, your family medical history, lab test results, medications, the results of operations—pretty much anything that has ever happened to you from a health standpoint from birth to the present. Today, a special database used by health insurance companies keeps complete (or as complete as possible) health records on *15 million Americans*. Databases only grow bigger with time, so if you are not in this database, it's entirely possible that you will be before long. More than 750 insurance companies use this database to issue insurance policies. You can visit this database website at www.mib.com, and for a mere nine dollars (what a deal!), they will provide you with a copy of your medical records.

Although theoretically your medical records are supposed to be private, there's one particular individual in your life who may well have signed away your rights to medical record privacy. That person is not your parent, your spouse, or your legal guardian, that person is you! When you go to the doctor and sign that mysterious form that's been photocopied 600 times to the point of illegibility, you're probably signing a waiver of your privacy rights. These waivers are known as *blanket waivers*, or general consent forms. These waivers permit doctors or other health-care providers to release information to insurance companies, government agencies, and others as well.

> **Taking Liberties**
>
> We never think about the privacy implications of the waiver forms we sign whenever we go for medical treatment. Some of the forms we're asked to sign are to protect the doctor from malpractice claims; others permit the release of your medical information. We sense that the receptionist will either deny us access to the doctor or just give us a hard time in front of the other patients in the waiting room so we always sign!

> **Legal Dictionary**
>
> **Blanket waivers—** General consent forms that permit doctors or other health-care providers to release information to insurance companies, government agencies, and others as necessary.

According to the San Diego-based Privacy Rights Clearinghouse (www.privacyrights. org), there are at least eight different ways in which your private health information can become public knowledge. Let's take a look at each in turn.

◆ **Insurance companies.** Good luck trying to get an insurance policy without them reviewing your medical records. And forget about them making a payment on a policy you already have without a new peek at your records. It makes sense, but you can be turned down for trivial and often inaccurate readings of your health information. And then those rejections become part of your records!

◆ **Government agencies.** The government is standing by, waiting to review your medical records should you file for Medicare, Social Security, disability, workers' compensation, or any other government-based program.

◆ **The Medical Information Bureau** (discussed earlier). Not only do they maintain a database on you, but if one insurance company lists information with them, all other insurance companies are free to peek as well.

◆ **Employers.** They usually get medical information about their employees by asking them to authorize disclosure of medical records. If your employer pays for your medical care, chances are that your application for medical insurance included a consent form that let them look at your medical records. Is your employer required to keep your medical information confidential? Only in a small number of states.

◆ **The courts.** Your medical records may be subpoenaed for court cases. If your medical condition is an issue in litigation—say, a car accident or a workers' compensation claim—the relevant parts of your medical record may be copied and introduced in court. But somebody's got to do the copying and also the deciding of what is relevant.

◆ **Hospital licensing procedures.** In order for hospitals to receive and maintain their operating licenses, they must make disclosures to the proper authorities of their patients' medical records. In theory, these records do not have names attached; we don't exactly know how to guarantee that your name doesn't somehow slip into the pile of documents that the overseeing agency is to review. Also, people with certain

Looking for Liberty

EPIC, the Electronic Privacy Information Clearinghouse (www.epic.org), is at the forefront of the fight to protect the privacy of medical records. EPIC points out that many individuals won't get treatment for their physical or mental illnesses if they fear that their employer or the government will have access to those records.

infectious diseases or other physical ailments will be of interest to public health agencies such as the Centers for Disease Control in Atlanta. Your records may be headed down to Dixie.

♦ **Informal health screenings.** We discussed these earlier. In order to protect your privacy when having your blood pressure checked or your cholesterol measured, the Privacy Rights Clearinghouse suggests that you ask what will be done with the information and who will have access to the health results before you agree to the procedure.

♦ **The Internet.** Anybody who logs on to, say, a cancer website is most likely either undergoing treatment for cancer or knows someone who is. If you were marketing products and services to cancer patients, wouldn't you want to just gobble up all the e-mail addresses, names, addresses, and phone numbers of such individuals that you could find? When you are going onto those sites, be careful not to identify yourself by your real name. There's truly no privacy in cyberspace, especially when it comes to medical issues.

Keeping Your Private Stuff Private

At this point, believe it or not, there is no comprehensive federal law that protects the privacy of medical records. Whenever a law is not in place that benefit consumers, there are two potential reasons.

HIPAA?
See
p. 108

First, the political lobbies of the groups that object to such a law may have been throwing their weight (and money) around state capitals and Washington, D.C. If that's the case, they are far more likely to get a hearing than the average citizen.

The Law of the Land

Naturally the Constitution doesn't speak directly about the protection of electronic medical records. Yet when jurists and attorneys seek to find answers about the constitutionality of a given practice, they start with the relevant clause in the Constitution or the Bill of Rights. You can make a strong case that the Fourth Amendment protection against improper search and seizure leads to limitations on how much private health information the government can maintain on its citizens.

This theory ties into the second reason why no such comprehensive laws may exist. It may well be that there is simply not a strong enough constituency for such laws.

Legislators are loath to expend political capital on a project that will probably annoy somebody if there is not a clear-cut constituency for that new law. If something is going to make it harder for insurers to get a peek at people's medical records, you can be sure that the insurers are not going to want that to happen. They have a lot of money and they donate a lot of money. So why would a congressperson or a state legislator willingly incur the wrath of big donors when there may be little or no payoff at the ballot box or, at least as importantly, in their wallets? That's the sad facts of politics.

So what can you do to protect yourself? According to the Privacy Rights Clearing-house, there are a series of steps you can take in order to limit the amount of medical information about you floating around in cyberspace, and then to limit access to the information that's out there. First, they suggest that you try to limit the amount of information released when you sign a waiver. A blanket waiver may read something like this: "I authorize any physician, hospital, or other medical provider to release to [insurer] any information regarding my medical history, symptoms, treatment, exam results, or diagnosis."

They suggest that you edit the waiver so it reads this way: "I authorize my records to be released from [X hospital, clinic, or doctor] for the [date of treatment] as relates to [the condition treated]." This will limit the chance that your entire medical record will suddenly find itself posted in some medical databank, open to the prying eyes of anyone with a modem and a knack for breaking through security provisions.

Taking Liberties

When I was a first year law student, my best friend was a medical student. Whenever he introduced me to his classmates, he'd always say, "Michael's a law student! Don't tell him anything! He could sue us one day!"

The Privacy Rights Clearinghouse also suggests that you use caution when filling out medical questionnaires. Typically, when you see a new doctor, you are given a multi-page questionnaire asking about everything that's ever happened to you medically, including the time you were caught playing doctor with the next-door neighbor. Instead of simply filling out the form to the nth degree, first ask if it's really necessary because once you release it to him or her and sign a blanket waiver, it can go anywhere. Also, ask exactly why you are being asked to fill out the form and who will have access to the information.

The Privacy Rights Clearinghouse urges individuals to be equally careful at informal health screenings—those times when you can get a free (or low-cost) cholesterol or blood pressure test outside a supermarket or at a county fair. What use will be made of that medical information? Who will have access to it? Do you really want a bunch of marketers to know that you have hypertension?

And finally, if you're visiting websites and participating in online discussion groups about a physical or mental condition, be sure to guard your own privacy. No one else is going to guard it for you.

Taking a Peek at Yourself

Mary Agnes Matyszewski, writing in the *Whittier Law Review*, Spring 2002, makes the entertaining point that patients often try to read upside down or look over their doctor's shoulder as he or she is writing case notes. It's much easier just to access your complete medical record. (And besides, they all have such terrible handwriting!) About half the states in the country permit complete access to medical records. You, your spouse, or your legal representative can sign a request for your medical records.

Let's say that a trial has to do with the emotional distress suffered by an individual who has witnessed a shooting. In this case, the entire psychiatric record of that individual, if there is such a record, would not be admissible in court. Instead, only the records pertinent to this specific situation would be admissible. In California, for example, the agency of the government seeking access to particular legal records is expected to use "the least intrusive means available" in order to find the specific information it needs, and is expected to "carefully tailor the subpoena to be so narrowly and specifically drawn as to avoid undue intrusion." That would be great if this were a perfect world. It's not. And that's why when it comes to medical records, we have fewer protections than we think.

> **Statutes of Liberties**
>
> The right to privacy comes into play when the state is seeking medical records for a trial. In that case, the judge has to weigh the right of privacy of the patient against the interest of the state in determining what sort of information is necessary to conduct the trial. The court will consider the relevancy of the records to the matter at hand, the medical condition that is involved in the litigation, and the reason why these medical records are sought.

Why Go Electronic?

There are many good reasons for electronically stored medical records. Amy M. Jurevic, writing in the *University of Missouri at Kansas City Law Review* in a health law symposium in the summer of 1998, lists some of those reasons:

- ◆ Electronic records allow health-care providers easy access to a patient's medical records and allow for continuity of care. In other words, all your doctors are on the same page.

◆ Paperwork can be reduced, which can save time and money (although don't expect to see any savings on your health insurance costs anytime soon).

◆ Speedy transfer of data between hospitals and offices of health-care providers.

◆ A reduction in time required to find missing records.

◆ Increased legibility of records. (Doctors' handwriting strikes again!)

◆ Expedited billing.

When everything works right, a patient who is in an emergency situation, whether at his or her local hospital, on a cruise ship, or even on the side of a mountain, can be treated much more quickly and effectively if the health-care provider has instant access to that patient's complete medical records. That's the upside.

> ### Looking for Liberty
>
> "Whatsoever things I see or hear concerning the life of men, in my attendance on the sick or even apart therefrom, which ought not be noised abroad, I will keep silence thereon, counting such things to be as sacred secrets."
>
> —The Hippocratic Oath

The problem with complete electronic medical records is that you may not want everybody to know what's on those records. Medical records often include family history of the patient (breaking the privacy of other family members), genetic testing, any history of drug and alcohol use, sexual orientation, and testing for sexually transmitted disease. Hackers can steal the information—or even alter it, out of a sick sense of entertainment.

In theory, the Health Insurance Portability and Accountability Act of 1996 created safeguards to protect the privacy of patient medical records. In fact, it's still a mess out there. A physician friend of mine says about herbal medications, "Anything you take in large enough doses to help you, you're taking large enough doses to hurt you as well." The same could be said of the benefits and drawbacks of electronically stored medical records. On the one hand, a lot of good can come when a medical practitioner can access your records in a timely fashion. The problem is that the appropriate medical care provider is not the only person who could find out about your case of mono in the ninth grade.

Another doctor friend once commented, "Half of all medical knowledge is wrong. The only problem is, we don't know which half." Once again, the same could be said about electronically stored medical records and patient privacy—a lot of what we are doing isn't helping, but the problem is that it's hard to identify exactly what needs to change in order to protect the rights of patients.

As Dana Carvey once said on *Saturday Night Live*, while doing an imitation of President George H. W. Bush: "My health plan? Don't get sick!" In other words, the best way to maintain confidential medical records is not to have any. (The only problem is, we haven't figured out quite how to do that yet.) Until then, be as careful as you can about what information gets into your medical records, and share only that portion of your medical history that is absolutely necessary. Dr. Big Brother truly is watching!

The Least You Need to Know

- There are at least eight different ways that your medical history can become public knowledge.

- People unwittingly give away more of their information than they realize.

- There are no comprehensive laws protecting the privacy of medical records.

- Electronic record keeping has its upside, but it makes unwanted retrieval of your information much easier.

Chapter 10

Your Credit Report: What Is It, What's on It, and Who Can Look at It?

In This Chapter

◆ For the record …

◆ Hey, that's *my* name!

◆ Online onslaught

Why is the government like an elephant? Just as an elephant never forgets, neither does the government.

Public Records Are ... Public!

The government—by which I mean federal, state, and local entities—has countless ways of compiling a biography about you. While we have not reached the point where all information about individuals is funneled to a single, secret dossier (at least, not that we know of), we surrender a wealth of evidence about ourselves from our first moments on earth until long after we have departed. For instance, your birth certificate reveals where and when you were born, your parents, and many other pieces of data. In theory, birth records are confidential. In theory, confidential records never fall into the wrong hands.

While you may be trying hard to forget about school, your schools have not forgotten about you. Your high school, college, and graduate school transcripts are still on file, and can be accessed by school districts to which you are transferring, state or federal education authorities, financial aid programs, law enforcement officials, or the general public, if a judge says so.

Unless you win the lottery or have very wealthy and generous parents, you probably have to work for a living. In that case, your employment data is on record with the Social Security Administration … forever. The right 14-year-old hacker can get you into Social Security Administration files before finishing a medium-size pizza.

Taking Liberties

If you're feeling nosy, you can find what your neighbors paid for their houses on many websites such as realestate.yahoo.com.

Get married? That's public knowledge. Your name, your spouse's name, the county in which the application was filed, and the date of the marriage are all available to anyone who cares to look you up, unless you are in a state that provides for confidential marriage certificates.

Buy a house? First of all, anybody with a modem can find out how much you paid for the house, when you bought it, how big it is, whether you have made additions to it, where it is located, who sold it to you, and so on. If you have bought a house, chances are you noticed those dozens of letters to you offering the services of mortgage brokers, carpenters, swimming pool cleaners, termite inspectors, and anyone else with the relatively small amount of money it takes to buy a list of new homeowners from list brokers. Not much privacy there.

Ever file a lawsuit? The facts of your filing became public record immediately. The one and only time I ever took a nonpaying client to Small Claims Court, I got a call that very same week from a producer of a reality TV court show who wanted to find out if we would litigate the case on national television, for a fee. We declined. (I lost.)

Get divorced? Public document. Arrest record? That's public, too. Change of address form with the post office? It's not supposed to be a public document, but it practically is, when you consider all the people the kind folks at the postal service sell your name and new address to.

Of course, if you receive Medicare or Social Security, that's *supposed to be* confidential, as are public library records and criminal history records. However, Privacy Rights

Clearing House (you can visit them at privacyrights.org) points out that information brokers can compile virtual "rap sheets" by searching arrest records and court files that are already public records.

From birth certificate to death certificate and everything in between, there is virtually no aspect of your life that goes unnoticed—and ignored—by some arm of the government. This is the price we pay for living in a technologically advanced society. If you truly want privacy, you may need to live on the beach, never seek medical care, never get married, never hold a job, never apply for a Social Security number, never take out a library book, and never rent a video. (If you're living on the beach, there's not much you can do with a video, but I think you understand where we're going with this.)

Since the above scenario is highly unworkable for most of us, we tend to accept, often unthinkingly, constant governmental violations of our privacy. Most of us go through life without tremendous interference from the government—but nonetheless it is somewhat disturbing to realize just how much they know about each of us. Let's look at cases where revelations of personal information could have very negative effects on our lives.

Credit Reports

There are three major private companies in the United States that are known as nationwide credit bureaus, or CRAs (consumer reporting agencies). They gather and sell information about individuals who apply for jobs, insurance, charge accounts, personal loans, or anything else where someone is extending credit or trust. These three companies—Equifax, Experian (formerly TRW), and Trans Union—maintain dossiers on millions upon millions of individuals. These dossiers include your payment history, where you work and live, whether you've been sued or arrested, and whether you have filed for bankruptcy. Whenever you apply for credit, the bank or company with which you are seeking to do business will contact one or more of these credit agencies to review, with your permission, your credit report.

Taking Liberties

Some states are acting to protect individuals from the release of driver's license identification. It's not hard to find an "investigator" on the Internet who can get you all the information you require about practically anyone, however.

Legal Dictionary

Consumer Reporting Agency (CRA)—A bureau that gathers and sells information about individuals who apply for jobs, insurance, charge accounts, personal loans, or anything else where someone is extending credit or trust. The three major nationwide CRAs are Equifax, Experian (formerly TRW), and Trans Union.

You do have a right to see what's in your credit report, and it is generally a good idea to review it at least once a year. You can contact the three credit bureaus, and it makes sense to contact all of them, because they do not all get the same information about you. For a fee of just under 10 dollars, they will send you a copy of your credit report. You can get a free copy if you have been denied credit or insurance and you request your report within 60 days of that negative action; inaccurate information might have crept onto your report. Perhaps you share the same first and last name as a person with a bad credit history, and some of their "dings" end up in your file. You have the right to demand, in writing, that each of the credit reporting agencies with that incorrect information check into the matter and fix your credit report. If you and the CRA are not able to agree on whether a disputed item should be removed, you can have your statement concerning that dispute added to your credit file. According to privacyrights.org, one study indicated that more than 50 percent of credit reports checked contained errors.

Negative information can remain on your credit report for seven years, with certain exceptions. Criminal convictions stay on forever. A Chapter 7 bankruptcy remains for 10 years. A Chapter 13 bankruptcy remains for only 7 years from date paid in full or 10 years if not paid as agreed. There are other exemptions as well.

Taking Liberties

The Social Security number we acquire either at birth or when we take our first job was never meant to be a national identification system. Opponents of national identification cards cite the Constitution's right of privacy as an important reason why such cards should never be issued.

Only people to whom you give your permission are supposed to see your credit report. If you want to rent an apartment, get a job, or apply for credit, the law allows that business to get a copy of your credit reports from each of the three agencies. (CRAs are governed by the Federal Trade Commission, which you can learn more about at FTC.gov.)

How private is your credit report? Not as private as you might wish it to be. The fact is that CRAs in the past have sold personal credit information to businesses that do marketing. Also, if you apply for a car loan with a bank, for example, that bank may share your credit information with all of its other departments.

There's an industry that specializes in "cleaning up" the credit of individuals. For the most part, they can do nothing more than you could do on your own, simply by requesting your credit records from the three credit bureaus. There is really no need to pay hundreds of dollars to a company to do what you could do for yourself.

Identity Theft

To what extent must the government protect your privacy by making violations of your privacy a criminal offense and a matter for the police? Let me offer a story from my own recent experience to illustrate this question.

One morning the telephone rang, and it was a credit agency, calling to see if I was seeking to open a charge account with K-Mart. I was not making such an application, and I told the person on the other end of the line as much. He said, "We didn't think so. You are a victim of identity theft."

Apparently, someone had gotten my name, Social Security number, and other personal data, either by the Internet, by combing through my trash, or through some other means. That person then sought to open up a charge account in my name. With no disrespect intended to K-Mart, I wondered why the individual had not aimed a little higher and tried to open an account at a Nordstrom's or a Saks Fifth Avenue. The caller from K-Mart security explained that I had to call all three of the CRAs and let them know that I had become a victim of identity fraud. I also had to go to the police station and report the crime to them as well.

I did so. I called Equifax (1-800-685-1111), Experian (1-888-397-3742), and Trans Union (1-800-916-8800). Identity theft is so prevalent today that all I had to do was follow the prompts ("push 1 if you are a victim of identity theft") and report the information to them. All three of my credit reports now indicate that I am a victim of identity theft, and any time anyone checks my credit record, they are obligated to call to make sure that I am really the person seeking to do business with them.

I went to the police station next. I live in Los Angeles, California, and one of my favorite pastimes is to listen to recordings of the old 1950s radio program *Dragnet*. One of the great things about *Dragnet*, outside of the snappy patter of the detectives, is the fact that the early 1950s were such a relatively crime-free time that detectives could spend as long as they wanted or needed to solve any crime, no matter how small.

Statutes of Liberties

In October 1998, Congress passed the Identity Theft and Assumption Deterrence Act of 1998 (Identity Theft Act) to address the problem of identity theft. Under this law, it's a federal crime when anyone "knowingly transfers or uses, without lawful authority, a means of identification of another person with the intent to commit, or to aid or abet, any unlawful activity that constitutes a violation of Federal law, or that constitutes a felony under any applicable State or local law."

Times have changed. When I went down to the police station in West Los Angeles, the person ahead of me in line was also filling out an identity theft report. People fill out these reports all day long. Apparently, there is an army of individuals who wake up, have coffee, watch *The Today Show*, and begin their daily routine of practicing identity theft. They open credit card accounts, establish cellular phone service, and open bank accounts in the names of total strangers. If it happens to you, remember that you are not alone.

The Federal Trade Commission suggests that to minimize your risk of identity theft you should make sure your credit record is up-to-date and accurate. Also, call creditors if you do not receive a bill on time. It doesn't mean stuff is free. It may mean that someone has diverted your bill to a different address to charge gobs of stuff on your account without your finding out. Also, don't use your mother's maiden name as a password on accounts—it's just too easy to guess. If you are the victim of identity theft, you can call the Federal Trade Commission directly at 1-877-IDTHEFT (438-4338), or visit their website at www.consumer.gov/idtheft/victim.htm.

Identity theft today is a federal crime and can be investigated by the U.S. Secret Service, the FBI, and the U.S. Postal Inspection Service, and prosecuted by the Department of Justice. Don't count on that, however. A few weeks after I filed my report, I received a letter from the police department explaining that they had put my identity theft on record. In that letter, they misspelled my last name. So much for the protection of my identity.

If you're a victim of identity theft and report it, the credit bureaus will send you a free credit report once a year for seven years, but only if you ask for it.

Keeping Your Privacy on the Internet

Following are some suggestions for how to protect your privacy in today's crazy world. Again, as we have noted, every time we reach any of life's milestones, from hatch and match through dispatch, we surrender a little bit more private information about ourselves. There are a number of steps that individuals can take in order to protect their privacy, both online and in the real world.

You can find out if your medical history is stored in the medical information bureau by contacting them at www.mib.com. If it is, you can get a copy of that report for nine dollars.

If you want to stop receiving pre-approved offers of credit, call 888-5OPTOUT (1-888-567-8688). Check the "opt out" box on any solicitation, over the Internet or through the mail, that requests your permission to share your name and personal information with marketers.

Only give out your Social Security number when it is required—as with banks, stock and property transactions, and the government. Businesses have the right to ask for it, but you have the right to refuse. Don't let merchants write your credit card number on your check when you are paying for something; that's a violation of your privacy. You can find a longer list of protections like this on the Privacy Rights Clearing House Privacy Survival Guide, which can be found online at privacyrights.org/fs/fs1-surv.htm. This is an outstanding resource for privacy.

Remember that the Internet was not designed for privacy. It was designed initially for conveying information among scientists. Before that, the original purpose of the Internet was to link together parts of the defense establishment in case an enemy attack brought down the U.S. phone system. The Internet was only opened to the public around 1990. (Thank you, Al Gore.) By that time, the technology for the Internet had already been put in place and was not geared to protect the credit card numbers of private users or the privacy of individuals who like to watch porn over the Net. Those uses were not really considered back when the Internet was created.

> **Taking Liberties**
>
> Don't enter sweepstakes! The Privacy Rights Clearing House says that people who enter sweepstakes and contests find themselves on "sucker lists." Your name, address, and phone number can be used for telemarketing scams, including get-rich-quick schemes. And besides, you never win!

> **Statutes of Liberties**
>
> The same FBI charged with protecting your privacy online also has the responsibility to fight terrorism. With resources limited, guess who loses?

Here are some online suggestions to increase your safety:

- Only give information that is *absolutely* necessary, i.e., those fields on Internet forms that are marked with asterisks. If it's not necessary to provide information about yourself, don't.

- Your browser can be set to maximize your privacy. Learn to clean your Internet cookie cache.

- Just say no to special offers. Any time a company is offering you "special offers," what they are really doing is getting you to release your name and address, and sometimes your phone number, date of birth, and names of children, to other marketers. Don't let them know anything more than what is necessary for the particular purpose you wish to achieve online.

◆ Look into "anonymous surfing" services that will give you a higher level of anonymity online. You can also install firewalls that protect your computer work and material from prying eyes.

◆ Finally, the Lakeland, Florida Police Department suggests that you go online right now to www.freeality.com or www.anybirthday.com and see just how much information is known about you online.

The Least You Need to Know

◆ You should check your file from all three major CRAs at least once a year.

◆ Technology has made identify theft quite simple and, thus, prolific.

◆ Protecting your child from online harassment is extremely difficult.

◆ Blocking software isn't 100 percent effective; monitoring your child's Internet use is the best solution.

Part 3

Lawmakers and Law Breakers

The subtitle of this section could be "Lawyers, Guns, and Money." We'll examine the intersection between the rights of the police and the rights of citizens. Can the police enter your home without a warrant? Can you shoot a burglar? Under what circumstances can the police stop your car and search it—and you? Can your kids be subject to a curfew? What happens to civil liberties when a person goes to jail? And what about new-technology intrusions on your privacy, such as hidden cameras in the changing room at the department store or when you undress at the tanning salon? Be prepared to be shocked—by the naked truth!

Chapter 11

Is Your Home Your Castle? Yes, But ...

In This Chapter

- ◆ Obtaining a warrant
- ◆ Do's and don'ts of warrant use
- ◆ Second Amendment issues
- ◆ Defining self-defense

Willie Sutton used to say that he robbed banks because "that's where the money is." Today people break into houses because that's where the money, VCRs, jewelry, TV sets, negotiable securities, laptops, etc., are. The other group of people who have a strong interest in coming into homes, whether or not they are invited, is the police, because homes are frequently the place where evidence of crimes can be found.

In this chapter, we're going to look at two sets of constitutionally guaranteed civil liberties that you enjoy. The first is the freedom from intrusion by the police who don't have a valid warrant, and the second is the freedom that some believe we have to own firearms.

"Open Up, It's the Police!"

"It's good to be the king." That must have been the sentiment of King George III, ruler of Britain, until he lost the American colonies. One of the reasons why Americans were literally up in arms about King George III was his insistence on the use of "general search power" for his police and armies. A British government official, such as a policeman or soldier, had the absolute freedom to enter the home of any American colonist, snoop around, and take whatever he considered objectionable or dangerous to the Crown. This approach to civil liberties sat rather poorly with the colonists, and when they drew up their own constitution, they made sure that the Bill of Rights contained language forbidding the state from warrantless searches in people's offices and homes.

The relevant language is found in the Fourth Amendment to the U.S. Constitution:

> The right of the people to be secure in their persons, houses, papers, and effects, against unreasonable searches and seizures, shall not be violated, and no Warrants shall issue, but upon probable cause, supported by Oath or affirmation, and particularly describing the place to be searched, and the persons or things to be seized.

The language may be legalistic and somewhat antique to our modern ears, but the sense of injustice that the authors of the Bill of Rights felt, dating from the era when the British could enter houses and do as they saw fit, continues today.

The Law of the Land

"The right of the people to be secure in their persons, houses, papers, and effects, against unreasonable searches and seizures, shall not be violated, and no Warrants shall issue, but upon probable cause, supported by Oath or affirmation, and particularly describing the place to be searched, and the persons or things to be seized."

—Fourth Amendment to the U.S. Constitution

Let's take a look at the process by which warrants are issued.

First a policeman gains evidence from one of three sources—informers, other police officers, or private citizens—that evidence regarding a particular crime can be found at a particular location. The police officer and then a magistrate or judge must weigh the quality of this evidence.

If the evidence is from a contact of the police officers in the underworld—a habitual offender who provides information to the police in exchange for monies or favors—then the quality of that information has to be weighed very carefully. Is it likely to be accurate? How accurate has this informant been in the past? If the evidence was developed by another police officer, there's a much higher likelihood that the evidence is accurate. Of course, a police officer does not need proof that evidence of a crime exists in a particular place to be searched.

The third source of potential information is a private citizen who is not a police informant. Although the police officer has to take into consideration the possibility that the private citizen is acting out of a grudge against someone, the fact is that individuals come forward all the time with information about crimes that they fear may be taking place in their own neighborhoods.

Once a police officer has information that indicates the likelihood that evidence will be found in a particular location, the police officer must then draw up an application for a *warrant.* Even today, the words of the Fourth Amendment of the Constitution come into effect: The warrant must be "particularly describing the place to be searched, and the persons or things to be seized." In other words, a warrant is not a statement that says, "Police officers can go into the house at 123 Main Street and do whatever they want. If they find bad stuff, it can be introduced in evidence." Instead, a warrant must be narrowly drawn; it must specify exactly which home, apartment, or office is to be entered. It must specify exactly what the officers expect to find there, and it must demonstrate that the police officer has a reasonable belief that such evidence will be found in that location.

Legal Dictionary

Warrant—An authorization or justification for a particular action; a judicial writ authorizing an officer to make a search, seizure, or arrest.

Once the warrant has been drawn up, the police officer cannot simply head over to the house where he or she thinks the crime is taking place, bang on the door, and get the evidence. Instead, another step precedes the execution of the warrant, the approval of the warrant by a "neutral and detached" magistrate or judge. The police officer can visit the magistrate or judge in person, fax the warrant over, or read the contents of the warrant over the phone.

The idea is that police officers want to stop crimes and catch people who commit them. While a police officer's first responsibility is to uphold the U.S. Constitution, sometimes, in the heat of tracking down a criminal or gathering evidence, the emotions of the moment may sway the police officer from protecting the rights of the person whose home is to be searched. For that reason, the American system calls for a cooler head to come and consider exactly what the police officer wants to do. That theoretically cooler and calmer head is on the shoulders of a judge or magistrate, someone not involved with the investigation of the crime. For example, if it turns out that the judge or magistrate issuing the warrant is actually involved in the criminal prosecution of the person whose home is being searched, the warrant is considered invalid and any evidence gathered under it cannot be introduced in court. (We don't make this stuff up; this was actually a New Hampshire case, *Coolidge* v. *New Hampshire* (1971) that ended up before the U.S. Supreme Court.)

Similarly, if it turns out that the magistrate gets a fee, say, five dollars, for every warrant he issues, and zero for every warrant he turns down, that magistrate cannot be considered to be "neutral and detached." (Again, I know you think I make this stuff up, but this is another Supreme Court case, *Connally* v. *Georgia*, decided in 1977.)

There is a practice called *magistrate shopping* whereby a police officer turned down by a magistrate or judge for a warrant will simply take that same warrant to another magistrate or judge, hoping for a different outcome. (This is a little like asking mommy after daddy has said no.) In theory, such a warrant would be considered invalid because public policy dictates that police officers should not be able to shop around until they finally get the answer they want. Instead the burden falls to the police officer to rewrite the warrant in such a way that it will comply with whatever requirements the law contains. For example, if the warrant is overbroad as to location, it can specify more clearly what area is to be searched by the police. If the warrant is overbroad as to scope, the warrant can specify exactly what sort of evidence the police are looking for. An unsigned warrant is generally an invalid warrant.

Legal Dictionary

Magistrate shopping— The process by which a police officer turned down for a warrant by one magistrate endeavors to seek approval of the warrant by another magistrate and another magistrate, until he gets the answer he desires.

Looking for Validation

Particularity is the Bill of Rights' way of saying that a warrant has to be specific about the place to be searched and the items or people that will be seized. There are three factors a judge should consider when deciding if a warrant meets this peculiarity standard: the description of the property to be searched, including *curtilage*; intensity of the search; and probable cause. Evidence discovered in violation of this principle is called "fruit of the poison tree" and is not admissible in a court of law. One of the first things a criminal lawyer will do is examine the warrants under which evidence about his or her client was discovered. The case law is full of examinations of warrants because the writing, signing, and execution of warrants is far from an exact science. Moreover, as times change, standards change, and a search or seizure that might have been considered acceptable in one era may be considered inappropriate in another.

The first key to a valid warrant is the description of the place to be searched. That sounds pretty simple, but it's not. What if the warrant says that the apartment to be searched is at 123 Main Street, Apartment 6, and when the police arrive, they find that there's an apartment 6 on every floor? Do they have the right to go through every single apartment number 6? Or do they need to have a more specific warrant? Chances are, such a warrant would be considered overbroad and would not give the police the right to inspect every apartment number 6 in the building.

Another issue that arises is whether a warrant permits the police officers to search not just the house or apartment at the given location, but also other places on the property, such as a car, a trash bin, or tool shed. The area surrounding the house is known in legal terms as the curtilage. A driveway or backyard would be considered curtilage. Generally, a warrant executable against a house implies the right of the police officer to inspect cars on the property, garbage bins, or anywhere else where they have a reasonable expectation of finding the evidence. This right extends into areas that are not visible upon inspecting the house from the outside and, therefore, are not specified in the warrant, such as an attic or basement.

The Law of the Land

To be constitutionally valid, a search warrant must be (1) based on probable cause, (2) precise on its face as to place to be searched and things to be seized, and (3) issued by a neutral and detached magistrate.

What if the apartment to be searched can only be entered through another apartment? Do the police need a separate warrant to enter that other apartment in order to execute the warrant? The answer is no, they do not. If the only way to enter an apartment is through someone else's apartment, the interest that society has in stopping crime outweighs the right of the tenant or owner of the other apartment to keep police from passing through.

Taking Liberties

In a criminal fraud case in the Bronx, New York, in the year 2000, all the evidence against the defendant was obtained via a search warrant. The warrant provided for a search of a basement apartment of a large building at 2114 Daly Avenue in the Bronx. However, there were three such apartments with three separate doors leading to three different basements of 2114 Daly Avenue, and the correct door was not specified in the warrant. The court found the warrant impermissibly overbroad and unconstitutional. Thus the evidence was thrown out and the defendant went free. Maybe next time the police will be a bit more specific in the area to be searched when requesting a warrant.

Finally, a warrant has to be specific as to just how thorough the search is going to be. For example, if the police are seeking to find a bale of marijuana, the police would not have the right to search through a medicine cabinet or cigar box. Those items would be too small to contain such a large amount of marijuana. Any evidence found in such places would not be admissible in court, because such evidence would indicate a more intense search than the warrant permitted. This issue is actually one of the most heavily litigated questions in the entire realm of warrant law.

The final consideration in the signing of a warrant is probable cause. Probable cause means that a police officer believes that evidence is, more likely than not, located in a particular place and that this evidence would be useful to a criminal proceeding. If both of these conditions are not met, the magistrate or judge should not sign a warrant. The concept of probable cause is to keep police from going on "fishing expeditions," in which they figure that a certain individual must be guilty of *something*, and if they just turn his house upside down long enough, they'll find evidence of some sort of crime. That's not the way the system works.

Statutes of Liberties

Under the "fruit of the poisonous tree" doctrine, if a warrant is proven defective for lack of probable cause, any evidence obtained via the warrant may not be used against the defendant in court.

Defendants who find themselves on trial because of evidence found in searches after legal warrants were issued are allowed to challenge the probable cause affidavit of the police officer. In other words, just because a police officer *says* that probable cause exists, that doesn't mean his statement will go unchallenged for all time. The U.S. Supreme Court has stated that defendants should have one "meaningful opportunity" to test the probable cause statement of a police officer. This operates as a check against unlimited police power.

Warrants Fresh and Stale

The judge or magistrate has signed the warrant. Now, the police officer has a certain amount of time in which to execute the warrant. Warrants not executed in a reasonable period of time—usually 3 to 10 days—are considered "stale" and evidence gathered pursuant to them cannot be introduced in court. The reason for prohibiting the use of evidence gathered under stale warrants is to protect individuals from a dilatory police force. It would not be fair to citizens if the police could simply stock pile warrants against anyone they considered suspect and then execute the warrants months, or even years, later whenever they thought some incriminating evidence might be found.

At this point, it starts to look like the movies or TV police dramas. The police officer knocks on the door, identifies himself or herself, and announces that the warrant is in hand and that a search is about to take place. If the occupant does not admit the police officer or if no one is home, the police officer can break down the door and enter, if necessary, subduing any individuals who may seek to interfere with the work of the police. There is a legal difference between detaining an individual—making the person sit quietly while a search is going on—and arresting them. Legalities generally make it easier to detain a person, and a detained individual does not have the same panoply of legal rights as someone placed under arrest.

With the human obstacles out of the way, the police go to work, searching for the evidence described in the warrant and searching in the manner that complies with the terms of the warrant. What happens if a police officer notices some evidence that potentially indicates criminal behavior while the search is going on? If the evidence that the policeman notices is in "plain sight," the police officer is entitled to take that evidence into custody, even though it is not listed on the warrant. If, for example, a police officer enters a home with a warrant because there is probable cause that the residence is being used as a methamphetamine lab, and the police officer walks in and sees a large stack of hundred-dollar bills on the table, he could take that money into evidence. If, on the other hand, the warrant only permits the officers to search one of the bedrooms, and a police officer goes into another bedroom, lifts up the mattress and finds the stack of hundred-dollar bills, that evidence would be excluded, because it was found in violation of the warrant—there is nothing related to a meth lab that an officer would have reason to suspect might be found under a mattress and the money wasn't in "plain sight."

There are other limitations surrounding warrants. For example, it is generally not permissible for a warrant to be executed at night; a nighttime intrusion by police is considered to be more emotionally upsetting than a visit during the day. Moreover, people have a higher expectation of privacy in their homes at night than during the day. Exceptions to this rule do exist, especially if there is a fear that the evidence will disappear by morning. On the other

Legal Dictionary

Plain view doctrine— Police may seize incriminating evidence if the initial police intrusion was constitutionally permissible and the incriminating nature of the evidence is readily apparent.

Statutes of Liberties

There is a "good faith" exception to the rule of excluding evidence found via a defective warrant. The exception applies if the official executing the warrant reasonably relied on the magistrate's determination of probable cause and the technical sufficiency of the warrant.

hand, police officers can pretend to be floral delivery persons, meter readers, or other relatively more welcomed guests in order to gain entry into a home. The courts prefer such ruses to a police officer having to force his way in.

Another limitation on warrants is that police officers do not normally have the right to conduct searches of individuals they find in a location for which they have a warrant unless they are planning to arrest those individuals. For example, police officers cannot go into a restaurant for which they have a search warrant and search all of the customers.

The Right to Bear Arms

There are two reasons why individuals want to own weapons (aside from the question of sport and committing crimes): the protection of oneself, one's family, and one's property; and the protection of one's nation. One of the most tortuous debates in American society, one that shows no sign of abating, is whether the Bill of Rights permits or prohibits federal, state, or local governments from passing laws that limit the rights of individuals to own guns.

The Second Amendment to the Constitution reads as follows: "A well regulated Militia, being necessary to the security of a free State, the right of the people to keep and bear Arms, shall not be infringed." How much ink has spilled over the centuries in trying to understand these 27 words? (And now, some more ink will be spilled!)

Taking Liberties

"My idea of gun control is a steady hand."

—Senator Lloyd Bentson, quoting his father

Many constitutional experts believe that the Second Amendment is one of the most poorly worded sections of the entire Constitution. It's just too vague. The sentence structure is somewhat tortured, and it's hard to understand exactly what Congress meant—at least from a simple reading of the text. Let's try to understand exactly what is going on here.

The first question is the relationship between a "well regulated Militia" and "the right of the people to keep and bear Arms." As with any aspect of American legal history, we need to begin our discussion with an understanding of what was happening in pre-Revolutionary America. At the time, the British did not want any of the American colonies to be able to rise up and overthrow their imperial masters. So, the British forbade Americans to come together in military units, knowing full well that those military units would one day be used against the British themselves.

The Americans, nonetheless, created militias—informal armies that consisted of able-bodied male landowners of military age. Each state had its own militia. Thus the explanation for the first half of the Second Amendment ("a well regulated Militia being necessary to the security of a free State"). If there had been no state militias, there would not have been a military force that could have been shaped together by the Continental Congress and General George Washington with which to defeat the British.

Article I, Section 8, of the U.S. Constitution authorizes Congress "to provide for calling forth the militia to execute the laws of the Union, suppress insurrections and repel invasions ..." This means that the federal government would take power over the militias and form them into an army.

The Law of the Land

"A well regulated Militia, being necessary to the security of a free State, the right of the people to keep and bear Arms, shall not be infringed."
—Second Amendment to the U.S. Constitution.

Now we come to the sticky part of the debate: What exactly is meant by "the right of the people to keep and bear Arms, shall not be infringed?" Most legal scholars agree that only state militias (the forerunners of today's National Guard) have the right to bear arms.

Instead the right "to bear arms" really means "the right to make war." That is, individuals do not have the right to start wars, or go into battle on their own. Only militias have that right. In other words, according to this line of thinking, the Second Amendment does not, and has not ever, granted individuals the right to own guns. "Bearing arms" does not mean "owning a weapon." It means, in fact, "going into battle."

Because of this interpretation, which the U.S. Supreme Court has always upheld, the government has the right to pass laws that limit the rights of citizens to own weapons. Such laws include making illegal the possession of concealed or unregistered weapons, purchase restrictions such as mandatory waiting periods, and laws that ban interstate transport of guns, and limitations on the sale of particular types of firearms, such as automatic weapons and machine guns.

How exactly does the federal government have the right to limit gun ownership on the part of individual citizens? In the 1939 U.S. Supreme Court case of *United States* v. *Miller*, the court held that the Second Amendment "must be interpreted and applied" only with regard to state militias—and there is no right to own guns.

The Law of the Land

"The Framers of the Bill of Rights did not purport to "create" rights. Rather, they designed the Bill of Rights to prohibit our Government from infringing rights and liberties presumed to be preexisting."
—Former Supreme Court Justice William J. Brennan

In part because of the continued strength of the *Miller* decision, the pro-gun owner-ship movement in this country does not appeal to the courts to overturn laws that limit the rights of individuals to own guns. Instead, the pro-gun lobby focuses its efforts on Congress to eliminate, or at least limit the effectiveness, of any law that limits the availability of guns in the United States.

The gun lobby draws on English common law and history for its position that the Second Amendment actually permits individuals to own guns, and that the Second Amendment prohibits the government from keeping individuals from doing so. In 1689, the English Parliament passed a law stating that Englishmen could own their own weapons and use them as they wished. There were a number of reasons for this position—and they are noted by Robert Harman in a note and comment in the *Whittier Law Review*, Winter, 1997. Those reasons are as follows: providing for the common defense of the people, self-defense, bating local law enforcement and cap-turing criminals, and protecting personal liberties from government encroachment.

Harman further notes that William Blackstone, the great compiler of England's laws, defined the right to bear arms as "as one of the great auxiliary rights necessary to ensure the three great rights of personal security, personal liberty, and private prop-erty." Such laws were carried over into the American colonies in the seventeenth cen-tury, where individuals were permitted and even expected to own their own guns and ammunition. Writes Harman, "Individual ownership of arms was both a right and a responsibility."

And there the matter remains. The antigun lobby has the U.S. Supreme Court clearly in its corner. The key phrase: "the right of the people to keep and bear Arms."

Taking Liberties

"The Second Amendment says we have the right to bear arms, not to bear artillery."

—Robin Williams

Who are "the people?" The antigun side of the debate says that "the people" is the army and the government. In other words, "the people" is a collec-tive noun. The pro-gun side of the debate says that "the people" means all the people, one by one, that each of us has a right to "keep and bear Arms." More ink is likely to be spilled before the debate is ever settled.

Ironically, one of the main arguments of anti-gun forces is that the fewer guns there are available, the fewer crimes will be committed, and the safer we will all be. Re-search today indicates, however, that those states that offer fewer restrictions on gun use actually have lower crime rates. The explanation is that people are far less likely to commit crimes if they fear that the people they will be attacking are themselves armed, which leads us to the question of self-defense: What can you do legally to defend yourself, your home, and your property?

Can You Shoot a Burglar?

The short answer: yes and no. (But you've probably come to expect that already.) It depends on where you live.

The basic rule in criminal law is that individuals can act in their own defense in a manner that is proportionate to the threat that they face. For example, George is walking down the street when a man thrusts a gun into his back and demands his money. If George happens to be carrying a weapon, it would be within his rights to turn around and shoot his assailant. Deadly force is acceptable where an individual has a reasonable fear of death or great bodily harm. When the case goes to court, there will be two tests: Did the alleged robbery victim fear death or great bodily harm, and would a reasonable person fear the same thing in that situation? If the answer to both questions is yes, our friend is not guilty of any crime. (George may live by the credo that it's "better to be judged by 12 than carried by six.")

What if that same individual had approached George from the front, and without carrying a weapon, made the same demand? In this case, unless George fears there would be great bodily harm, deadly force would not be acceptable in the eyes of law. George would have to make some kind of retreat, if possible. If no retreat were possible, George would then have the right to use the same level of force that he thought might be inflicted on him. What happens if this same scenario plays out in one's home?

In our homes, we have a very high expectation of privacy, much more so than in the street. We have, therefore, the right to defend our homes to a much greater degree. If a burglar enters a home, an individual has the right to attack that burglar on the grounds that there is a serious expectation that the intruder is likely to cause death or great bodily harm to someone in the home. Many states have laws that expressly offer this right to individuals in their homes; they are known as *"Make My Day"* statutes.

There's a big difference between "I'll punch you right now" versus "if you do that again one more time, I'll punch you." The former statement implies immediacy, that the harm is about to happen right now and triggers the right to self-defense. If someone makes the latter statement, then self-defense is probably not appropriate, because the threat of the use of force is not immediate. Above all, the response has to be proportionate, which means that if someone threatens to slap you, you cannot take

Legal Dictionary

"Make My Day" **statutes**—Laws that permit you to shoot and kill an intruder inside your home if you have a reasonable belief that the intruder has committed or intends to commit a crime in the dwelling.

out a gun and shoot them. There's a certain lack of proportionality in this that even New Yorkers would recognize. The concept of the necessity to retreat from the assailant before one takes an action in self-defense is quite controversial, and only about half the states have this requirement. Finally, if the assailant withdraws from a confrontation by either leaving or giving a verbal indication that the conflict is over, the self-defense right disappears. In the eyes of the law, it is not acceptable to chase after an individual who has made a threat and then ran off without making good on that threat.

Statutes of Liberties

It is generally not permissible to devise booby traps in your home to harm unauthorized intruders.

In your home, in non-Make My Day states, you can only use deadly force when violent entry is made or when there is a reasonable belief that it is necessary to prevent a violent attack on yourself or someone else in the family. This means that you can shoot a burglar, but only if he's about to shoot you, unless you are in a Make My Day state.

What constitutes a threat? It may be verbal, or it may be a push. You do not have to take the first hit in order to receive the self-defense protection. However, you do have to have a reasonable expectation that you are about to be hit.

One of the most intriguing cases in this entire area of the law concerns an individual who kept a collection of glass bottles in an unoccupied building on his property. He set up a "spring gun" that would shoot an intruder who entered the property. One such intruder did enter that out-building and was duly shot by the spring gun, but survived. He sued in the state of Kansas, where this took place, claiming that his rights had been violated and that the homeowner had no right to protect unoccupied property with potentially lethal force. The intruder won, and the homeowner ended up having to sell his home in order to pay off the 30,000-dollar award that the court awarded the intruder. This is a powerful illustration of the fact that in the United States, human rights are considered far superior to property rights. Is it part of your civil liberties to protect your property with deadly force? Apparently not.

There you have it: the ins and outs of the laws of self-defense. Perhaps the only good thing about getting into a jam in which the above laws would come into play is the fact that you get to stare your assailant in the eye, give him a steely look, and say, in your toughest voice, "Feeling lucky, punk? Then make my day!" (The editors of *The Complete Idiot's Guide* series and the present author do not actually recommend the above course of conduct; it's just a figure of speech.)

The Least You Need to Know

◆ A warrant can only be obtained through a stringent process.

◆ The requirement for probable cause acts as a check against unlimited police power.

◆ Freedom from improper searches and seizures is one of the most important limitations on governmental power.

◆ The wording of the Second Amendment leaves it open to various interpretations.

Chapter 12

What a Nuisance!

In This Chapter

- ◆ Torts in flux
- ◆ Varieties of nuisances
- ◆ Technology strikes again
- ◆ HIV and the law

Commentators on the Constitution give the Founding Fathers generally high grades for predicting the sorts of situations that Americans would find themselves in, even decades or centuries after the Revolution. And yet, there are some things that even the Jeffersons and the Madisons could never have imagined. How about, say, peeping-toms with Internet-ready digital cameras? Or knowingly passing HIV to an unsuspecting sex partner? No, the Founding Fathers never could have foreseen those sorts of situations. In this chapter, we're going to take a look at some of the modern twists on "nuisance law."

The fact is that when people live cheek to jowl, as we do in modern society, it is sometimes very hard for us all to get along. The way we wish to use our property sometimes conflicts with our neighbors' desires, as in the cases of barking dogs, nudist neighbors, junked automobiles on the front lawn, spiked walls (walls or fences that neighbors build strictly out of a sense of spite), and so on. We have trouble getting along when our neighbors spy on us, when television "reality" shows intrude in our homes or workplaces with hidden cameras, when perverts and other miscreants seek to take still photos or videos of us when we are in compromising positions, and on and on. Then there are the cases where individuals spread sexually transmitted diseases, including HIV, to unknowing bed partners.

With all these ways to cause harm to each other, it's no wonder that we all cannot get along. In this chapter, we are going to examine the areas of nuisance law and other ways in which our conduct can be disruptive, dangerous, or even life threatening to those around us. Specifically, we are going to look at five areas:

◆ Nuisance law

◆ Peeping Toms, old-fashioned and Internet-savvy

◆ Intrusions by "Tabloid TV"

◆ Recording phone calls and reading other people's e-mail

◆ Passing sexually transmitted diseases to others without their knowledge

Defining Black and White

Before we get into these issues, I'd like to tell you a story from my own law school experience. I saw an intriguing article in the newspaper that presented a set of facts that I thought would make a fascinating legal case. I was a first-year law student at the time, and I ran with the facts of the case to my tort professor and man who employed me then as a part-time researcher, Daniel Polsby. I breathlessly set out the facts for Professor Polsby (it's been so long that I have no recollection what the case was about, unfortunately). I waited eagerly for him to tell me how a court would decide the case.

He shrugged. "No idea," he said matter-of-factly. I was shocked. Professor Polsby was one of the nation's leading authorities on torts, the sort of "civil wrongs" we are discussing in this chapter. How could a man as erudite, accomplished, and wise as he not know how a judge would decide a case?

"Are you sure?" I asked. "Is there something I might have left out from the case?"

"No," he replied. "You described it perfectly. But I have no way of knowing what a judge would do. Nobody knows what judges will do … until they do it. That's how the legal system works."

The conversation was a rude awakening. As a first-year law student, I harbored the romantic notion that if you studied enough law, you would be able to predict with certainty how any given case would be decided. The fact is that you never know how a judge is going to decide a case until he or she decides it. There are no absolute black-and-white situations in the world. The study of law is about understanding how to think about the shades of gray in any given situation, how to apply what legal precedent or previously decided rules or cases come into play, that's about it. You simply do not know how a judge is going to rule until the ruling comes down.

You might argue that *The Complete Idiot's Guide to Your Civil Liberties* has already demonstrated countless situations in which a clear rule of law exists. But those rules of law had to come from *somewhere*. Many came about when a judge decided that he or she didn't like the previous way the law handled a given situation and so overruled the previous decision, ignored it, or distinguished it and then came up with his or her own new approach.

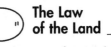

The Law of the Land

The doctrine of precedent states that lower courts in subsequent cases involving similar facts must follow prior decisions of the higher courts.

We've seen repeatedly how the pendulum swings in various areas of the law, reflecting changing mores. As society became more liberal in the 1960s, so did many civil liberties and civil rights laws. As society grew more conservative in the 1980s and 1990s, those laws changed yet again. In an overarching sense, it's very hard to predict whether a given rule of law will last for a short or long time. On any given day, in any particular case, it is practically impossible to determine how a judge will come out on the issue. That's why we call them judges—they get to decide which rules apply in any given case.

As we discussed earlier, if a litigant thinks that he or she has been cheated by the judge's decision at the trial court level, he can appeal that decision to state appellate courts all the way up to the U.S. Supreme Court. However, judges generally dislike overruling each other. One of my law professors explained that they keep running into each other at the same cocktail parties, and it's very awkward if an appellate judge runs into a trial court judge whose decisions he consistently overrules. But it does happen. The same case can lead a trial court judge to conclude one thing, an appellate court judge to conclude something entirely different, the state supreme court to side with the winner of the trial court case—but for different reasons altogether, only to be overruled by the U.S. Supreme Court for reasons that no one had even begun to consider when the case first went to trial.

Taking Liberties

Although it sounds schizophrenic, it can happen that a trial court decision is reversed by the appellate court, the appellate court is later reversed by the state supreme court, and the state supreme court is eventually reversed by the U.S. Supreme Court. Can't you people make up your minds?

I mention all this because in each of the five areas that we are about to discuss, it's entirely possible that the rules will change drastically in the next three to five years. These areas of the law are especially in flux because they deal with relatively new areas of the law—how to handle questions involving the Internet, e-mail, AIDS, and new technologies for snooping in other people's businesses and affairs. When you see what the law says in some of these sensitive areas, you may come to the same conclusion—that the law surrounding these issues has a long way to go before it can begin to produce settled rules by which everyone can live.

Let's jump in.

What a Nuisance!

Nuisance is a legal term that dates back so far into English history that it's actually French in origin. The word "nuisance" derives from a French word meaning "to injure or harm," which in turn is derived from the Latin prefix "necro-," which science-fiction fans will recognize as a word meaning "death." If you cause grave injuries to another person, in a legal sense, you may well be committing a nuisance.

Nuisance law traditionally governs an individual's right to enjoy his or her land free from interference. Most traditional nuisance cases have to do with things that offend the senses, such as an especially smelly pigsty, a tannery (a place where animal hides are turned into leather, not a tanning booth), a house of prostitution (need we say more?), or a saloon. The law used to hold that whoever got there first, wins. In other words, if you moved next door to a pig farm, you had no right to sue in nuisance to get them to turn those pigs into bacon as rapidly as possible. In the eyes of the law, you were "coming to the nuisance," and since you knew what was going to be your next-door neighbor, you had no right to complain. That aspect of the law has changed in recent years; the fact that a plaintiff (the person doing the suing) has "come to the nuisance" is considered just one factor in the decision-making process of the judge, not the determining factor. The biggest problem with nuisance law is that it can be very hard to determine what is a nuisance and what is a legitimate use of land. The way you use your property may make great sense to you, but it may be highly offensive to your neighbors. Courts are loath to step into such neighborly disputes, especially when legitimate cases can be made on both sides for continuing or abating (the legal term for ceasing) the behavior being termed a nuisance.

There are different kinds of nuisances. A public nuisance is something that interferes with the public health, safety, comfort, convenience, or other subjects that affect the public as a whole. Private nuisances take place when a neighbor does something that has little or no effect on the entire community but has a tremendously negative effect on the resident next door.

What happens in a nuisance suit when it goes to trial? Generally, the judge seeks to determine how valuable the behavior being called a nuisance is to the person who is practicing it, and how destructive it is to the person who is complaining about it. If a person does prove in court that someone else is creating or maintaining a nuisance, the judge can order one of two things: financial damages, to make the injured party whole; and/or *injunctive relief*, legalese for a ruling that forces the other person to cease the nuisance behavior. When people sue over a nuisance, they may claim that the property value of their home or land is diminished by the presence of a nearby nuisance. Or they may claim that they have suffered a loss because they are not able to enjoy their property to the fullest. Or they may claim that the situation is upsetting their children, or keeping friends and relatives from visiting, because it is simply too disturbing.

> **Statutes of Liberties**
>
> Nuisance law does not exactly have an untroubled past. In the nineteenth century, there were actually places where white individuals sued in nuisance when a black family moved into their neighborhood.

> **Legal Dictionary**
>
> **Injunctive relief**—A ruling by way of a court order requiring an individual to do or omit doing a specific action. You may be found in contempt of court if you fail to follow the court order. Those held in contempt may be fined and/or imprisoned.

John Copeland Nagle wrote in the *Emory Law Journal* of Winter 2001: The easiest nuisance cases to decide are those involving environmental issues, such as when your ground water is contaminated by your neighbor's water pollution. An environmental nuisance can be on an even larger scale, such as when the health of a community is affected by emissions from a factory or plant (think of the movie *Erin Brockovich*).

The more difficult nuisance cases involve situations where the damage is harder to quantify—or is a matter of some debate. For example, a married couple buys their dream home only to find out that the public uses a beach immediately adjacent to their property as a nude beach. Thousands of people come every summer to drop trou and enjoy nature in the buff. The couple sues the state in which they reside for failing to enforce laws forbidding nude beaches. They claim that the presence of this nude beach is a nuisance that affects their ability to enjoy their own property, that their children are negatively affected by the presence of the nudists, and that none of their friends want to visit. (Obviously, their friends are different from my friends.)

The court held that the public nudity in this case did violate the right of the home-owners to enjoy their property. (However, keep in mind that this decision is only binding in Oregon and that it's possible that another trial or appellate judge could overrule the decision at a later date.) Then there's the question of aesthetic nuisances. An aesthetic nuisance occurs when a neighbor does something that violates the taste of another individual. For example, if Ralph likes to litter his front lawn with rusted frames of deceased automobiles, and his neighbor Stuart thinks this is likely to drive down property values, Stuart can go to court. Would Stuart win? Hard to say. Courts are only beginning to recognize the concept of aesthetic nuisances, which do not fall into any of the traditional areas of nuisance law—noise, odor, dust, or safety hazards.

Taking Liberties

When I was in law school, my favorite nuisance case, *Nova Mink* v. *Trans-Canada Airlines* (1951), involved the owner of a mink farm who sued an airline for its low-flying flights, which, the plaintiff claimed, made the minks so nervous that they would eat their young. The airline won.

In the past, the courts generally held that one man's garbage was another man's gold, and that aesthetic, subjective issues of taste were matters into which the courts did not want to venture. But this is starting to change. Courts in Colorado, New Hampshire, Virginia, and other states have begun to recognize that aesthetics matter, that it's not fair to Stuart if Ralph keeps his front lawn littered with car parts. Today, zoning ordinances handle many of the questions that used to be decided in terms of nuisance law. Zoning gives very clear guidelines to homeowners and renters as to what sort of behavior is permitted. In some residential communities, covenants or rules recorded on the deeds exist that place strict limits on what property owners can and cannot do. However, this does not mean that Stuart would definitely win his case against Ralph. He won't know until a judge tells him, and by that time, he will have spent a small fortune in legal fees. Is it worth it? If your neighbor won't abate the nuisance, it may make more sense just to close your eyes—or, if appropriate, hold your nose.

Taking Liberties

Nudity itself may constitute a nuisance. In *Mark* v. *Oregon State Department of Fish and Wildlife* (1999), beachfront prop-erty owners claimed the presence of nude people on the beach diminished the value of their home. The court agreed.

Other cases involving aesthetics and nuisance law concern cemeteries built adjacent to homes. In these cases, courts generally rule that while cemeteries have to be located somewhere, they are generally not permitted to be built alongside residential neighbor-hoods. Other such cases involve neighbors suing over the use of a private residence as a "group home" for individuals with a particular disability or disease, or for the treatment of addicts and alcoholics, or even for religious groups. There are no hard and fast rules in these areas, although courts often take the position that you do not have a right to choose your neighbors or regulate how they behave. That's because you'd then be infringing on *their* civil liberties.

Peeping-Toms

Traditionally, a peeping-tom was a lonely sort of individual not likely to share the fruits of his snooping with anyone else. Even if a peeping-tom had a camera, with how many people could he realistically be expected to share that photograph? Not all that many.

The Internet changed everything for peeping-toms. First instead of using an analog camera that would require a trip to the One-Hour Photo hut, the modern peeping-tom uses a digital camera, thus shielding him from the dirty looks that he might have received from the clerk. Instead he can take those photographs and upload them right to the web, where a theoretically innumerable audience could see his naked neighbor. Or he could do far worse things.

As Lance E. Rothenberg writes in the *American University Law Review* of June 2000, "Modern electronics have transformed the deviant, usually solitary act of peeping into a booming and perverse online industry, built specifically upon the exploitation of non-consensual pornography."

Until the Congress or the U.S. Supreme Court makes a decision, the same case can come out differently when decided in different states. For example, Rothenberg described a situation in a New Jersey mall in which an odd-looking individual was seen placing a shopping bag under the feet of women wearing skirts while riding the mall's escalators. After the eighth such incident involving an unaware female shopper, the individual was stopped by mall security. It turned out that the bag contained an 8mm camera with which the tom was shooting footage to be uploaded to a website as "upskirts." In other words, women who were simply going about their day had no idea that their private parts were about to be exposed

> **Statutes of Liberties**
>
> Whether you have an expectation of privacy in a given situation will depend largely on the decisions of judges in the state in which you live. In 2002, a case from Washington, *State* v. *Glass;* a video voyeur was successfully prosecuted after he used a shoe camera to take upskirt pictures of women in a shopping mall. The court found the women had a legitimate expectation of privacy in public.

online. In another case, the owner of a Missouri tanning salon surreptitiously taped more than 100 naked women in the company's changing room while they were getting ready to enter a tanning booth. What makes these two cases so extraordinary is that neither violated the law.

How can this be? One of the themes throughout this book is that your right to privacy in a given situation is governed by your *expectation* of privacy in said situation. As we discussed elsewhere, you have a much higher degree of privacy in your home than you do in your car, at school, at work, or while walking down the street. Traditional privacy laws offer virtually no protection to anyone in public—in a mall, in a store, or anywhere else where it can be expected that other people can see them dressed as they are. On a moral level, there is no question that the Montclair Mall peeper was committing an act that would shock the conscience of any member of society. From a legal point of view, he had not broken any laws—because there is no expectation of privacy in public.

You may have heard of other such violations of privacy on the Internet in terms of photographs of people on roller coasters or water rides at theme parks. Individuals sometimes station themselves near such rides at places where people are upside down or very wet, and therefore more vulnerable to the prying eye of the camera. Such photographs do find their way onto the Internet. The owners of amusement parks may have a right to sue such photographers for trespass—but only if they can find them.

 Taking Liberties _____

The company for "Girls Gone Wild" is known for filming young women who are intoxicated and coaxed into undressing in public. A student brought suit after a "Girls Gone Wild" cameraman secretly filmed her at a Mardi Gras festival. The student found out when her friends reported seeing her on television commercials for the videotapes. She appeared on the cover of the video and even had her full portrait plastered on billboards across Europe with the caption "American Girls"—all without her prior knowledge or consent. The case was still pending at the time of publication.

Ironically, according to Rothenberg, states are seeking to catch up with "video voyeurs." However, the language states are using in their anti-video voyeur laws falls back on the traditional concept that a right of privacy only exists where an individual has a reasonable expectation of privacy. Since you have no right to privacy in public, you are not protected from video voyeurs by the new laws. After all, they are shooting you in a public place, not in your home.

Two other authorities in this area, H. Morley Swingle and Kevin M. Zoellner, writing in the *Journal of Missouri Bar* for November/December 1996, suggest that the newly written anti-peeping-tom laws might not even apply to tanning salon owners who secretly videotape their customers. State laws generally prohibit eavesdropping, listening in on communications between two people, such as a telephone conversation. That's because in the old days, prior to the advent of modern TV technology, the only way to violate someone's privacy was to listen to them. So this is yet another area of the law that is far from settled. While some state statutes do prohibit stores from videotaping their customers in dressing rooms or changing rooms, the bottom line is that most don't. If you really need to go to a tanning salon, you may want to change at home.

Tabloid television is a major part of the society-wide cultural race to the bottom of the barrel. Under the guise of informing people, these shows humiliate and embarrass individuals, couples, and businesses without any regard for privacy rights, decency, or the pain and discomfort they often cause. As far as everyday citizens such as you and I are concerned, pretty much everyone agrees that tabloid TV goes too far.

Everyone, that is, except the courts.

Is it legitimate for reality TV show cameramen to ride along with police to tape—and then broadcast—the arrest of a citizen? Can a camera crew enter an apartment along with the fire department to videotape someone receiving CPR? Can an investigative TV news program send hidden cameras "behind the scenes" to show that a business is dishonest?

The answer, most of the time, is yes. The courts of law held that newsgathering is a protected activity under the U.S. Constitution. Courts are very slow to deny First Amendment rights to newsgatherers, unless their conduct is so egregious that it truly shocks the conscience. Courts occasionally justify behind-the-scenes cameras in workplaces by comparing them with food critics who visit restaurants without revealing the purpose of their visit.

A personal note here: I've been on both sides of this particular issue. As a researcher for CBS News's *60 Minutes* broadcast, I was once sent on an assignment to get a job as a cold caller with a bogus company that would call local businesses, claiming to be representing the Police Department, and offering to sell them ads in a police yearbook. Not too many businesses turned down a pitch like that, and they would rake in tons of money before moving to the next town. One day, I was sent out to their office and was hired. The plan was that I would work there the following Monday until 3 P.M., when Dan Rather, himself, accompanied by a camera crew, would bust through the door that I would unlock and videotape the entire group of bad guys ducking for cover under the desks.

I got the job with them on a Friday, and was going to start work on Monday. That Friday night, however, the producer of the segment called my home and left a message: It turned out that it was against CBS's Standards and Practices to have their own employees pretending to work for companies in this manner. Instead of me, they used a man who worked at the Better Business Bureau. He went and applied for a job at the same place, got hired, and let in Dan Rather and crew at the appointed hour. I saw the episode on TV, and I witnessed my punitive boss and would-be colleagues, all doing the dive-under-the-desk bit. Afterwards, a grateful Dan Rather interviewed the man from the Better Business Bureau, who recounted his tale of adventure working for this boiler room operation. My 15 minutes of fame, gone forever.

Taking Liberties

I found myself on the opposite end of this privacy issue several years ago while skiing in Switzerland. I'd taken a pretty nasty fall and needed to be removed from the mountain by sled. To my dismay, there were no St. Bernards with miniature barrels of whiskey to come to my aid. Instead, a photographer skied up along with the rescue team, and began to take pictures of me, in my agony. He either spoke no English or pretended not to, and kept taking pictures of me until I jabbed him with my ski pole. Score one for self-help, American style!

In such "undercover" operations, there are no hard and fast rules as to legitimacy. The leading case in this area involves some staffers at ABC's nighttime newsmagazine *Prime Time Live* who secretly made videotapes of practices in the meat department of a major supermarket chain. The court in that 1997 case, *Food Lion, Inc.* v. *Capital Cities/ABC, Inc.*, held that the reporters were guilty of trespass and a breach of a "duty of loyalty" to their employer, Food Lion. ABC was not liable for fraud or unfair trade practices. In other words, ABC was found to have committed some but not all of the improper practices with which it had been charged.

This case was decided by the Fourth Circuit Court of Appeals, which, although just one step below the U.S. Supreme Court in the federal court system, makes decisions that are only binding on the states within its region, not the rest of the country. So there is no clear federal law on whether or not it is legitimate for news programs to use hidden cameras. Courts do not want to put themselves in the position of determining whether a given TV show is news or entertainment. Presumably, shows that are clearly for entertainment value, as opposed to news value, would not be able to get away with hidden camera-type tactics. But who's to say where the line can be drawn between news and entertainment, especially in a world where "infotainment" rules? The courts want no part of that debate, so it's more likely than not that the media can continue to abuse the privacy of Americans with impunity.

Living in the Age of AIDS

Jane had been a top producer in her region, and as a result, the company was flying her to the national sales conference in Ixtapa, Mexico. The idea of a free trip to Mexico in February sounded awesome to Jane, who lived in Buffalo and faced that city's harsh winters. At the sales conference, Jane, who was single, met a company executive named Tom who was based in southern California. Jane and Tom hit it off over the free margaritas at the opening night party, and were something of an item throughout the five days of the sales conference.

Jane was fairly conservative in her private life. If it weren't for the sun and the tequila, she might never have become romantically involved, however briefly, with Tom. But she felt a certain safety in the sense that although he was a total stranger, he did work for the same company; he was not some guy off the street. And although he did work for the same company, he lived far enough away that any chance of a long-term relationship, which Jane was not really looking for, seemed remote. Their fling lasted the five days of the sales conference, and when it ended, they returned to their respective regions of the country. They exchanged a few e-mails, but even that level of communication petered out after a few short weeks.

Taking Liberties

Notable sports figure Earvin "Magic" Johnson was sued by a former female sex partner when he transmitted the HIV virus to her.

Tom was nothing more than a distant memory until the moment when, six months later, Jane went to the Red Cross to donate blood. Normally, she was able to circle N for No to all the questions relating to sexual practices that might have put her at risk for HIV. When she reached the question, "Have you had sex with anyone with the HIV virus?" she circled N, but she felt a slight twinge that she could not identify.

Three days later, the Red Cross called and asked whether she could make an appointment to come in and talk about the results that followed the testing of her blood. When she came in for that conversation, the news was not good.

Although apocryphal, Jane's story is not uncommon. For centuries, individuals have passed sexually transmitted diseases (STD) on to other people, sometimes knowingly, sometimes not. The question in the law is whether passing a sexually transmitted disease to another person is a criminal act, or whether an individual who gets an STD from someone else can sue that person in a civil action. This is not a classic civil liberties issue, but it's worthy of our attention nonetheless, as it relates to the right of the individual to pursue his or her life as that person sees fit.

Many states have laws making it a crime to knowingly infect another individual with a sexually transmitted disease. These laws have come to the fore in the last 20 years since the spread of the HIV virus. Individuals who are infected with an STD can also bring civil actions against the person who gave them that disease, as long as it can be shown that the defendant knew or should have known that he or she had the disease at the time of transmission. Individuals can bring civil actions on a variety of bases. They can claim battery, which is defined in the law as a "harmful or offensive intentional contact" with someone else. They can also claim fraud—the sex partner denied having the disease but concealed it. There is also a right to sue for intentional infliction of emotional distress; it is, of course, extremely distressing to learn that one has acquired a sexually transmitted disease, especially one that is most likely incurable and fatal, as in the case of AIDS.

> **Statutes of Liberties**
>
> Civil liability for the sexual transmission of diseases has been founded on actions for battery, misrepresentation, emotional distress, and negligence.

The defendant in such a case can claim that he or she had no knowledge of the disease at the time of sexual transmission to the plaintiff. This defense becomes especially complex given the nature of the HIV virus. People with HIV are often asymptomatic for months or even years before the onset of any AIDS-related illnesses. From a policy perspective, it can be argued that society encourages at-risk to get tested. On the other hand, the fact that they were tested could be used against them in a case where they are being criminally prosecuted for spreading HIV.

There is also the possibility that an individual *should have known* that he or she was infected with HIV at the time of intercourse. That knowledge could be construed from the fact that the person is experiencing AIDS-related illnesses, such as Karposi's sarcoma, certain forms of pneumonia, and other illnesses that are most often found in young people only when they are HIV positive.

The question of legal action in the transmission of an STD is not an easy one to answer, as it requires the plaintiff to prove that the defendant knew or should have known that he or she was HIV positive at the time that they had sex. Society also has to decide whether it wants to afford a right of privacy to HIV-positive individuals—should they have to disclose that they are in fact HIV positive to every potential sex partner? Or do they have a right to keep such private information to themselves?

This area of the law, as with the others discussed in this chapter, is far from settled. It does seem clear, however, that an HIV-positive individual who fails to inform potential sex partners of his or her condition runs afoul of both criminal prosecution and civil suits.

The Least You Need to Know

- ◆ Because of varying factors in each case, it is nearly impossible to determine how a judge will rule on an issue.

- ◆ Due to changes in societal mores, many laws are in a constant state of flux.

- ◆ Once e-mail has been opened by the recipient, it is no longer considered a private matter.

- ◆ Knowingly transmitting an STD can result in criminal or civil prosecution.

Chapter 13

Rights on the Road

In This Chapter

♦ Driving while black

♦ What's the problem, officer?

♦ Licensed to give out personal data

♦ Red light district

After bed and work, the place where most of us spend the most amount of time is our automobiles. Cars represent both freedom (mobility to go where we want when we want) and restriction, (you need to have a license, insurance in most states, and vehicle registration and you need to follow motor vehicle rules). So it's not surprising that autos symbolize another important crossroad between the rights of the individual and the needs of society.

In this chapter, we're going to examine what civil liberties are involved when it comes to you and your automobile. Specifically, we'll address the questions of racial profiling, legal and illegal stops, searches and seizures (and what to do if you're pulled over), drunk driving, and those pesky new cameras that photograph drivers speeding through red lights. Let's hit the road!

Racial Profiling

Racial profiling is the police practice of pulling drivers over based on their race, national origin, or ethnicity. Racial profiling is commonly known as "DWB" or "driving while black." The practice is not only morally wrong; it's illegal. Harvard Law School Professor Randall Kennedy describes it as "a type of racial tax for the war against drugs that whites and other groups escape."

The police justification for racial profiling is that many police officers and their superiors believe that people of color commit a disproportionate amount of crimes. Therefore, by pulling over a driver who is of color, they are increasing the likelihood that they are going to find that the driver is guilty of something—a weapons violation, drug possession, or some other illegal activity. Because the Fourth Amendment and case law demand that police officers have at least a particularized and reasonable suspicion that a crime is being or is about to be committed before they can stop and search someone, racial profiling is unjustifiable.

Legal Dictionary

Racial profiling—The police practice of pulling drivers over based on their race, national origin, or ethnicity.

The Law of the Land

Racial profiling violates the Fourteenth Amendment right to equal protection under the law, as well as the Fourth Amendment right to freedom from improper searches and seizures.

Racial profiling has been so prevalent in the United States that there are laws or proposed laws, lawsuits, and reporting requirements for police departments in virtually every state of the union. Some police departments that have been found guilty of racial profiling are required to keep data on traffic stops, often precinct by precinct, so as to indicate whether they are pulling over a disproportionate number of minority drivers. Additionally, some police departments require racial sensitivity training for their police officers, to attack the notions that people of color are more prone to committing crimes than whites.

Racial profiling is not just ineffective; it is psychologically damaging for those millions of Americans who experience it. Among blacks, it is very difficult to find a person who has not experienced racial profiling at some point in his or her life. Racial profiling triggers fear, anger, rage, and a sense of being outside the system, which leads to a pervasive sense of alienation.

Ironically, in the landmark 1996 case *Whren* v. *United States*, the U.S. Supreme Court actually strengthened the hand of those who continue to practice racial profiling. The *Whren* decision permits "pretextual stops," stops that police officer makes on the "pretext" of some minor driving violation, such as changing lanes without signaling or having a tail light out. The real reason that the police officer is stopping the car has to do with the officer's suspicion that the occupants of the car are committing some sort of crime. In *Whren*, the U.S. Supreme Court said that pretextual stops are legitimate and legal, and that any such traffic stop gives police officers a right to search the car.

Mind If I Take a Look?

There is a stepping stone process to searches of motor vehicles/When we are driving, we have a reduced expectation of privacy compared to when we are sitting in our homes. On the road, anyone can look in the window of our car and see us. Since our expectation of privacy is lowered, the police have a greater right to examine your car and its contents—without a warrant—than they would in your home.

The Fourth Amendment forbids unreasonable searches and seizures. Normally, if a police officer were to search your home, he or she would have to obtain a warrant.

Because the Supreme Court recognized that it is not possible to get a warrant every time a police officer pulls over a car, it is legal for an officer to stop a car with a driver who appears to be committing a traffic violation or other crime. It is also legal to search the car and its occupants in proportion with the officer's reasonable suspicion.

Taking Liberties

The greater the level of suspicion on the part of the police officer, the more elaborate the permissible search.

Remain Calm!

If you are stopped, the wisest course is to turn on your interior light, put the keys on the dashboard, and put your hands on top of the steering wheel. A police officer approaches a stopped car warily, because any such encounter could be a fatal one. Politely ask the officer why you have been stopped. Don't give attitude or ask a question like, "What's the problem, officer?" No matter what your friends have told you, don't ask for a badge number. There's no reason to antagonize the officer, who derives little pleasure out of these encounters.

Stay in the car, and make no sudden movements. Don't say anything more than they ask, and above all, don't argue. If you have been injured in a car accident, try to get photos. It is a very good idea to keep a small disposable camera in your glove box, so that you can have photos to document your side of the story in an accident case. If you don't like the way the police officer treats you, you can file a written complaint with the Internal Affairs Department of your police force or the Civilian Complaint Board.

What can police officers do? They can ask you to get out of the car and present your license and registration, ask questions, ask for your consent to search your car, determine the VIN (Vehicle Identification Number), and control the car and its occupants for the length of time of the stop.

Let's say that the officer pulls the driver over and suspects that something is amiss. The officer can then ask the driver to get out of the car. Let's say that the officer now notices a bulge in the waistband of the driver. If he believes that the bulge is a gun, then it is legitimate for the officer to frisk or pat down the driver (or occupant) for reasons of officer safety. If, in fact, the driver appears to be carrying a gun, it would now be legitimate for the police officer to arrest the driver. Similarly, let's say that a police officer sees a marijuana cigarette in the ashtray. Such a violation of the law would permit the officer to move to the next stepping stone and perform a complete search of the car. And so it goes. The greater the level of the police officer's suspicion, the greater the level of intrusion into the privacy of the vehicle and its occupants.

> **Looking for Liberty**
>
> Surprisingly, you can say no to a police officer's request to search your car and you can't be arrested for saying no. Most people don't realize this. As attorney Raymond A. Cassar comments, "If they have to ask your permission, you may assume they have no right to search your car."

Generally, if a police officer were to find a marijuana cigarette burning in the ashtray of a car, the officer would arrest the occupants and then call for the car to be towed to the nearest police station, where it would be searched. If a pound of cocaine were found in the trunk at that time, that search would be considered legitimate and the evidence would be admissible in court. On the other hand, if a police officer had simply pulled over a driver for failing to change lanes and then demanded that he or she open a locked trunk, such a search would be considered an impermissible violation of the Fourth Amendment.

The Vehicle Exemption

Back in 1925, the courts developed what is known as the "vehicle exemption" to the Fourth Amendment. This exemption is the most far-reaching justification for police officers searching cars without a warrant. As we said earlier, we have a diminished expectation of privacy when we are driving in our cars. In addition, cars are mobile (duh!), which means that a driver could drive off with the evidence if a police officer had to go out and find an impartial judge or a magistrate to issue a warrant before he could search and seize.

Finally, cars are burdened with a great degree of regulation to begin with. You have to have a car registered and insured in most states, and you have to be licensed in order to be driving legally. Since a car is essentially an environment replete with a high degree of regulation, it's understood that you don't have as much freedom in your car as you do in your home.

Put all those factors together—a diminished expectation of privacy, mobility, and an atmosphere of regulation—and you have a situation where it is legitimate for police officers to search vehicles without a warrant. Police officers do need probable cause, which is to say that if they did have time to present the evidence for searching a car to a detached, neutral magistrate or judge, that magistrate would indeed issue a warrant. The bottom line: Police don't have free reign to turn your car upside down, but if they have a reasonable suspicion that you're doing something illegal, they are free to search your car without a warrant.

> **Statutes of Liberties**
>
> Since cars can get away quickly, taking evidence of a crime with them, warrants are not required for many kinds of automobile searches.

There are several other kinds of legitimate reasons for searching cars. There is the vehicle pat-down, or frisk. A police officer with probable cause is allowed to search your car for weapons. Not the whole car, and not the trunk or your locked glove box, because there is no instant access to those places and therefore a police officer's life would not be threatened by a gun in such a place. However, any area of the car to which the driver or a passenger would have instant access can be searched for weapons—no warrant necessary. If a police officer finds a weapon or other contraband, the vehicle exemption is triggered, and a full search is now legitimate.

If a driver or occupant of a car is arrested, a police officer may make a "search incident to the arrest." This search must be contemporaneous with the arrest, and only allows the police officer to search the passenger compartment and any unlocked containers therein before the car is impounded. Once the car is impounded at a police station, a full search is legitimate.

This is called an *inventory search*. This is a search for valuables such as jewelry or money. The police do not want people coming up to them after a car has been impounded only to be told, "You guys stole all our money!" Therefore, police officers are entitled to perform inventory searches to look for valuables. On the other hand, an inventory search cannot be a pretext for a search for evidence such as guns or drugs.

The best way to avoid trouble with the police is to drive under the speed limit, while wearing a seat belt, and without drugs or weapons in your car. It sounds so obvious. Would that more people followed those simple suggestions.

Secrets of a Driver's License

Your driver's license provides a fair amount of information to the police. Specifically, your license reveals your name, birth date, address, physical description, social security number, instances of failure to appear in court or pay fines, and the status of your license (whether it is valid, revoked, suspended, or expired). The information contained on your driver's license also reveals any major traffic convictions you have had in the last seven years or any minor offenses in the last three years or at least what the website Privacyrights.org claims.

Taking Liberties

Some states, such as California, have a magnetic strip, similar to that of a credit card, on the back of the license. These magnetic strips contain lots of personal information. Civil libertarians are concerned that these strips could be coded with considerably more information about individuals, thus violating their privacy rights without their even knowing it.

Departments of Motor Vehicles can and do release driver information to marketers and even casual requesters. Today, however, some states require notification to a driver before his or her driver's license information can be revealed to a stranger. This new legislation is in response to a California case in the late 1980s in which an actor was murdered by an obsessed fan who found her home address simply by contacting the DMV.

One for the Road?

Drunk driving is a huge problem in American society, and laws have become increasingly strict in terms of dealing with it. In the eyes of the law, when you accept the privilege (it's not a right!) of driving, you've also accepted the rules of the road with regard to drunk driving. This acceptance on your part means that police officers can arrest you for drunk driving based on observation, sobriety tests, or, depending on the state in which you are imbibing, a blood-alcohol level as measured by your breath, urine, or even your blood. Depending on the state, from .08 to .10 percent of blood alcohol concentration means that you are legally drunk. For individuals under the age of 21, the level of blood-alcohol concentration is much lower; .01 to .02 percent blood-alcohol level means you are legally drunk. The courts can suspend a driver's license for one year if a person refuses to take a test and a prosecutor can so inform a jury at a trial.

Drunks have few rights—police officers can actually ask drunk drivers questions without offering them their Miranda rights. (Presumably, they are too drunk to understand exactly what the Miranda rights are all about.) In the case of felony drunk driving, in which a person hits or kills a pedestrian or other driver or commits some other serious crime while driving high, police can use reasonable force in order to draw blood from the driver. In short, one for the road just is not that great an idea.

Say Cheese!

In many communities across the country, the police have instituted a new way of catching individuals who run red lights. The new-fangled speed trap uses one or more cameras mounted at intersections where it is common for individuals to speed through traffic lights. Why is it so important to catch these drivers? Statistics indicate that over a million people are injured every year, and 8,000 are killed, at intersections, and a very high number of those injuries and deaths are attributed to drivers running red lights. In addition, more than one out of five accidents in urban areas are due to drivers who run red lights.

Many drivers don't like the idea of cameras observing them from on high. There's something creepy about it, almost Orwellian in nature, about the government using unmanned technology to spy on its citizens. Are red light cameras a violation of your civil liberties?

> **Statutes of Liberties**
>
> People who argue that red light cameras simply raise funds for municipalities miss the point. There is an epidemic of danger-ous driving today, especially as more drivers use cell phones. Any law that protects lives is a good thing. Otherwise, why have stop lights at all, if people feel they can ignore them with impunity? Some see red light cameras as beneficial to society while others see them as a pro-found violation of civil liberties.

Not according to the courts. In keeping with the due process clause of the Fourteenth Amendment, there is a requirement that drivers must be notified about the placement of such cameras. Due process has two prongs: first, an individual must have notice that a right is going to be taken away and second, the individual has the right to a hearing to determine whether the government action is fair. In the case of red light cameras, cities provide notice to drivers in two ways: through publicity in the media prior to the installation of such cameras, and through the use of signs warning motorists that red light cameras are present.

Do you get a hearing after you get such a ticket? If you want one, of course. Many people find it easier to simply write the check for the fine than to fight the ticket. The drivers who think they were unfairly penalized by a red light camera do have the right to a hearing before a traffic court. Is there a privacy right that's violated by the use of red light cameras? Again, the test is what sort of expectation an individual has as to his or her privacy in a given situation. As we've discussed, drivers have a lower level of expectation than do people sitting in their homes. Since you could be observed by a police officer—or another driver—as you speed through a red light, you have no privacy right in so doing. Thus, there is no privacy issue from a civil liberties standpoint.

Here's how the cameras work. If your car runs a red light, an automatic sensor takes four digital pictures, which are included along with the citation. The pictures show the car crossing against the red light, a close-up of the license plate, a close-up of the driver, and a broad shot of the intersection. You are also offered the opportunity to purchase wallet-size photos or blowups for your living room wall.

Although that last statement is not entirely true, it does bring up another challenge to red light cameras. Many wonder whether such cameras exist in order to stop red light violators or to simply make money for towns and cities. They certainly are a cash cow, there's no question about that. Red light cameras catch thousands and thousands of violators in the act, and the overwhelming majority of them do not challenge the citations, thus generating great revenue for the city. On the other hand, if you don't want to pay a fine, use your break pedal. That's what it's for.

> **Looking for Liberty**
>
> Police Officer William Potts of Detroit, Michigan, is credited with inventing the first traffic light, which was installed in 1920 at the intersection of Woodward and Michigan Avenues in that city. His concept was to modify train signals for use by automotive traffic. A true unsung hero; we should be calling traffic lights "Potts Lights."

In some states such as California, the Department of Motor Vehicles can place a hold on a red light violator's registration to compel the payments for unpaid citations. The only legitimate challenges to red light tickets are if the driver of the car is not the person in the picture, and if the pictures are too blurry to offer recognizable images of the driver, the license plate, and the traffic light.

The Least You Need to Know

- ◆ People have a lower expectation level of privacy in their cars than at home, and so their right to privacy is less as well.

- ◆ Racial profiling violates the Fourteenth Amendment right to equal protection under the law.

- ◆ Courts have ruled that the use of red light cameras does not violate your civil liberties.

- ◆ The greater the level of suspicion on the part of the police officer, the more elaborate the permissible search of a vehicle.

Chapter 14

Right of Association?

In This Chapter

- ◆ Imposing curfews
- ◆ Kids' rights?
- ◆ Public assembly
- ◆ Flag-burning: legal or not?

In this chapter, we're going to examine three fundamental questions of civil liberties as they affect the rights of individuals to gather, demonstrate, take actions such as burning the American flag in public, or even just hang out or wander around after dark. Each of these issues is a civil liberties "hot button," and powerful emotional issues drive both sides of these debates. We will begin with the question of city-ordained curfews for minors, and then consider the question of public demonstrations and how First Amendment rights of speech and freedom of assembly are legally regulated, and then we will take up the issue of whether it is constitutionally permissible to burn the American flag.

City Curfews for Kids

There is something disturbing about the idea of kids of all ages out late into the evening, away from parental supervision, at risk. No parent needs reminding about what a dangerous world we live in. With increasing haste, cities and towns across the United States have therefore passed curfew laws that essentially confine to their homes children who are not accompanied by adults, not running errands, or not engaged in First Amendment activities such as attending church.

Taking Liberties

Several California cities have daytime curfew laws. School-age children seen in public during school hours may be fined or sentenced to community service.

Statutes of Liberties

Las Vegas implemented a curfew as a means to combat underage prostitution.

These curfew laws specify the times during which unaccompanied children must be off the streets. Although highly popular across the country, the laws also indicate that children must not be seated in cars by themselves or hanging out on street corners, in public places, or anywhere other than where they live. Most ordinances contain punishments for children who violate the curfew. Some ordinances also punish parents of children who break curfew or who are repeat offenders.

Cities that pass curfews for minors offer the following reasons for doing so. First, they want to do something about the problem of teenage crime. In theory, by having a curfew, police have a valid reason for challenging the presence of any young person on the streets after dark. Without a curfew, the police might be able to pull over and talk to such a teen, but would have no automatic grounds for taking that person into custody or driving him or her home. The theory is that a curfew for young people reduces teen crime, although there are no clear statistics that such is the case.

The second reason for passing curfews for kids is to protect the kids themselves from becoming victims of crime. City streets are dangerous places at night, no matter what your age. By passing laws that limit the rights of children to be out after a certain time, cities are working to protect their young people from becoming victims of crimes.

A third reason is the concept of enhancing parental authority. The idea here is that parents have more control if their kids cannot be out after a certain hour of the evening. As for this point, many parents disagree, and say that *they* want to make decisions about when and where their children are free to go outside the home, and that they do not want the assistance—or interference—of the town or city when they are so deciding.

The question of whether curfews for minors are valid is surprisingly complex, touching on many different aspects of American legal history, constitutional rights, and the courts.

Kids Have *Some* Rights

According to the U.S. Supreme Court, the U.S. Constitution and Bill of Rights apply to children as well as adults, but come with significant limitations when it comes to children. For example, it is constitutional and permissible to pass laws that forbid the sale of pornographic materials to minors. Although such laws could be construed as violations of their First Amendment rights, the lawyers who so argue are generally told by the Supreme Court to go home and wash their mouths out with soap.

Looking for Liberty
"One of the hallmarks of a free society is the law abiding citizen's ability to go about unchallenged by state authority, secure in the assumption that the presumption of innocence protects him from inquiry or interference without clear and just cause. Curfews contradict this ability, and contribute to the slavish state of mind that characterizes people who live under totalitarian systems, and who must be prepared at all times to give state authorities some explanation even for their innocent pastimes." —Alan Keyes

Furthermore, it is constitutionally permissible for states to make it more difficult for teenagers to get abortions than adults, especially without their parent's knowledge. The theory is that children are more vulnerable than adults and thus need a higher degree of protection. Children also do not have the life experience with which to decide important issues, and therefore need protection and guidance on the part of society. Finally, it is public policy in the United States that parenting matters, therefore parents get a "boost" from the legal system by backing up their decisions within a legal framework. The most obvious example is that most of us take for granted that movies should be rated depending on their content.

The question arises: What rights do kids have? The most important rights that children, or anyone in American society, can enjoy are those preserved in the First Amendment—specifically the right to freedom of speech, freedom of assembly, and freedom of religion. Children do not have absolute rights in these areas; witness the antipornography law we discussed a moment ago. But state and federal courts are loath to trample on First Amendment rights of minors when it is possible to avoid doing so.

In addition to these, there are other special rights afforded parents and children. These rights are guaranteed by the Fourteenth Amendment, and they include the right to travel, and the rights of parents to raise children as they see fit. So when a town or city passes a curfew for children, it does not pass that law in some sort of legal void. There is actually a great deal of history regarding curfews that the courts will consider when examining the constitutionality of a given curfew ordinance. There are social issues that ought to be taken into consideration as well.

A Sorry History

America indeed has a sorry history when it comes to curfews. For centuries, race-based curfews were in effect in Washington, D.C., and other major cities throughout the United States. It was illegal for a black person to go about in a city at night unless he or she was serving a white person at that time or driving the equivalent of a taxi. These race-based curfews lasted well into the twentieth century.

During World War II, American citizens of Italian, Japanese, and German origin were subject to curfews on the grounds that they posed potential security threats to the nation. Indeed, Japanese citizens were interned in military base concentration camps up and down the West Coast during World War II. Only in the last decade or so has Congress finally passed legislation apologizing to the Japanese, Italian, and German citizens of the World War II era for subjecting them to curfews and essentially suspecting their patriotism.

Statutes of Liberties
Governments have imposed curfews for years, and not only against minors. In the days before the Civil War, whites regulated what times colored people could be out on the streets.

In more recent times, even into the 1960s and 1970s, curfews existed on college campuses—but they only applied to women. The idea was that if women were off the streets and paths of college campuses at night, they would be less subject to sexual assault or other crime. These rules were challenged in court and were found to be unconstitutional. (Perhaps it would have been wiser to let the women walk around freely at night and impose a curfew on the men.)

In Chapter 12, we discussed the concept of "driving while black," the phenomenon of racial profiling by police on our nation's highways. It has been shown throughout the country that police frequently exhibit discriminatory attitudes toward drivers who are black or Latino and pull them over in numbers far higher than those of white drivers, suspecting them of crimes, or simply harassing them. It could be said that curfew enforcement offers examples of "walking while black," because in city after city, data indicates that black and Latino youths are far more likely to be stopped, frisked, or arrested for curfew violations compared to white kids. Furthermore, curfew enforcement for the most part takes place in cities, where poor and black residents are the majority in many neighborhoods. Critics of curfews point out that the mere fact of curfews is discriminatory when poor, black children are confined to apartments while middle-class or upper middle-class white kids can enjoy backyards, basements, and front lawns.

Critics also charge that curfews are only selectively enforced; that white neighborhoods are seldom targeted for curfew violations, while areas where black youths congregate are far more likely to be scrutinized by police. The sense of unfairness that this brings causes a terrible stigmatization of black and Hispanic youths.

> ### Statutes of Liberties
>
> When curfew laws were first introduced in Europe several hundred years ago, they were used by the upper classes of society to control the lower classes. The theory was that crime originates from those in the lower class and thus placing restrictions on poor people would reduce the amount of crimes that they have an opportunity to commit.

The Constitutionality of Curfews

On *Saturday Night Live* during the 1970s, Father Guido Sarducci summarized constitutional law in this manner: "Anything we don't like is unconstitutional." We would like to think that there is a more rational way for courts to determine what laws are constitutional and what are not. Unfortunately, many judges will tell you that it comes down to a question of gut feeling. They sense whether or not a law should be constitutional, and then they provide a method of backing up their gut feeling with the kinds of legal words and phrases that other courts and legal commentators will find acceptable. This process appears to be particularly true when it comes to curfews.

Let's take a brief trip to a constitutional law class in any law school's first-year program. Here you will find the professor telling the students that there are three ways by which a court can determine whether a given law is constitutional or not.

The first method is called the *rational basis* test. Until the 1960s and the civil rights era, this test was the most commonly used method of determining constitutionality of a given law. If a law treated one group of people differently from another—kids versus adults, women versus men, blacks versus whites, all that a court had to determine was if there were some sort of rational connection between the intent of the law and the classification it was imposing. In other words, it was not unconstitutional for states in the South during the Jim Crow era to say that blacks had to sit in the back of the bus.

> ### Looking for Liberty
>
> In 1955, the city of Montgomery, Alabama, had a municipal law that required blacks to sit at the back of the city's buses. Rosa Parks is known for her incredible courage to stand up against racism when she took a front seat and refused to move to the back of the bus.

Although it seems clear that such a law denied blacks equal protection, under the rational basis doctrine, the law could distinguish between whites and blacks as long as there was some sort of important public policy that was being met. In that era in the South, the important public policy was the honoring of the greater rights of white people. Since there was a rational basis between putting blacks in the back of the bus, and allowing whites to enjoy superior rights, that law was considered constitutional.

Fortunately, by the 1960s, this way of thinking was replaced by a new method of analysis. It is rare today that a law is considered constitutional or unconstitutional based on the test of rational basis. Instead, courts examine a law that distinguishes on the basis of race using a *strict scrutiny* test. When a court subjects a law to this analysis, it asks this question: Is the discrimination that this law permits "precisely tailored" to a compelling government interest? Curfews provide an excellent example of how this might work: Curfews distinguish between children and adults. When a curfew law for minors is passed, then the legal system is clearly discriminating against people under a certain age and is clearly giving more rights to adults. In order for it to be legitimate for the state to discriminate in this manner, that discrimination must be precisely tailored, or exactly what's necessary in order to meet a "compelling government interest." The state must also prove that the means it uses to meet this interest is the least restrictive means available.

Supporters of curfews, as we have seen, say that there are three compelling government interests in having night curfews for kids: to reduce crime by young people, to reduce the number of young people victimized by crime, and to enhance parental authority. So if you're going to apply strict scrutiny to curfew laws, you have to believe that limiting the rights of young people matches up perfectly with some or all of those governmental desires.

Legal Dictionary

There are three tests for determining whether a law is constitutionally permissible:

Rational basis—The law is constitutional if it is rationally related to some legitimate government interest.

Intermediate scrutiny—The law is constitutional only if it is substantially related to an important government interest.

Strict scrutiny—The law is unconstitutional unless it is necessary to achieve a compelling government interest, and the law uses the least restrictive means necessary to advance that interest.

Many courts today apply the strict scrutiny test to curfews—but come out with different results. Some courts say that curfews do advance a compelling governmental interest, while others state the exact opposite. We are all waiting for the U.S. Supreme Court to come down from its perch and make a definitive ruling, one way or the other.

Intermediate scrutiny requires an "important" governmental aim. For example, the pattern of the U.S. Supreme Court indicates that racism is more odious than sexism. Laws pertaining to racial issues receive "strict scrutiny"—the highest standard of analysis. Gender-based laws, on the other hand, only receive "intermediate scrutiny" and they are harder to declare unconstitutional.

Public Speech

The question often arises as to whether a particular group has the right to use a public space like a park or a street for a demonstration, concert, or march. The law in this area initially developed when the U.S. Supreme Court began to consider cases involving Jehovah's Witnesses and their rights to go door to door with their religious materials. The Supreme Court held repeatedly that "little people" like Jehovah's Witnesses had no other alternative if they wanted to get their message out to the public. They could not afford mass mailings or advertisements, so if their right to go door to door were taken away, they would have no ability to share their message with the world.

In the 1941 case of *Cox* v. *New Hampshire*, the U.S. Supreme Court created the framework by which all public demonstrations, concerts, and speeches are judged today. That test is called the "time, place, and manner" rule. In other words, a city or town seeking to impose restrictions on speech would have to justify its actions. A locality would have to balance the First Amendment Rights of those who sought to use a public space for a speech, demonstration, or concert against three requirements. First, the regulation must be content-neutral—in other words, you can't make a rule to limit points of view you don't like. Second, it must be narrowly tailored to serve a significant governmental interest. That is, you can't simply pass a rule saying "No speeches on Main Street, ever." And third, it must leave open alternative channels for communication of information. If you're going to

The Law of the Land

The time, place, and manner rule is a doctrine that enables government officials to implement reasonable content-neutral regulations on speech that is considered harmful. The regulation must be narrowly tailored to serve a significant government interest and should leave open alternative channels of communication.

forbid a group the right to gather in the park, you must make some other arrangement for them to get their point across.

meets the 3 criteria

Decisions by cities and towns about issuing permits for demonstrations, concerts, speeches, or other events in public places have to be content-neutral. In other words, the government cannot approve or deny a particular group a right to a permit simply because the government likes or dislikes the group's message. It is permissible, however, to decline to give a permit to a group if the demonstration would have a bad effect on, say, the park where the event would take place, the neighborhood, public safety, or even the sound levels involved in the concert or demonstration.

For example, there is a group called Rock Against Racism that sought to have public concerts in New York City. Neighbors complained about the high sound volume at the concerts. When Rock Against Racism refused to lower its sound volume, the city actually "pulled the plug" on one of its concerts and silenced the affair. Rock Against Racism went to the Supreme Court and lost—(*Ward* v. *Rock Against Racism*) because of its own stubborn unwillingness to work with the city and balance its First Amendment right to put on a concert against the rights of the surrounding neighbors to a little peace and quiet. Indeed, other musical groups frequently used the same performance space, but always complied with city regulations about volume. Rock Against Racism in many ways was its own worst enemy; if only it had sought to work with the city to balance its rights against those of the neighboring residents, its concerts might have been permitted to go forward.

Another important case regarding time, place, and manner took place in late 1977, when a group sought to sleep overnight in Lafayette Park, opposite the White House in Washington, D.C. In *U.S.* v. *Thomas*, the Supreme Court held that it was not legitimate to conduct that sort of protest because the park department had a legitimate interest in keeping the park free of people at night, so that the park itself could continue to flourish. We see this balancing test in effect whenever an organization seeks a permit for any gathering to take place in a public space.

The Nazis March in Skokie

In 1982, Nazi leader Frank Collin sought to receive a permit to conduct a march in the predominantly Jewish town of Skokie, Illinois. The permit request took on national and international significance because Skokie was the home to many Jews who had survived the concentration camps. The case pitted two fundamental American rights: the right to freedom of assembly and speech and the right to freedom from troubling political speech. In our society, freedom of speech is not an absolute; it isn't permissible, of course, to yell "fire" in a crowded theater. Nor is hate speech permissible under the U.S. Constitution. There was nothing clear-cut about whether the Nazis should have been given a permit to march in Skokie, exercising their First Amendment rights at the expense of the rights of the residents, including Holocaust survivors, to be free from hateful speech.

The American Civil Liberties Union entered the fray on behalf of the Nazis. Although the ACLU helped the Nazis to win four separate court contests, they ultimately lost 30,000 members as a result of their support for the controversial group. The ACLU, of course, was not supporting Nazism; they were supporting individuals wishing to exercise their First Amendment rights.

> **Looking for Liberty**
>
> The American Civil Liberties Union was founded in 1920 by Roger Baldwin to champion the freedom to express unpopular ideas. The organization seeks to defend the constitutional rights of every individual in the United States. In that effort, sometimes they must defend individuals whose ideas are blatantly offensive to many, such as the Ku Klux Klan.

Can a society really have First Amendment rights if the majority can pick and choose who can enjoy those rights? Probably not. Ultimately, a compromise was reached, and a small Nazi march was permitted to take place in another part of Chicago, far from the Holocaust survivors of Skokie.

The bottom line: Exercising one's First Amendment rights in a public setting like a park or a city street depends on the time, place, and manner in which the organizers intend to make use of public facilities.

Burning the Flag

Flag burning is considered *symbolic speech* protected by the First Amendment. Symbolic speech enjoys the same protections as actual speech, according to the U.S. Supreme Court, which most recently addressed this issue in the case of *Texas* v. *Johnson* in 1989. Five years earlier, at the Republican National Convention in Dallas, an individual named Gregory Lee Johnson burned an American flag while President Reagan was making a speech in the nearby conventional hall. Johnson was convicted under a Texas law that criminalized the "desecration" of "a venerated object." He appealed to the Supreme Court, and a divided Court held that the American system is strong enough to permit individuals to challenge it, either verbally or, as in this case, nonverbally.

The resulting uproar led to a call from then-president George H. W. Bush for legislation prohibiting the burning of American flags. Such a law was passed and it was subsequently declared unconstitutional by the U.S. Supreme Court when it promptly came up for review. Although there was much talk of a new constitutional amendment to protect the flag from being burned, any such patriotic furor eventually petered out.

Taking Liberties

The defendant in *Texas v. Johnson* was facing a one-year prison sentence and $2,000 fine for burning the American flag. Until the 1989 Supreme Court decision, 48 states and the federal government had laws on the books prohibiting flag desecration.

Reason prevailed, and it is understood that while the desecration of the American flag is indeed a repugnant act, it is protected by the U.S. Constitution. Indeed, the fact that our constitutional system permits such symbolic challenges as flag-burning only serves to indicate its strength. News reports often show demonstrators in other countries burning American flags as a means of protest against Uncle Sam. One wonders what would happen to those same mobs if they were to burn flags of their own nations. Probably nothing good.

The Least You Need to Know

- ◆ The Constitution and Bill of Rights apply to children, but with significant limitations.

- ◆ Critics of curfews argue that the laws are unconstitutional due to racial discrimination.

- ◆ Public demonstrations must undergo the "time, place, and manner" rule.

- ◆ The Constitution's allowance of such defiant acts as flag burning only serves to emphasize its strength.

You've Got Jail: Civil Liberties Behind Bars

In This Chapter

- ◆ The reality of prisons
- ◆ Arguments for incarceration
- ◆ Inmates' rights
- ◆ "Hot button" issues

Nobody wants to go to jail. We recoil at the idea of confinement, of regimentation, of the intimidating, oppressive atmosphere we intuitively expect prisons and jails to present. In the 1980s film *The Gods Must Be Crazy*, one of the characters said that when Africans are jailed, they often die within 30 days because they cannot see the sky. In most prisons and jails, we're not exactly talking river views. What little natural light there is flows in through narrow slits of reinforced glass reminiscent of gunwales on medieval castles. Jail is not a place where most of us would like to spend a night, let alone a period of years.

Yet, prisons and jails are not as horrifying in modern America as we often might imagine. Many of us derive our expectations about correctional institutions and penal officers from movies such as *The Shawshank Redemption* or *Birdman of Alcatraz*. Contrary to the Hollywood image, most prisons and jails are not the kind of gloomy, cavernous, nineteenth-century atrocities that were most likely built with the thought of breaking the spirit of those who entered. Similarly, most penal officials, from wardens down to guards, are not sadistic individuals who like to make the inmates suffer over grievances real and imagined.

Elementary, by Design

Penal officials have significant limitations on the way they may manage the lives of those for whom they are responsible. Correction officials, by and large, are not the abusive "tough guys" we see in the movies. Rather they are indistinguishable from other law enforcement agents such as police officers or highway patrolmen and women—they are dedicated individuals with a fairly thankless task to perform, one that is unpredictable and occasionally highly dangerous, and one for which society offers little in the way of recognition or thanks, financial or otherwise. No one gets rich working in a prison. The men and women who take on the task of regulating the behavior of inmates are generally very courageous individuals performing a public service without which our society would cease to function.

Taking Liberties

Many civilians—neither prisoners nor corrections officers—go to prison every day. Attorneys, members of religious groups, members of Alcoholics Anonymous, and volunteers who teach (among other things) writing and acting often visit prisons. It's a powerful experience; you might want to see the inside of a prison or jail for yourself! (But not as a customer, of course!)

Statutes of Liberties

Inmates must have access to the courts and most prisons are equipped with law libraries so that inmates can learn how to write their own appeals. Most inmates are far too poor to engage lawyers on the outside to litigate on their own behalf.

Do abuses take place in prisons and jails? Of course they do. Correctional institutions are run by human beings, and human beings do fall short of their highest capabilities from time to time. This is true in virtually any field one can imagine, be it business, politics, entertainment, or even religion. Yes, people are fallible, but the problem is that we tend to paint with a very broad brush anyone who is a member of a group containing individuals who have, on occasion, done the wrong thing. The majority of the time, corrections officers do the right thing every day.

Throw Away the Key?

One of the reference sources for this chapter quotes Dostoyevsky as saying that you can judge a society by the way it treats its men and women in prisons and jails. By that standard, we in America don't come off half bad. The fact is that when people are imprisoned, we don't forget about them and throw away the key. Rather, although the civil liberties of inmates are severely restricted, many rights of prisoners still remain. Corrections officers do a fairly credible job of upholding the rights and civil liberties of inmates. When they fail to do so, prisoners' rights organizations, the American Civil Liberties Union, law school legal clinics, and other individuals and groups step in to publicize these lapses, and to win redress for affected prisoners.

The whole point of incarceration is to deny rights to individuals who have committed crimes. The American penal system uses incarceration as a tool to accomplish many aims. First there is the concept of punishment. Committing a crime leads to loss of liberty.

Second is the notion of rehabilitation. Behind bars, individuals have opportunities to reflect on their actions, and even start new lives. It is possible to complete an education behind bars, gain computer training, learn new trades, attend 12-step programs that combat drug and alcohol addiction, to attend religious services provided by a wide variety of outside groups, and to engage in counseling in order to reflect on one's life and one's acts. While the rate of recidivism—the return to crime post-release—for inmates is quite high, nonetheless, many do go on to lead productive lives involving work, family, and community, without a return to penal institutions. In other words, a stint in a prison or jail can be the beginning of a new life and the end of an old one.

The Law of the Land

The Eighth Amendment protects prisoners from "cruel and unusual punishment." This is often cited by death penalty opponents. In fact, the Eighth Amendment prohibits abusive prison conditions of all types.

A third aspect of the use of incarceration is the notion of retribution. In prior eras, if one individual committed a crime against a member of another family or tribe, the resulting blood feud could last for years, or even generations. Prison is a way to offer a sense of vengeance and retribution not just to society as a whole but to the particular individuals who have been harmed by another person. When all in a society agree that the state and not individuals has the right to punish and seek retribution, society becomes a much more stable and healthy place.

The fourth and final reason for incarcerating offenders is to protect society from further criminal acts by these same people. Theoretically, prison and jail terms are set in a framework whereby the severity of the crime dictates the severity of the sentence. In many states, aggravating and mitigating factors are considered when setting an individual prisoner's term. *Aggravating factors* may include the use of a weapon or the terrorizing of victims in addition to robbing or attacking them. *Mitigating factors* may include the low intelligence or family background of the defendant. The basic idea, or hope, is to put an individual out of society long enough for that individual to cease to be a threat to society. The high rates of recidivism in our society indicate that it's no simple task to rehabilitate a prisoner, no matter how long he or she remains behind bars.

Legal Dictionary

Aggravating factors—Additional circumstances in the commission of a crime that call for a higher degree of punishment, such as torturing a person prior to killing him or her.

Mitigating factors—Additional circumstances in the commission of a crime that call for a lower degree of punishment, such as cooperating with authorities to identify other potential defendants.

Sources of Inmates' Rights

A Texas sheriff, quoted in *The Wall Street Journal*, once defended his right to treat prisoners harshly with the explanation: "They didn't get there by singing too loud in the Sunday choir." No, singing at high volume in church may annoy one's fellow parishioners, but it surely doesn't merit a term in the joint. Based on anecdotal experience and conversations with corrections officers in prisons and jails across the country, the surprising truth is that drugs and alcohol are involved in at least 80 to 90 percent of the inmates in our penal system. This indicates to me that the easiest way to clean up the prison problem in America would be to clean up the drug and alcohol problem. Since that isn't going to happen overnight, prisons and jails will be with us well into the future. And since that's the case, it is vital that prisoners are

Looking for Liberty

Prisoners' rights groups have come together to form the Prisoners Rights Unity Project. Among their free services are a guide for wives of prisoners who are going to visit their incarcerated spouses for the first time. You can find that guide at www.geocities.com/valkryja/prisoners_wife/index1.html.

entitled to enjoy the rights guaranteed them by the U.S. Constitution and by federal and state laws.

Inmates do not have full constitutional rights. The deprivation of freedom entails a deprivation of civil liberties, for two reasons: as punishment, and as a means of permitting corrections officials to run an orderly institution. The primary sources of prisoners' rights in our society are the Fifth, Eighth, and Fourteenth Amendments to the U.S. Constitution. Let's examine each in turn and see how these amendments relate to the specific rights of inmates.

The Fifth Amendment states four specific rights that individuals enjoy when it comes to the question of criminal proceedings. First, there can only be a criminal trial on a felony charge after a grand jury has indicted an individual or a process such as a bill of information. The indictment process requires a prosecutor to make a good faith showing to a grand jury (usually 23 citizens called to serve by lottery) that if this matter were to go to trial, there's a strong possibility that the prosecution would prevail. This constitutional protection means that an individual cannot be pulled from his or her bed in the middle of the night and whisked off to a trial. Such actions can and do take place under totalitarian regimes.

The second right that individuals enjoy under the Fifth Amendment is freedom from *double jeopardy*. This means that if a person goes to trial for a particular crime and is found not guilty, the government cannot put the same individual on trial for the same crime.

You may recall that after the criminal trial of O. J. Simpson, there was a civil trial as well. It would appear that Simpson was being tried twice for the same crime—allegedly murdering Ron Goldman and Nicole Simpson. This is not so. Simpson could not be brought up again on criminal charges for those same crimes after he had been acquitted. The civil trial, although it grew out of the same circumstances (the deaths of Goldman and Nicole Simpson) related to violations of civil law for which O. J. Simpson could not have been imprisoned or executed.

Legal Dictionary

Double jeopardy—A violation of the constitutional freedom from being tried or punished twice in criminal court for the same crime.

The fact is that the first trial was a criminal trial, brought by the people of California against Simpson, for the crime of murder. The second trial was a civil matter, brought by the parents of Ron Goldman against Simpson for depriving the civil rights— especially the right to continue living—of their son Ron. The standards of evidence are different in criminal and civil cases. In a criminal case, one must prove "beyond a reasonable doubt" that the individual is guilty of the crime with which he or she is charged. In a civil trial, the standard is much lower. One need only prove by a "preponderance of the evidence" that the plaintiff's case has been made.

The Law of the Land

Not all unpleasant punishment rises to the level of the "cruel and unusual" standard of the Eighth Amendment. Courts give prison officials a great deal of latitude in terms of running their institutions.

The difference between the criminal standard of "beyond a reasonable doubt" and the civil standard of "preponderance of the evidence" might be described in percentage terms as the difference between, say, 85 to 95 percent on the criminal side and only 51 percent on the civil side. Goldman's parents were able to prove that the evidence indicated that there was at least a 51 percent chance that Simpson had in fact killed Goldman. Thus, the Goldmans were able to prevail in court and win large damages against Simpson.

A not guilty verdict in a criminal trial does not preclude a civil case that arises out of the same set of facts. In this situation, the first case—the criminal case—was brought by the government, and the second case—the civil case—was brought by individuals, Goldman's parents. So technically, the U.S. government was not trying Simpson twice for the same crime. Simpson was only in jeopardy of losing his freedom in the criminal case, so technically he suffered no "double jeopardy" even though he underwent two trials.

The third protection afforded individuals under the Fifth Amendment states that an individual shall not "be compelled, in any criminal case, to be a witness against himself." In other words, if the government is going to bring charges against an individual, an individual cannot be forced to testify in his or her own defense. The burden is on the prosecution to prove criminal charges and a defendant does not have to do the government's work for them.

Legal Dictionary

Miranda rights—The rights a law enforcement officer must read a suspect in order to make sure that any statements or confessions were not coerced.

There are many safeguards against the use of improperly obtained confessions. For example, when a person is arrested for a crime, he or she is "Mirandized"—they are read their *Miranda rights* by the arresting officer. The phrase "Mirandized" comes from the landmark U.S. Supreme Court case of *Miranda* v. *Arizona*, decided in 1966. In that case, the defendant Ernest Miranda had been arrested and was denied the right to remain silent and have access to an attorney.

There are six points to a "Miranda warning." They are as follows:

1. You have the right to remain silent and refuse to answer questions.

2. Anything you do or say may be used against you in a court of law.

3. You have the right to consult an attorney before speaking to the police and have an attorney present during questioning now or in the future.

4. If you cannot afford an attorney, one will be appointed for you before any questioning, if you wish.

5. If you decide to answer questions now without an attorney present, you will still have the right to stop answering at any time until you talk to an attorney.

6. Knowing and understanding your rights as I have explained them to you, are you willing to answer my questions without an attorney present?

The reading of these rights to an individual—sometimes done repeatedly prior to questioning and sometimes done on videotape and in writing to make sure that any statements made are admissible in court—is an essential method of safeguarding the Fifth Amendment right against self-incrimination.

The fourth and final aspect of criminal law covered by the Fifth Amendment is called the "due process" clause. We discussed this earlier; it reads that no individual shall "be deprived of life, liberty, or property, without due process of law." "Due process" is generally understood in the law to mean notice and a hearing. Notice means that an individual is afforded adequate notice that some right is about to be taken away.

For example, there is the concept of eminent domain, by which a local government condemns property and takes it in order to build something for the public good. The government cannot simply send a wrecking ball over to your home, knock it down, and ask questions later. Instead

Taking Liberties

In the post-September 11 environment, it is possible for the government to hold individuals suspected of terrorist crimes for lengthy periods, often without any contact with their lawyers. Such governmental actions may be constitutionally dicey, but there is a far greater tolerance for them during times of national crisis or war.

the government has to provide fair notice to the affected individual of the government's intentions. That notice has to be followed by a hearing to determine whether the government is within its rights in taking the property. The same thing is true if the person is to be denied, say, Social Security benefits, schooling for immigrant children, or any of the other rights and privileges that Americans enjoy.

In the criminal sphere, the due process clause means that there has to be a trial before a person's freedom, property, or life can be taken away. It is constitutional for the court system to hold individuals without bail if the individual is considered a flight risk (someone who is likely to flee the jurisdiction or the country prior to trial) or if the person is considered likely to commit another crime prior to trial.

The Fifth Amendment in Prison

Once a person is tried, convicted, and sentenced to a term in a correctional institution, the Fifth Amendment still pertains. As we shall see, prisoners have rights behind bars—not the full panoply of rights that you and I enjoy on the outside, but some. Those rights cannot be abrogated or denied by penal officials without due process, in accordance with the Fifth Amendment.

The next part of the Constitution that pertains directly to prisoners is the Eighth Amendment, which prohibits cruel or unusual punishment. Keep in mind that in the late eighteenth century, when the U.S. Constitution and the Bill of Rights were becoming law in the United States, France was still using the guillotine to lop off the heads of both criminals and those who dared to disagree with the reigning authorities. (They tell the story about the malfunctioning guillotine in France. Two prisoners had been forced to put their neck on the line to have their heads chopped off. Since the guillotine malfunctioned, they were set free. The third prisoner, an engineer, placed his neck on the line, studied the machinery, and shouted, "I see the problem!" Which shows that what you say can and will be used against you.)

Taking Liberties

Is there a precedent for keeping dangerous al Qaeda and Taliban prisoners at Guantanamo Bay? Yes, there is! Intriguingly, John Jay, a Founding Father and a leader of the counterintelligence movement during the Revolutionary War, stationed prison ships in the Hudson River to house the most dangerous British prisoners.

Today, France has eliminated the guillotine, and capital punishment is outlawed in many U.S. states. But there are many other ways to treat prisoners in "cruel and unusual" ways. The Eighth Amendment to the U.S. Constitution forbids such practices, and when such abuses occur, prisoners are guaranteed—or, at least, are supposed to be guaranteed—access to the courts in order to plead their cases.

The final constitutional amendment that relates to prisoners' rights is the Fourteenth Amendment, which applies the due process obligation to the states as well as to the federal government. The Fifth Amendment to the U.S. Constitution makes it unconstitutional for the *federal* government to deprive individuals of life, liberty, or property without due process. The Fourteenth Amendment extends that obligation to all *state* governments as well as to the federal government.

Conditions of Confinement

Jail is no picnic. Nevertheless, prisoners are entitled to the basic necessities of life—food, shelter, health care, and personal security. I'm sure you don't look back with great fondness on the meals they served in the cafeteria. (Does "Mystery Meat Monday" ring a bell?) Prison fare is not especially appealing. Your author has eaten hamburgers made by inmates at Riker's Island in New York City. The guards call these hamburgers "murder burgers," and with good reason: They make you long for McDonald's.

If you take the tour at Alcatraz, you are told that the prisoners were fed gourmet meals, in part as a means of keeping them happy and nonviolent. Whether that is truth or myth is hard to determine. It is certainly true that prison fare at most institutions is nothing to scrawl home about. On the other hand, prisoners do have a right to have their basic nutritional needs met. Prisoners are also entitled to meals that comport with their religious beliefs. Jewish prisoners who wish kosher meals are entitled to receive same, and Muslim prisoners are entitled to pork-free meals. Courts strike down as frivolous challenges to prison meal plans when petitioners claim that they have started a religion requiring them to eat filet mignon and drink good Scotch three times a day. But there is a fundamental right to nutritious (if not delicious) prison fare.

Statutes of Liberties

Proper shelter is a vital issue in jails and prisons today. We live in times of budget crises and overcrowding. Frequently, you can see bunk beds arrayed in dayrooms of prisons and jails, simply because there are not enough regular bunks for the inmates. Inmate overcrowding leads to all kinds of problems—discipline problems all the way through large-scale rioting. Organizations supporting prisoners' rights frequently litigate when the number of prisoners in a given area far exceeds the number of persons for which it was built.

It is similarly unconstitutional for prison authorities to deprive individuals of proper health care. In prisons and jails, inmates have access to nurses, doctors, dentists, and other specialists. One of the features of the prison or jail day is "pill call," when inmates line up to receive whatever medications they're supposed to be taking. Inmates who do not receive the medication or medical treatment they need are entitled to litigate in order to enjoy proper health care. According to the American Civil Liberties Union, if a prisoner wishes to challenge his medical care, he or she should offer sick-call requests for medical attention or records reflecting the following facts:

♦ When was medical attention requested?

♦ To whom were the requests submitted?

♦ What was the medical condition that the prisoner complained about?

♦ What was the effect of delay in treatment?

> **The Law of the Land**
>
> In June, 2000, the U.S. Supreme Court, by a 7 to 2 vote, upheld the constitutionality of the Miranda warnings. Chief Justice William Rehnquist wrote that the original Miranda case was a constitutional decision of the Supreme Court that could not be overridden by an action of Congress.

> **Taking Liberties**
>
> There is no "bright line" test of what level of force violates the Constitution. It depends on the circumstances. *De minimis* (minimal or insignificant) force is held not to be a violation of the Eighth Amendment, which guarantees freedom from cruel and unusual punishment. The problem is that courts disagree as to what constitutes de minimis force. Even lethal force can be constitutional if it is an appropriate response to a given situation.

Personal security is the final point concerning issues of confinement that frequently becomes a matter of litigation. Prisons and jails are, often, violent places, and it is not possible for corrections officials to prevent every act of inmate-on-inmate violence. Nevertheless, prisons and jails are expected to segregate especially violent individuals and to house prisoners in such a way that conflicts along racial or ethnic lines are prevented or at least minimized.

There are also severe limitations on the use of force by corrections officials on inmates. It is understood that prison guards occasionally need to use force in order to enforce the rules and regulations of the institution. Nevertheless, corrections officers do not have absolute freedom in how they exercise the use of force.

There are times when force is considered unreasonable or excessive, especially with regard to the Eighth Amendment. A federal court will consider these issues to determine whether a prisoner's constitutional rights have been violated: Why was force necessary? Was the level of force used appropriate or excessive? How much injury was inflicted? And was force applied in a "good faith effort" to keep prison discipline, or was it applied "maliciously and sadistically" in order to cause harm?

Prisoners are entitled to spend "adequate" amounts of time with their counsel. The courts do not like to interfere with the way penal officials run prisons and jails. This means that penal officials are entitled to promulgate reasonable limitations on the amount of time prisoners can spend with their lawyers. However, it is unconstitutional to deprive an inmate the right to see his or her attorney. In addition, prisoners usually enjoy access to law libraries in the facility. Some of these libraries are quite sophisticated and offer access to Lexis, West Law, and other computer legal search services.

Just because a person is in prison does not mean that he or she loses the right to petition the courts for redress of grievances. The U.S. Supreme Court case *Bounds* v. *Smith*, decided in 1977, held that prisoners have a constitutional right of meaningful access to court. This means that if a prisoner cannot afford a lawyer, the legal and correctional systems must provide legal services to that prisoner. Other U.S. Supreme Court decisions reinforce the rights of prisoners to adequate assistance so they can attack their sentences or challenge the conditions of their confinement.

Prisoners also are allowed to communicate with their attorneys without eavesdropping by prison authorities; this applies to law students and legal assistants as well as members of the bar. Frivolous claims by inmates, in some states, lead to "three strikes" situations—three consecutive frivolous, malicious, or nonsensical court claims that result in deprivation of access to courts for that prisoner. In other words, the court system does not feel obligated by the Constitution to entertain silly claims by inmates.

Limits on Prisoners' Rights

There are, of course, many limitations on the rights of prisoners. Prisoners lose their First Amendment right to free speech where it conflicts with the need of prison officials to run their prisons in a safe and secure manner. Corrections officials can limit access of prisoners to news media. Prisoners do not have the right to object to transfers to other facilities. Since there is no reasonable expectation of privacy in a jail cell, searches and seizures are generally permitted—the Fourth Amendment right to freedom from such searches and seizures does not hold in prisons.

Incoming mail to prisoners as well as mail between inmates is fair game for prison officials to examine for contraband. The need, obviously, is to regulate the sorts of things that find

> **Looking for Liberty**
>
> One of the most important books about prisoners' rights is *Gideon's Trumpet* by Anthony Lewis, which details the story of an indigent Florida prisoner and his struggle to receive adequate legal counsel.

their way behind prison walls. Yet prison officials cannot read mail that comes from an inmate's attorney to that inmate. Also, there is no specific right to visitation, let alone to conjugal visits. And there are limits to a prisoner's ability to marry behind bars. On the other hand, many rights are lost, often forever—such as the right of a convicted felon to vote.

In short, while prison is a depressing and dispiriting environment at best, the U.S. Constitution and rights afforded by federal and state laws do pertain behind prison walls. While the rights of inmates are substantially limited compared to those of us on the outside, this is still America, and the rights they do have are up to corrections officials and the courts to protect.

DNA Databank

Since 1988, American courts have admitted, under certain circumstances and with certain limitations, DNA evidence. Such evidence is only admissible in cases where DNA is available and at issue. Blood, semen, or hair samples must be found at the crime scene, collected, preserved, and tested to be admissible evidence. This biological "fingerprint" indicates with a high degree of accuracy—although without absolute certainty—the likelihood that a particular person committed a crime, fathered a child, or is otherwise the individual sought by the police or the courts. DNA evidence by itself is not probative; it does not prove 100 percent that a particular individual is the culprit. Rather, it provides a high degree of likelihood that an individual in question is the "right" person.

The civil liberties issue regarding DNA has to do with nonconsensual DNA testing of prisoners. Some states have begun to collect the DNA of inmates, without their consent, in order to create databanks for future use. The theory is that people in prison are highly likely to go out and commit more crimes once they are released. So, if you want to maintain a database of a group of individuals likely to commit crimes, who better than inmates? They are all locked up, so it's very easy to get at them. There is the reduced expectation of privacy that offers a constitutional justification for taking their DNA. And they are hardly in a position to complain.

> **Statutes of Liberties**
>
> Under California law, all felons convicted of violent crimes are required to provide blood samples. Refusal is a misdemeanor, punishable by an additional year in jail or a $500 fine.

It is true that the DNA may be used to solve future crimes, but most DNA databanks were originally created to clear past unsolved crimes. The DNA of a criminal in crime "A" is placed into the databank—If it matches a prisoner, then law enforcement officials conclude that they have now solved crime "A."

Thus, the theory is that many prisoners behind bars have committed other past crimes for which they have not been charged.

But others are complaining on their behalf. The question of whether it is legitimate to take the DNA of prisoners without their consent raises a number of important constitutional issues. Does an individual have an inviolate privacy right in his or her DNA? Does the state ever have a right to take a person's DNA? When there is a new form of technology available, courts generally look back to the most similar situations they can find in order to make decisions. In this case, courts have looked to the issue of blood testing to see whether or not it is legitimate for the state to compel individuals to give DNA samples. There are in fact circumstances in which the state can compel individuals to give blood samples. The Supreme Court has held that individuals do have a privacy right in their own blood. And yet, that privacy right can be weighed against the state's need, if any, to maintain order or solve crimes. As a result, the Supreme Court has concluded that the Fourth Amendment prohibition against unreasonable searches and seizures means that a warrant is necessary in order to have a nonconsensual blood test performed on an individual. If there is no time for a warrant, as in the case of a drunk driver whose blood alcohol level is likely to diminish before a warrant can be issued, a nonconsensual blood test is permissible if there is probable cause to indicate that a crime has in fact been committed.

Applying this reasoning to DNA cases, courts have held that individuals do have a privacy right in their DNA. And yet, there are circumstances under which DNA testing can be done even without the consent of the individual. Indeed, prisoners have a much lower expectation of privacy in jail than do private citizens in society. But the analysis does not stop here. The real question is this: Is it fair to invade the privacy of individuals, even in prison, on the grounds that they *may* commit crimes at some point in the future? The gut instinct of most people would be that the answer is no. It doesn't seem fair to suspect that someone *might* commit a crime and then take investigatory actions based on that belief.

Taking Liberties

Via use of the DNA data-bank, Virginia managed to find culprits for 750 unsolved crimes.

Yes, the government issues warrants and wiretaps against organized crime figures or others suspected of committing crimes, but in those cases, the individuals are already in the process of committing crimes. The government is seeking to prove that they have broken the law and is seeking to stop them from committing further criminal acts. Here, you have individuals who certainly have broken the law, or at least they have been convicted of breaking the law. That's why they landed in jail. But once they are there, is it fair to assume that they are going to commit crimes in the future? It's true that our nation's prisons and jails do have high rates of recidivism—many people who commit crimes go on to commit more—but does this mean that they must suffer the indignity of a DNA test on the grounds that they might commit more crimes in the future?

While prisoners do have a lower expectation of privacy in jail, and while their possessions and their bodies can be searched for the possession of illicit contraband, there's something chilling and almost science-fiction-like about making assumptions about an individual's behavior once he or she has left a penal institution. Theoretically, prisons and jails are supposed to rehabilitate individuals so that they will not commit crimes in the future. Creating a DNA databank of prisoners seems to be an admission of failure on the part of the criminal justice system. It's as though corrections officers are saying, "Look, rehabilitation is a sham. We all know these people are going to commit more crimes. So let's get some identification material from them right now." If anything seems like a violation of civil liberties, it would be this.

Taking Liberties

DNA testing originally gained national prominence when used to exonerate prisoners of crimes they didn't commit. Today it has become an accepted form of evidence, with certain limitations.

Chemical Castration of Sex Offenders

Sex crimes are endemic in American society. The question today is whether new scientific techniques and medical breakthroughs can possibly alter the physiology of sex offenders to the point where they will not want to commit sex crimes in the future. The State of Oregon has introduced a process of *chemical castration*, following the lead of countries such as Denmark, Germany, Norway, Sweden, and Switzerland.

According to Caroline M. Wong, writing in the *Oregon Law Review* in the spring of 2001, such chemical castration techniques in Europe have proven very successful. Whereas two thirds of sex offenders will commit further sex crimes if they do not undergo chemical castration, just 15 percent of those who undergo it commit further sex crimes. Wong points out that Thomas Jefferson argued for surgical castration for offenders convicted of sodomy, rape, or polygamy, pointing to the fact that sex offenders in other times and places have faced castration as a treatment or punishment. The question, for civil liberties purposes, is whether such treatment constitutes cruel and unusual punishment outlawed by the Eighth Amendment to the U.S. Constitution.

In Oregon, and so far, only in Oregon, some sex offenders are being treated with antiandrogen medication, which is intended to reduce their appetite for committing further sex offenses. Such individuals are treated with a female contraceptive, Depo-Provera. This practice has sparked an enormous controversy far beyond the borders of the state. Those who support Oregon's experiment with chemical castration suggest that there is no violation of the Eighth Amendment because different forms of castration have been considered acceptable throughout much of American history and because the medication causes only minor side effects, most of which cease with the end of treatment. In addition, since individuals receiving this treatment have already served jail sentences, some argue that the law violates double jeopardy because, in essence, the offender is being punished twice for the same crime. Opponents also argue that chemical castration violates the individual's freedom of thought, as it affects the thinking process of the individual. Other problems with chemical castration: It is coerced, and it can trigger punishment of an individual who refuses to take part in the program.

Legal Dictionary

Chemical castration—A drug treatment used to reduce the amount of male hormone testosterone the body produces.

The Least You Need to Know

◆ Even in prison, individuals enjoy civil liberties, limited as they may be.

◆ The primary sources of prisoners' rights in our society are the Fifth, Eighth, and Fourteenth Amendments.

◆ The Fourth Amendment does not apply to inmates.

◆ DNA databanks and chemical castration are two "hot button" topics still under debate.

Part 4

Liberties at Home, Work, and School

The rights to live where you want, work where you want, raise your child as you want, and get the education you want are crucial in the American legal system. But what rights do you really have, how are they enforced, and how have your rights and your children's rights been whittled away over the last 20 years?

In this section, we'll examine civil liberties in three crucial areas of life: the home (including adoption and divorce), the workplace (including getting hired and getting fired), and school (including the facts about just how many rights kids really have).

Chapter 16

Property Rights

In This Chapter

- What's yours is theirs
- The Fair Housing Act
- Seize and desist
- "Superfund" sometimes isn't

One of the oldest clichés in the English language states that "a man's home is his castle." Although it's the twenty-first century and we guard our castles with security systems instead of alligators, we still have the right to protect our property, at least to a certain extent. In this chapter, we discuss your rights as a property owner as well as the rights of people who come upon your property with or without your permission.

The American Way?

It used to be that you could not even build a house if it blocked the view of an older house. This was known as the legal doctrine of *ancient lights*. As the United States grew more industrial during the nineteenth century, it became apparent that people would be living closer together and that society could no longer permit individuals the freedom to limit their neighbors' houses in certain ways. So today, unless zoning regulations say otherwise, it is entirely legal to build a building that blocks the view of another—the owners and tenants in the older building cannot stop you from putting up the newer one. Without the repeal of the doctrine of ancient lights, no city in the United States could possibly have been built. Not entirely true. In many cities, a zoning ordinance may still prevent you from building that second story to your house.

Living Where You Want

All the rights that you have as a homeowner, renter, or business owner are meaningless if you cannot buy or rent the home, piece of property, or business location of your dreams. In the past, in the United States, it was legal to discriminate in terms of race, religion, ethnicity, marital status, etc., when determining whether a person had the right to buy or rent a home. These laws, called restricted covenants, were actually part of the deeds on properties and forbade owners from selling those properties to, say, blacks, Jews, or single people.

Legal Dictionary

Ancient lights—The early- to mid- nineteenth century American legal doctrine that prohibited the construction of buildings that blocked someone else's sunshine. This doctrine was overturned later in the nineteenth century as America grew economically and new, larger buildings had to be built.

Such covenants persisted into mid-twentieth-century America, and some members of the U.S. Supreme Court, while they were young attorneys, actually drafted covenants as part of deeds for their real estate developer clients. This shocking piece of American legal history began to change with the passage of the Civil Rights Act of 1968, also known as the Fair Housing Act.

The Rights of Home Buyers

The Fair Housing Act of 1968, along with the Civil Rights Act of 1866, prohibits discrimination in the world of real estate. It is illegal to discriminate against members of any of seven protected classes: race, color, national origin, religion, sex, family status, and disability when it comes to the rental or sale of houses, the obtaining of homeowner's insurance, and the process of getting a home loan. The Fair Housing Act makes the following practices illegal:

◆ **Refusal to sell or rent.** It is a violation of federal law as defined by the Fair Housing Act to refuse, for reasons related strictly to race or color, to sell or rent to an individual who is a member of one of the seven protected classes mentioned previously. A seller or lessor (a landlord) does not have the right to refuse to sell or rent to a member of one or more of those categories who makes a bona fide, or legitimate, offer. The text of the law reads as follows: It is illegal "to refuse to sell or rent after the making of a bona fide offer, or to refuse to negotiate for the sale or rental of or otherwise make unavailable or deny a dwelling to any person because of ... membership in a protected class."

◆ **Discrimination in the terms or conditions of sale.** It is illegal for an apartment manager to require a higher security deposit from families with children than from single people or married couples who have no children. It is also illegal to demand a higher application fee from minority applicants. This practice is just as illegal as refusing to sell or rent in the first place. Multi-family dwellings today must provide the following seven design and construction standards: accessible building entrance on an accessible route, accessible and usable public and common use areas (such as laundry areas), useable doors, accessible room into and through the apartment in question, light switches, electrical outlets; thermostats and other environmental controls in accessible locations, reinforced walls for grab bars, and useable kitchens and bathrooms. Today, virtually all apartments and condos have been built with these standards in mind.

◆ **Advertising.** It is illegal to publish the fact that a landlord or seller will not deal with individuals in any of the protected classes. An interesting sidelight: While it is well known that, until the 1960s, many hotels and restaurants would not offer accommodations or meals to blacks, it is less well known that Jews were often denied service as well. Hotels that accepted Jewish guests would display a large H in their advertising (for Hebrew). That letter told Jewish clients that they were welcome without alerting the rest of the world to the fact that the hotel accepted Jews.

◆ **Denying availability.** It is against the law to lie to a member of a protected class and say that there are no units available for sale or rent when such is not the case. This law applies to real estate agents, apartment managers, or anyone who might be in a position of power with regard to renting or selling homes.

◆ **Blockbusting.** *Blockbusting* is one of the most disgusting tactics that the real estate industry, not always a bastion of ethical behavior, has ever created. Blockbusting means that a real estate agent will go to a house in an all-white neighborhood and

Legal Dictionary

Blockbusting—The practice of scaring homeowners into selling their property because an "undesirable" family, usually members of a minority, is about to move in.

tell the homeowner, "A black couple is about to move in down the block. If you don't sell your house quickly, your property values are going to plummet." Such information can trigger a stampede of house sales, often at below-market prices, as neighbors compete to leave a community into which they fear a black couple will move. Sometimes, blockbusters will even install a black family in a white neighborhood, in an effort to hasten the process of getting listings from panicked, racist, white homeowners. A realtor might tell homeowners that because of the change in complexion in the neighborhood, there will be more criminal or other antisocial behavior, the schools may decline in quality, or it may be too dangerous to take one's children to the park.

- **Steering.** Steering means what it sounds like—a real estate agent directs, or steers, white homebuyers to white neighborhoods and black homebuyers to black neighborhoods, failing to inform potential homebuyers (or renters) that houses or apartments are available for sale or rent in neighborhoods where the predominant number of people have a different skin color.

- **Failure to make reasonable accommodation.** As we mentioned earlier in this section, individuals with disabilities are protected by the Fair Housing Act. A disability is defined in the Fair Housing Act as a physical or mental impairment that substantially limits one or more of a person's major life activities, or a record of having such an impairment in one's life. A landlord is obligated to make "reasonable modifications" to a dwelling if a person with a disability wants to live there. The question of what exactly is a reasonable accommodation is a very complicated issue and more can be learned about it at www.fairhousing.com.

- **Redlining.** The term redlining comes from the (now illegal) practice of literally drawing a red line on a map around certain neighborhoods, either because they are predominantly minority occupied or because they are less than desirable. Bank loan officers traditionally considered those homes within the red lines to be poor risks from the point of view of lending. The practice of redlining, or making a blanket condemnation of a neighborhood and refusing to make housing loans in that neighborhood, is illegal under the Fair Housing Act, but the practice has taken decades to abate. Organizations such as Los Angeles' Operation Hope work with bankers to bring them into neighborhoods they might otherwise have avoided, out of fear or ignorance, and also help tenants make the step to home ownership by assisting them with their credit record and explaining to them the process of buying a home and getting a home loan. (You can read more about the process of antiredlining behavior at www.operationhome.org.) Red-lining is a serious barrier to fair housing; those who cannot get a home loan generally cannot buy a home.

How bad is it today? It's still pretty bad. The problem with housing discrimination is that it can be very difficult to prove. Unless a black renter has his offer rejected and then discovers that the home or apartment is still available, how would he know, or prove, he was the victim of discrimination? The practices of redlining, steering, and discrimination in general can be very hard to detect. After all, the individual home-owner is not privy to the inner decision-making process of banks, so how would you or I know whether a particular house is in a redlined neighborhood? Banks today no longer have big maps with red lines hanging on their walls for anyone to see. If any-thing, housing discrimination has "gone underground," and it is much harder for individuals to tell whether their rights are being protected.

How can an individual tell if he or she is being "steered" from all-white (or all-minority) neighborhoods? Brokers would not come out and say, "You don't want to live there, that neighborhood is all black, or all white." Instead, they might use certain code terms such as indicating that the neighborhood is "transitional"—a signal that one group is moving in and another group is moving out. Today, anyone with Internet access can search the Multiple Listings Service (MLS) that realtors use when looking for properties. But unless you take the trouble to do this, how can you be sure that you are not being steered away from or toward certain neighborhoods?

Also, many individuals are simply not aware of their rights. For example, a broker could tell a prospective purchaser that he or she would not be "comfortable" or "compatible" with the other residents in a neighborhood because of race—that's a crime. But how do most people know that such a statement is illegal? If a member of one of the protected classes makes a bona fide offer and is turned down, how exactly can that prospective buyer be sure that he or she was turned down because of race, religion, or disability? If there are multiple bidders on a property, sellers do not have to give reasons why they turned down one buyer and accepted another, especially if the bids were identical. And finally, how can a black renter or buyer know that he or she is being charged higher rental fees or sales charges without speaking to a white individual who is seeking to buy or rent in the same area?

In short, illegal discriminatory conduct must often be inferred from circumstances or statements. Most people who discriminate may be evil, but they aren't stupid enough to come right out and do something that is clearly actionable. So the courts step in, after an individual has filed suit, to determine whether or not a violation of the Fair Housing Act has occurred.

Righting the Wrongs of Discrimination in Housing

If an individual goes to court seeking redress for discrimination that he or she has suf-fered, here's how it works: The individual must show four different points: (1) he or she belongs to a protected group; (2) he or she applied for and was qualified to obtain the housing in question, which was in fact available at that time; (3) he or she was rejected for that house; and (4) the housing remained available even after their rejection.

If an individual can make a showing of all four of these points, the burden then shifts to the defendant. The defendant then must show that there existed some "legitimate, nondiscriminatory reason for its action" according to the Fair Housing Act." The act does not require that the plaintiff—the person who feels that he or she has been discriminated against—show that discrimination was why they did not get the property. As long as it can be shown that a racial or other discriminatory motivation was possible, the plaintiff can go forward with the lawsuit.

It's very hard to put a dollar value on the loss of one's civil rights. How exactly do you measure that kind of damage? It's not like the loss that occurs when a house burns down or a business is robbed, where a dollar amount can be used as compensation. A person's civil rights are intangible and extremely important, and for that reason, jury verdicts and pre-jury settlements are often extremely high.

Attorney Edward G. Kramer, writing in the Association of Trial Lawyers of America Annual Convention Reference Materials (Volume I, Civil Rights Section, July 2001), lists seven recent cases in which juries and judges awarded large amounts of money in compensatory and punitive damages to individuals whose rights were violated under the Fair Housing Act. The verdicts and settlements ran from 765,000 dollars in one case into the millions—and in the largest case of all, Nationwide Mutual Insurance Company, Inc., there was a jury verdict of 500,000 dollars in compensatory damages and 100 million dollars in punitive damages in an insurance redlining case.

It shocks the conscience that it took the civil rights era of the 1960s to make fair housing the law of the land. According to one report, there are still as many as two million cases of housing discrimination every year in the United States. Whether this figure is inflated or not is impossible to know, simply because it's so hard to determine what goes on in every single real estate transaction. If you think that you have been discriminated against in the process of obtaining a residence, you may want to consult a lawyer and see if your Fair Housing Act-guaranteed rights have been violated.

The Government Giveth ...

... And the government taketh away. There are circumstances under which the federal, state, or even local government can deprive a property owner of all or part of his or her property. In this section, we're going to examine four ways in which the government can restrict the rights of property owners, or even deprive them entirely of their property. These four possibilities are:

◆ Eminent domain (also known as "condemnation"), when the government wants your land

◆ Regulatory takings, where the government passes a law restricting the use of property

◆ Criminal and civil forfeiture, when the government takes property because of criminal misdoings

◆ Superfund, the Environmental Protection Agency's mechanism for cleaning up major toxic waste sites.

Eminent Domain

The government does not have the right to take private property unless there is an extremely good reason for doing so. However, under the doctrine of eminent domain, the government has the power to acquire property for public use as long as it pays the owner "just compensation." Let's say the government wants to build a freeway and your building happens to be in the way. Even if you do not want to sell your property, the government can make you do so, as long as the public use to which the government would put the land is important enough and as long as they pay you for it.

I'm sure you've heard the expression, "You can't fight City Hall." Never is this more true than when it comes to eminent domain. You can delay but not prevent eminent domain. If the government is set on taking your property, it will.

If the government does commence an eminent domain action against your property, it cannot simply take it and wave goodbye to you as it kicks you off your land. Instead, the Fifth Amendment of the U.S. Constitution declares that private property may not be taken for public use without fair payment, the legal term for which is just compensation. You can and should be paid for the real property—the actual land and/or building sitting on it; the improvements you've made, such as fixtures and equipment; and if it is a business location, *good will*.

If there is a tenant in a building being taken by eminent domain, that tenant may also share in the proceeds from compensation payments from the government. Many leases contain a compensation clause that states exactly how the money is to be split between the landlord and the tenants.

Legal Dictionary _____

Good will—The reputation a business has in a community for doing good work at fair prices and its patronage. If the business could move down the block and have a similar location, there would be little or no damage to the good will of the business. If, on the other hand, it would be impossible for that business to relocate in the neighborhood, then the government would be obligated to determine the value of the good will and pay the business owner that amount.

The government is responsible for paying fair market value for the property that it takes. What is fair market value? Let's say that you own that property, and you are in no particular hurry to sell. You're willing to sell, but you don't feel any particular obligation to do so. If the right price came along, you would take it. Let's say that a buyer for that same property came along, and was willing to make an offer on that property. The highest price to which you and that buyer would agree in an arm's length transaction is considered fair market value for the purposes of eminent domain. An arm's length transaction refers to a deal in which the buyer and seller do not have a motivation to make the price artificially low or high. A nonarm's length transaction might be one in which a parent transfers a property to a child for a nominal amount, such as one dollar.

Taking Liberties _____

In Queens, New York, you can find a Macy's store that is almost entirely round, except for one small piece. The store looks like a large, white doughnut from which someone has nibbled a small bite. One of the property owners on the residential blocks where this Macy's was built simply would not sell his property to the store, no matter how much they offered. So Macy's had to build around the individual, since a private business or individual does not have the right to compel others to sell or lease their land.

Generally, as soon as the government makes a deposit of probable compensation into court—the day the government writes a check, getting ready to pay you for the land it's taking—is the day upon which the value of the property will be determined, for the purposes of valuing it. Alternatively, the day the eminent domain complaint is filed in court—the day you decide to fight the case—or even the trial date can be considered the date in question.

Let's say the government only needs a part of your property, perhaps to widen a road, install cable TV lines, or construct access to a beach or other public area. In that case, the government will pay *severance* damages, the amount of money that you would lose because this piece of property is being taken, or severed, from the rest of your property.

Once the government entity—the city, the town, the public agency involved, etc.—makes the decision to go ahead with a project, that entity will contact all of the property owners involved and offer them compensation for the properties that will be taken. If no such accommodation can be reached, then the government will turn to the courts. If your property is taken, you do not get a bonus or extra amount because of the fact that you are forced to sell. You only get the fair market value of that land. Similarly, the government cannot impose a penalty or require you to take a lesser price simply because it is the government, and you're not.

Regulatory Takings

Regulatory takings are a slightly different animal than eminent domain. In a regulatory taking, the government passes a regulation that has a negative impact on your ability to live on or use the land.

Let's say you own a coal mine, and the government passes a regulation severely limiting your ability to mine coal. They passed the regulation in order to protect your neighbors, whose houses were in danger of sinking into the ground because of your coal-mining operations. Such were the facts in a leading U.S. Supreme Court case, *Pennsylvania Coal Company* v. *Mahon*, decided back in 1922. The Supreme Court held that if the government passes a regulation that seriously disrupts a person's ability to use his or her property, the government has to compensate that individual. Such a regulation is said to "take" from the individual property rights (one or more of the sticks we like to talk about) without compensation. The Fifth Amendment to the U.S. Constitution forbids such takings where there is no compensation.

Remember that one of the chief reasons for the founding of the United States was to move away from the British government's ability to act without scruple when it came to the property rights of Americans. So this concept of a limitation on the government's power to take property, either by eminent domain or by passing regulations (regulatory takings), is deeply enshrined in the law of the United States.

The key question surrounding a regulatory taking is whether a law "goes too far." The expression "goes too far" implies that the government does have a certain amount of power to regulate land use, water use, and just about everything else under the sun. But there are times when a law is said to be overreaching.

When does a law go too far? When a judge says it does. If a regulation or law wipes out the entire value of a piece of property, there is generally no question—an unconstitutional regulatory taking has occurred. But what if only a part of the value of the property has been taken away? Does that mean that the government should be forced to pay as much as it has damaged? Hard to say. Regulatory takings cases are not easy to decide, and there is no absolute rule of thumb in order to predict how they will come out.

Justice Oliver Wendell Holmes wrote in the aforementioned *Pennsylvania Cole Company* v. *Mahon* decision, "government could hardly go on if the values incident to property could not be diminished without paying for every such change in the general law." But neither Justice Holmes nor anyone else has been able to provide a precise definition of what a regulatory taking is. Today, courts look for the economic impact of the regulation, the extent to which the regulation has interfered with the expectations of investors (you bought the coal mine because you wanted to mine coal and now find you can't), and the character of the government action.

Forfeiture

When the government goes after drug dealers, organized crime kingpins, or other assorted bad guys, one of the side benefits of putting those people away is that the government gets to keep their stuff. And frequently, bad guys have really nice stuff. Boats, planes, fast cars, houses—the government gets to keep all these goodies. They sell some and use the rest, such as very fast boats, for fighting crime.

Legal Dictionary

Forfeiture—The process by which the government takes possession of property belonging to individuals who run afoul of the law.

The *forfeiture* process often places the U.S. or state government in an odd position, as it sometimes has to own and operate assets that one does not normally associate with typical governmental functions, including such things as a card casino, and a brothel. Most of the time, items that the government takes by forfeiture are not normally quite so, shall we say, intriguing.

There are two kinds of forfeiture—criminal and civil. Criminal forfeiture happens as a means of punishing individuals who have done bad things. If a person is convicted of a crime and it turns out that the defendant either used a particular piece of property—a house, a boat, a plane, whatever—in the committing of that crime, or if they bought the item with proceeds from that crime, the government can seek to impose criminal forfeiture and thus take possession of the property. If other entities believe they have a property interest (for example, if a bank financed a car, boat, or plane that was used in the commission of a crime and is now subject to criminal forfeiture), that entity may seek a hearing before the judge in order to be made whole. Criminal forfeiture often comes into play in cases where individuals possess equipment to create counterfeit money, or they own explosives, illegal firearms, illegal gambling equipment, and drug cases.

Civil forfeiture is another tool at the government's disposal to confiscate property that was used in furtherance of a crime. This leads to intriguing case names that can sound like *United States of America* v. *$5.2 million*, or the state of *Michigan* v. *Porsche Boxster Convertible*. It's not that the cash or the car is going on trial. Rather, the government is bringing a proceeding not against the criminals but against the material goods themselves to determine whether the government should be entitled to take them from the wrongdoers. The same high standard of criminal cases—evidence that proves the case "beyond a reasonable doubt"—exists in civil forfeiture actions as well.

Our Hero, Superfund

As President George H. W. Bush once said, "Pollution … bad." Almost everyone would agree with him. And yet, for decades, businesses (even some individuals) poured all kinds of toxic chemicals and other destructive material into the earth. The result: locations around the country so dangerous that they require expensive cleanup far beyond the capacity of an individual homeowner in order for the site—and nearby areas—to be safely inhabited, by businesses or by families.

The United States established the Environmental Protection Agency (EPA) in part to supervise the identification and clean up of these toxic waste sites. The EPA created a method of holding polluters liable for the cost of these cleanups. That law is known as the Superfund Law, also known as the Comprehensive Environmental Response, Compensation, and Liability Act, enacted by Congress in 1980.

Legal Dictionary

Superfund—A fund created by the government to pay for the worst waste disposal and hazardous-substance sites endangering either human health or the environment.

The Superfund Law created a tax on chemical and petroleum businesses, and the tax money collected goes into a large trust fund called the *Superfund*. Superfund is intended to pay for the worst waste disposal and hazardous-substance sites endangering either human health or the environment. As time passed, the chemical and petroleum businesses must have done some pretty sharp lobbying work on Capitol Hill, because the tax on those industries went away. Now, your tax dollars and mine go to work as part of the Superfund cleanup efforts.

If your property is located on or near a Superfund cleanup site, your right to sell—or, in some cases, even use—property on or near Superfund sites can be severely limited or, in some cases, withdrawn from you, even for a period of years.

Superfund works this way. The Environmental Protection Agency finds a site that it determines to be highly dangerous to people and/or the environment. The EPA then has the option of doing the cleanup itself using Superfund money and then recovering costs from the polluters, forcing the polluters to perform the cleanup themselves by going to court, or entering into settlement agreements with the polluters that require them to clean up the site or pay for the cleanup. That sounds fine—but who are the polluters?

The former owners and operators, current owners and operators, people who arranged for the disposal or treatment of hazardous substances on a given location, or people who chose a given site as a hazardous waste dump are all considered PRPs, or Potential Responsible Parties. (Any resemblance of the phrase PRPs and the police term "perps," short for perpetrators, is highly noncoincidental.) If Sludge Incorporated either owned or operated, now or in the past, that big, brown, bubbling, smelly piece of real estate across from your house, or if they trucked hazardous waste to that location, or picked out that location as a good place to dump hazardous stuff, then Sludge Incorporated is a PRP.

Congress passed the Superfund Law with the provision for *strict liability*, which means that it's not necessary for the government to prove that Sludge Incorporated was the actual company that created the hazardous waste situation. Maybe Sludge Incorporated was completely blameless in the way it operated the parcel of land, and maybe it was the Disgusting Company that's truly at fault. Under the Superfund Law it doesn't matter. The EPA can go after any PRP it chooses. If Sludge Incorporated thinks it has been wrongly prosecuted by the EPA, it can then file its own suit against the Disgusting Company in order to retrieve the money that it had to pay out to Superfund. If the Disgusting Company, which was actually the cause of this hazardous waste dump, no longer exists or cannot be found, Sludge Incorporated is out of luck. If this sounds a little like playing musical chairs in a toxic waste dump, you wouldn't be far from the truth.

Here's how you fit into the picture. Let's say you own Smelly Fields, a 500-acre tract adjoining the parcel that is now a Superfund toxic waste cleanup site. You want to sell the land to real estate developers, who will build 50 homes and rename the tract Fragrant Acres. You know that your parcel is across the street from a Superfund site. Do you have to disclose this information to potential buyers? It depends on the state, but the answer is probably yes. If you don't tell the real estate developer, he can very likely come after you when he finds out that he is not permitted to build on that land.

You might think about cleaning the land adjacent to Smelly Fields yourself, but don't think too long. Not only is the cost of performing a toxic waste cleanup incredibly high, but once you do, *you* become legally responsible for any future pollution problems as a result of the cleanup you did—forever.

Once the EPA declares a piece of land a Superfund site, the property values of nearby land drops dramatically. However, unlike with regulatory takings, the government doesn't have to pay you a penny. The EPA's attitude is that when the thing is finished a few years from now, property values will rebound. (Ask the people at Love Canal how their property values are doing and they may be singing a different song.)

If you ever wanted to see the "government shrug" in action, take a look at the property values FAQ (frequently asked questions) section of the EPA's website (www.epa.gov/superfund/tools/today/prop3.htm). For every question, there is a buck-passing reply.

Basically, all the EPA will do is come in, destroy your property value for a potentially extended period, shift the blame, and refer you to everybody else under the sun. Let's take a look at a case study, from the Houston Chronicle, May 12, 1991, "Superfund Site 'Traps' Homeowners." According to the story, dateline Aspen, Colorado, 1,200 people living on 110 acres below an abandoned silver mine could not sell their houses because the mine had been declared a Superfund cleanup project by the EPA. The mine, in Smuggler Mountain, had been used only from 1887 to 1893.

The initial claim of the EPA, that the cleanup would only take two years, turned out to be rather optimistic. According to the EPA itself, completion on the site was not completed until September 1996, a full *10 years* after the EPA placed the site on its Superfund National Priorities List in 1986. To add insult to injury, the site was not even deleted from the Superfund National Priorities List until September 23, 1999. Once again, you've got rights … unless the government steps in and decides that you don't. Is this a great country or what?

The Least You Need to Know

- Private property may not be taken for public use without fair payment.

- The Fifth Amendment offers protection from certain kinds of property seizures.

- The Fair Housing Act offers protection from discrimination based on seven categories, including race.

- The government owes you no compensation if a Superfund site negatively affects your property values.

17

Getting Hired

In This Chapter

- ◆ Unfashionable genes
- ◆ When your parachute fails
- ◆ Lies, all lies!
- ◆ Corporate downsizing

In today's technologically advanced world, employers have a wide variety of techniques for screening potential employees. The traditional standbys of polygraph or lie detector tests, along with personality tests, still exist. The problem with those tests is that they are not always successful at predicting which employees will work out—and worse, from a civil liberties point of view, they can be unreasonably intrusive into the private lives of potential hires. Another new technology with an impact on employment is DNA testing. Employers are now using genetic testing and genetic screening in order to determine which potential employees might develop illnesses that would require either high disability or insurance payouts, and are making hiring decisions based on that information. Is that fair? More importantly, is it legal?

Finally, employers take two other considerations into account, sometimes rightly, sometimes wrongly, the physical appearance of the potential employee, specifically with regard to weight. Should a moderately overweight person be less likely to get a job than a person in great physical condition should? Should that moderately overweight person be entitled to special legal protection, so that he or she is not discriminated against because of those excess pounds? And what about an obese person? What sort of rights should the obese have—those who have no control over their weight and those who simply eat too much? Believe it or not, these issues are litigated on a regular basis in society, with no answers in sight.

This Is Only a Test

You've probably heard about the human genome project, the purpose of which is to map out the entire structure of human DNA to predict, prevent, and treat medical problems. There are many moral debates surrounding the use of genetic testing. One civil liberties concern involves the question of whether or not employers should be permitted to conduct genetic testing on potential employees before they hire them. Does the employer have the right to such information, or does such a pre-employment requirement place an unconstitutional invasion of privacy upon job seekers?

The purpose of genetic testing is to reveal three possible facts. First, genetic testing can reveal whether an individual has a disease or health problem due to genetic anomaly defect, which would indicate that the person either has the disease now or will develop it in the future. Genetic testing can also reveal whether a person is a carrier for a genetic defect. In this case, the individual will never contract that disease him or herself, but could very well pass it down to future generations. The third condition genetic testing can detect is whether an individual has a predisposition toward developing a particular disease. In this situation, the individual does not have the disease now, but may develop it in the future. It's not certain that the person will develop such a disease, but there is a decent chance that he or she will.

Legal Dictionary

Genetic testing—The examination of genetic material, usually a blood or urine sample, to determine the presence of mutated or abnormal genes.

There are certain bona fide uses for genetic testing. For example, if a person has a genetic predisposition to developing cancer if there are certain toxic materials in his environment, it makes sense for companies that deal with such toxic materials to test potential employees to screen out those who would be seriously affected. Such employers are actually required by the Occupational Safety and Health Act (OSHA) to perform such genetic testing. Commentators Jared Feldman and Richard J. Katz, writing in the spring 2002 issue of the *Hofstra Labor and Employment Law Journal,* note that other groups of employees, such as airline pilots or operators of heavy machinery, could be screened for the potential for heart attacks, the development of Alzheimer's, or other conditions that would involve neurological deterioration. There are some legitimate purposes for genetic testing in the workplace, and Congress has actually mandated that sort of testing in certain situations.

Some employers seek to use genetic testing for a very different purpose. They wish to determine which potential job candidates either currently have or are likely to come down with the sort of expensive medical conditions that would trigger higher insur-ance costs down the road. Once again, the civil liberties issue here consists of balancing two sets of rights. On the one hand, there is the right of the individual to have his or her privacy safeguarded. In this case, the question is whether a person's genetic makeup should be information to which a potential employer has access. On the other side of the equation is the right of the employer to do what he or she thinks is best in order to lower the costs of insur-ance and ultimately keep the business profitable.

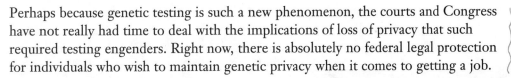

Taking Liberties

Have you ever called in sick to work? With genetic testing, employers can determine which potential employees are more likely to take advantage of all their sick leave.

Perhaps because genetic testing is such a new phenomenon, the courts and Congress have not really had time to deal with the implications of loss of privacy that such required testing engenders. Right now, there is absolutely no federal legal protection for individuals who wish to maintain genetic privacy when it comes to getting a job.

Although there are some health-related laws that protect individuals in the workplace—such as the Americans with Disabilities Act, which prevents most employers from discriminating against individuals who currently have disabilities—there is nothing in the act that addresses the question of asymptomatic individuals with genetics that indicate possible future disabilities. So the Americans with Disabilities Act does not cur-rently help individuals whose genetic screenings indicate a potential for serious illness or disease.

Statutes of Liberties

To circumvent application of the Civil Rights Act, in the 1970s, employers used genetic testing to deny jobs to African Americans who carried a gene mutation that predisposed them to sickle-cell anemia.

Title VII of the Civil Rights Act of 1964 also prevents individuals from discrimination in the workplace. Yet this law, which deals with factors of race, ethnicity, religion, and others, does not speak to the idea of genetic testing. First, genetic testing could not even have been imagined back in the early 1960s when the law was written. Second, the Civil Rights Act of 1964 only speaks to situations that exist presently time—a person's race, a person's religion, and so on. The authors of the law had not conceived of a world in which a reason for prejudice might not be detectable now but might come into existence in the future. Because of these two factors, no one has ever brought a successful genetic discrimination claim under Title VII of the Civil Rights Act.

The most important current federal law that actually discusses genetic testing is the Health Insurance Portability and Accountability Act of 1996. This law prevents individuals who are changing jobs from losing their health insurance coverage because of any preexisting condition, including genetic defects. Authors Feldman and Katz point out three problems with this law:

- It allows insurers to request or require genetic testing, which means that the results of one's genetic tests are no longer private information.

- The law does not protect individuals who are not covered under groups.

- It allows insurance companies to view the records of genetic information for group plan members. But the law in no way addresses the question of whether an individual can be forced to undergo genetic testing when seeking a new job.

Some states make it illegal for employers to discriminate on the basis of genetic information, and it is now the policy of the federal government, in its own hiring, to forbid discrimination due to genetic information. But there are as many as two dozen states that currently have no protection at all for workers who are required by their employers to seek genetic testing before being hired. Over the years, Congress has considered several different versions of laws that would offer such protections, but it has yet to pass such a statute. For the time being, if you wish to get a job, depending on the state you are in, you may be required to undergo genetic testing before anyone hires you.

> **Statutes of Liberties**
>
> Insurance companies may use genetic testing to discriminate against those individuals more likely to develop serious illnesses.

Personality Tests

Personality testing is a very troubling aspect of the hiring process, and it is a very sticky situation in terms of individual civil liberties. There are no federal laws against personality testing by private employers before the grant of employment, nor has Congress spoken on the issue, which means that it is legal for employers to require personality testing of employees before they make job offers.

There are many problems with personality testing. First of all, they don't always work very well. Anybody who has ever sat through a standardized test of any sort knows that there are ways to "game" the tests, or skew the results in a way that is going to be most favorable to the test-taker. It's fairly obvious if you have a choice of appearing compliant or aggressive on an employer's personality test you are going to give them every reason to think that you'll be an absolutely model employee. There has not yet been a personality test devised that cannot be outsmarted by individuals of even moderate intelligence.

Legal Dictionary

Personality test—Usually an exam composed of a series of questions used to identify marked characteristics, such as nervousness or creativity.

The second problem is that even if an employer could come up with a test that could not be gamed, there is a very big difference between taking a test and acting in the real world. While a testing situation is stressful, it's not nearly as stressful as when an angry customer is on the phone, a business decision must be made, or a negotiation must be completed. Personality tests fail to mirror the source of stressful situations that occur in the real world. This means that employers are paying to get results that have little or no validity when the rubber hits the road.

Taking Liberties

In a personality test recently given by a large corporation seeking a new vice president, the following question was asked:

You are stopped in your car at the light, waiting for it to turn green. To your right, you see three people seated at a booth waiting for the next city bus. They are, (1) your best friend who saved your life, (2) the woman of your dreams, and (3) an old injured lady. You have a small two-seater convertible; who do you give a ride to?

Of 200 applicants, only one answered correctly: Give the keys to your best friend who saved your life and let him drive the old injured lady to the hospital. Then stay behind with the woman of your dreams.

A third problem with personality tests is that they are often biased against members of minority groups. For example, one well-known personality test used as its "norm" a group of people who were most likely entirely Caucasian from a city in the Midwest. The "norms" of that group may be entirely different from the "norms" of individuals who come from minority groups, other parts of the country, or countries other than the United States. It would be a violation of an individual's civil rights if a personality test were found to be biased against his or her ethnic, religious, or racial group, especially if that test is used as a determining factor in whether or not the individual should be hired.

Yet another problem with testing is that it can be very expensive for employers, especially if they have to keep track of how various racial and ethnic groups perform on the test relative to groups of Caucasians or others, which is sometimes required by law. Also, how do you test individuals with disabilities? What about testing foreign job applicants?

In short, there is virtually no end to the number of flaws that personality tests possess.

From a civil liberties perspective, personality screening is even more problematic. Many of the questions used in personality tests deal with the religious beliefs and even the sexual practices of potential employees, areas into which employers have no right to explore. It's simply not fair for individuals to have to answer questions on personality tests that they would be legally absolved from answering in face-to-face interviews. Not only that, an employer who flat-out asked some of the questions on personality tests in interviews would actually be violating the law and liable to be sued!

When we talk about the right to privacy in general, we have to keep in mind that nowhere in the Constitution does it say, "You have a right to privacy." Instead, as we have discussed elsewhere in this book, the U.S. Supreme Court has "discovered" the right to privacy by taking together the various freedoms granted by the Constitution and the Bill of Rights. So there is never a bright line constitutional test to indicate whether a particular practice violates the privacy rights of individuals. Each issue has to be considered case-by-case. The question of personality tests in general has never been addressed directly by the Supreme Court.

Statutes of Liberties

The closest the Supreme Court has come to ruling on the question of personality testing came in a case involving individuals who sought to become firefighters. They were challenging the requirement to undergo psychological testing, which, they said, constituted a violation of their privacy rights. The Court agreed that such testing did "forbid" their privacy rights, but since firefighting is such a dangerous and stressful profession, the government's need to know which firefighters would handle the pressure well outweighed the privacy right of the individuals to keep from undergoing psychological tests. That case did place some limits on the validity of personality testing in the employment setting, but it failed to declare unconstitutional the issue of personality testing in general.

Individuals can sue over violations of privacy rights when employers use personality tests that are considered psychologically invasive—that is, they delve into the private areas of the mind that are off-limits to employers and truly none of their business. However, there are many limitations on the ability of individuals to maintain such lawsuits. First, it's expensive to sue. Second, employers may be savvy enough not to keep records of psychological testing and can therefore claim that an individual was not suitable for some other reason. Most people in America simply cannot afford to take the time or spend the money to bring such a lawsuit, especially when the results are so uncertain. It's been said that in America you get all the justice you can afford. Unfortunately, that may be the case here. Members of minority groups may have better luck bringing actions against personality tests on the grounds that such tests discriminate against members of their group, but even those suits are very difficult to win.

Lie Detectors

The basic rule about lie detector tests, also known as polygraph examinations, is "Fuggeddaboudit." In 1988, Congress passed a law stating that private employers cannot use lie detector tests to screen potential new employees, nor on a random basis to verify the honesty of current employees. The only circumstance under which polygraph testing is legitimate is if a particular employee is suspected of a crime, such as theft or embezzlement.

The basic problem with lie detector tests is that they are not 100 percent accurate.

According to Paul D. Seyferth, writing in the September-October 2001 issue of the *Journal of the Missouri Bar*, polygraph tests measure and record physiological changes in the body of the person being examined. The theory is that your heartbeat, blood pressure, pulse rate, breathing, and perspiration change when you lie. Is this true? Hard to say. Law enforcement agencies like to use polygraph tests in the process of criminal investigations. The problem is that we cannot be sure whether the polygraph tests themselves are accurate or whether a suspect's belief in the accuracy of polygraphs causes him or her to vary subconsciously blood pressure, perspiration, or other factors. In other words, polygraphs may be akin to the "trials by ordeal" of yore, in which the guilty conscience of the individual would cause that individual to "fail" a test. The court system is so suspicious of polygraphs that polygraph evidence cannot be introduced in a court of law.

Some companies (including security firms or drug manufacturers) and many government agencies (including the CIA, the FBI, and the Justice Department), are entitled to perform polygraph tests before granting employment. The law prevents private companies from denying employment, firing, or otherwise discriminating against any employee based solely on the results. In other words, no one really knows just how accurate they are. Polygraph expert Seyferth quotes former President Nixon as saying, "I don't know much about polygraphs, and I don't know how accurate they are, but I do know they scare the hell out of people." If they had polygraphs in the mid-eighteenth century, would the young George Washington have been subjected to one when they found the cherry tree chopped down? Would that have disqualified him from making the run at the presidency were the media of the day to find out about it? Those are two American history questions that luckily never arose.

Legal Dictionary

Polygraph or lie detector—A machine that records the pulse, heart, and breathing rates of the applicant during a question and answer session. Chan-ges in those rates are recorded and used to determine truthfulness.

Obesity and the Law

Surveys indicate that good-looking people make more money than average-looking people do, that tall people make more money than short people do, and that thin people make more money than fat people do. It's very hard to say exactly why this is the case. Maybe people who take better care of themselves inspire more confidence in others. Maybe people just like to do business with good-looking people, for any number of reasons. There is no legislating personal preferences. However, there is a legal question if individuals are discriminated against because of their physical appearance.

It is illegal for businesses to discriminate against individuals with disabilities, as we have discussed. The question now arises: Does obesity count as a disability? Does an employer have a right not to hire an individual simply because he or she is obese?

Statutes of Liberties

A San Francisco ordinance required a fitness center to hire a 240-pound woman as an aerobics instructor.

The law recognizes three different levels of overweight. The first level is the category into which millions of Americans unhappily find themselves: a few pounds over their "ideal" weight, as determined by their height and insurance companies. The second category includes individuals who are significantly overweight, which means that they are 20-30 percent above their ideal weight. These individuals would be considered fat by their fellows; so writes Donald L. Bierman, Jr. in the Winter 1990 issue of the *Santa Clara Review*. The third category are the morbidly obese, individuals who are 100 pounds over than their ideal weight or twice their ideal weight. Bierman writes that obese individuals—either those who are significantly fat or morbidly obese—face discrimination in the hiring arena.

Obesity is not considered a disability under current federal law or in most states. If a person is moderately or dangerously overweight, he or she may be turned down for a job. Is this a violation of their civil liberties? In an abstract sense, most likely. In a legal sense, no. The courts generally do not consider obesity a handicap or disability. As with genetic testing, employers sometimes discriminate against the obese due to the fear that they will trigger greater insurance costs, long-term care needs, or disability payments in future years.

Whether obesity should be considered a disability for the purpose of state laws is very much an open question today. While some commentators have sought to make "appearance discrimination" a violation of federal civil rights law, this has not yet happened. For the time being, the medically obese and the significantly overweight have no special legal protection when it comes to seeking employment.

The Least You Need to Know

- ◆ Depending on the state you are in, you may be required to undergo genetic testing before going to work.

- ◆ The Supreme Court has never directly addressed the legality of personality tests.

- ◆ Because the validity of polygraphs is questionable, they are not permissible in criminal proceedings.

- ◆ Overweight people currently do not have special legal protection when it comes to seeking employment.

Rights on the Job

In This Chapter

- ◆ The inappropriate interview
- ◆ Procreate = recreate?
- ◆ Hostile work environments
- ◆ Master and servant

In this chapter, we're going to examine your civil liberties in the workplace. Today, the employer and employee, whether in the private sector or in government job, are bound together in a complex web of rules, regulations, and limits on both sides. There exists today a delicate balance between the needs of the employer to conduct business in a successful and profitable manner and the needs of the employee to have his or her privacy and dignity respected.

Getting the Job

What exactly is a potential employer allowed to ask a potential employee within the context of a job interview?

Let's see: It's fair for an interviewer to ask you where you want to be in five years, or why you are attracted to work at XYZ Corp., but there are a lot of questions that are not just unfair but illegal. You don't have to answer questions with regard to your race, your housing status (whether you rent or own), your marital and family status (including whether you plan to marry or have kids), your political leanings, your religion, or your age (unless it's simply a question of whether you're 18 or over). The key test is this: If a question feels too personal, it probably is.

An interviewer also cannot ask you about child-care arrangements, whether your spouse minds if you travel, or whether your spouse is disabled. Employers cannot require medical examinations, photographs, military discharge status information, or your financial status. In addition, the fact that friends or relatives of the interviewee work for the same employer cannot be examined or held against you, unless there would be a conflict of interest.

The Career Center offers an excellent suggestion about how to handle questions that you may think are illegal. They write, "[R]emember that the employer may not be aware that he or she is asking an illegal question. Rather than telling your interviewer that he or she is asking an illegal question, you can simply say, 'I do not feel comfortable answering that question at this time.'"

If your refusal keeps you from getting the job, it may be just as well. After all, if they're so intent on violating your privacy at the job interview stage, do you really think this is the place you're going to want to spend the next few years or the rest of your career?

Drug Testing

As this book is written, one of the most prominent national issues is the question of whether baseball players should be tested for steroid use. Steroids, of course, are an illegal method of enhancing athletic performance. The debate over testing involves balancing the privacy rights of players to refuse to undergo urine testing with the right of the baseball leagues' desire to maintain the integrity of the national pastime.

While most of us are not likely to be challenging Barry Bonds for his single-season record of 73 homeruns, anyone who goes to work today may face the possibility of being tested for drug use. Employers want to test employees for drug use because the hidden cost of drug abuse runs into the billions of dollars annually in this country. That hidden cost involves disruption to employers and worksites and the difficulty of firing people. It's very hard to fire a person simply because he or she is an addict, and employers do not want to have to go through the rigmarole of seeking to terminate an employee on such grounds. Also, the health and safety of the individual worker and his or her co-workers may be threatened if that worker shows up on a job site high or otherwise out of control. In such cases, it's understandable that employers would want to test their employees.

Courts have held that corrections officers, people who work in nuclear power facilities, and air traffic controllers, for example, have a lower expectation of privacy than other government workers. If you work in a nuclear power plant or if you're handling incoming and outgoing flights at an airport, your right to privacy comes second to the public's right to safety. That's just how it is. In prison, corrections officers are used to having a lower expectation of privacy as they go about their business. For that reason, and because of the importance of helping to make prisons and jails as drug-free as possible/corrections officers, nuclear power workers, and air traffic controllers are subject to random drug testing.

Taking Liberties

The kind of job you hold dictates the level of privacy you can expect when it comes to random drug testing. The more it involves matters of security or safety, the greater the likelihood of testing.

When it comes to other areas of public trust—teaching, firefighting, police work, and army civilian employees—there has to be reasonable suspicion of an individual before that person can be tested. In other words, because their work is not quite as sensitive as the fields of corrections, nuclear power, or aviation, these individuals are entitled a higher degree of privacy. The courts are in doubt as to transit workers. On the one hand, transit workers are performing an important public service. On the other hand, it's tough to compare the importance of driving a city bus to working as an air traffic controller.

There are several problems with drug testing, the main one being that it violates the presumption in this country that we are innocent until proven guilty. By demanding drug tests, either at random or on a regular basis, the employer is implying that the employee is violating the drug laws. There is simply an issue of fairness that the U.S. Constitution requires.

The second problem with drug testing is that it is not always accurate. In fact, the most common drug tests administered by employers today result in false positives—they mistakenly indicate the presence of drugs in the urine when no drugs are present—as high as 66 percent of the time. Moreover, drug tests can determine the presence of marijuana and other drugs in one's system, but they cannot detect alcohol or beer. This means that if you smoke a bud, it may be

Statutes of Liberties

Many things about you are simply none of a prospective employer's business. The only questions an employer can ask in a job interview relate to how well you can perform the work.

detectable, but if you drink a Bud, you're in the clear. More expensive tests exist, and they are more accurate, but since they are more expensive, you guessed it—employers don't want to pay for them.

The laws in this country are different if you are a public employee—that is, if you work for the government—than if you work in the private sector, meaning you work for a private business. How could this be? Well, the Bill of Rights, specifically the Fourth Amendment to the U.S. Constitution, protects individuals against intrusion into their lives or "search and seizure" by the government. If you are a public employee, the Bill of Rights forbids the government (your boss) from violating your rights by making you submit to a drug test. In the private sector, since the boss is not the government, it's much easier for private sector employers to require drug tests, either at the interview stage or on the job.

Taking Liberties

You have more rights if you are employed by the government than if you are employed by a private citizen, because many of the safeguards that the Constitution and Bill of Rights provide only pertain to the government—not to private employers.

The private employee-employer relationship is actually based originally on the master-servant relationship. If you've ever felt that your boss is a slave driver, that's because it's in his genetic coding to act that way! The trouble with the master-servant relationship, from the point of view of the servant, is that you have no rights. Our modern-day American employment law, in the private sector, is actually rooted in the master-servant mentality, which means that the employee has no rights unless the government specifically says otherwise.

So the question becomes, under what circumstances is a drug test a search? And if it is a search, when is it justifiable? This becomes a legal issue that goes beyond the scope of this book. It's something that the courts have not been able to make a definite decision about, as simple a question as it seems.

A drug test can be justifiable if two conditions are met. First, when the test begins—before any results come in—there must be some sensible justification for it. And second, the drug test the employer is requiring must be "reasonably related to the circumstances which justified it." For example, it's okay to test a bus driver for the presence of drugs if he's been involved in a recent serious accident.

On the other hand, courts have held that there is no right to privacy with regard to bodily fluids. While a court order may be required in order to take blood from a suspect in a criminal matter, urine is considered less important, because, not to get too clinical about it, but we pass urine every day. (I'm not making this stuff up, this is your legal system at work.) Warrants are not usually necessary for drug tests, for the simple reason that the evidence may be gone before a warrant can be secured.

Does this mean that you have absolutely no rights if your employer wants to institute or continue random drug testing in your workplace? If you work in the private sector, your rights are extremely limited. First of all, if you are applying for a job, you have a lower expectation of privacy than someone who currently has a job. Second of all, anything urine reveals about a person's drug-taking habits is not considered "self-incrimination." Blood, urine, and DNA are all considered physical evidence, and they are therefore in a different category than testimony you might give about a crime you may have committed. The only ways in which a person who does not like drug testing can sue would be in one of the following four ways:

Legal Dictionary

Physical evidence—Any form of tangible evidence that may tend to prove a point; not just evidence that comes from a human body (bodily fluids).

- ◆ **A violation of privacy.** Your employer is snooping into your off-duty life (which we'll discuss further later on) or too many people or the wrong people are watching you give a urine sample. Of course, a drug test by nature snoops into your off-duty life.

- ◆ **Defamation of character.** The boss tells people you have failed a drug test when this is in fact not the case; these people could be your co-workers, the human resources department, or anyone else who might have a stake in your character.

- ◆ **Negligence.** Your test turns up a false positive and they take action against you.

- ◆ **Wrongful discharge.** They fire you without regard for your rights.

The trouble with the American legal system is that you get the best justice money can buy. This means, unfortunately, that if you cannot afford to sue an employer who punishes you or fires you for inaccurate results of a drug test, you have no recourse unless you can afford to hire an attorney or find one who will take the case on a contingency basis. Once again, your rights are not everything they should be.

Nice Cubicle: Dating in the Workplace

The Bill of Rights guarantees Americans freedom of association, which means we can spend our time with people we like and avoid those we don't like. The right to freedom of association relates to the question of dating on the job. Let's see just how.

Most of us spend more time at work than we do anywhere else. In the morning, we leave our home and get in our car or onto public transportation, get to work, often eating at our desks, leave when the workday is done, perhaps stop off at the gym, and then go home.

For many workers, the workplace becomes the engine for social lives simply because they have virtually no other place during their days to meet people. Employers are not big fans of employee dating, simply because issues from favoritism (when relationships are working well) to workplace violence (when things go sour) afflict the office when love strikes on the job. Gary Vikesland, writing on Employer-Employee.com, notes that it's not just impractical but sometimes even counter-productive for employers to try to ban co-worker dating. After all, Vikesland writes, Bill Gates met Melinda French when she was a Microsoft employee. Fish got to swim, birds got to fly, and co-workers are going to find love around the water-cooler, no matter what an employer does.

Looking for Liberty

WorkplaceFairness.org is an online clearinghouse of information dedicated to protecting employees' rights. Since employers have the paychecks and the lawyers on their side, groups like this help level the playing field.

So what's an employer to do?

Guidelines, guidelines, guidelines. A wise employer puts into place guidelines about workplace dating—and then enforces them with consistency across the workforce. Selective enforcement of any employer-employee rules is a recipe for disaster; nowhere is this quite so true as in the area of co-worker dating. It makes sense for employers to ban relationships between bosses and subordinates, for reasons relating to sexual harassment (which we'll discuss shortly).

There are legal reasons why employers should not seek to bar such relationships. First of all, individuals enjoy a right to privacy and a right of association, meaning that what they do when they're away from the office is their own business. A serious concern for employers—and employees as well—is the issue of statutory rape. If there are individuals below the age of 18 in a workplace, dating them may have serious legal consequences both for the employee getting involved with an underage person and for the employer.

Statutes of Liberties

Sometimes, when individuals are fired or demoted for dating someone at the office—or even a competitor—the lawyer representing the discharged or demoted employee might sue the employer on the grounds of "intentional infliction of emotional distress." This is a legal way of saying, "You hurt my feelings, so pay up, bub." Not all courts accept the theory of intentional infliction of emotional distress, but since you never know, employers need to walk on eggshells when it comes to this issue.

Vikesland offers the following employee dating guidelines:

- Before asking a co-worker out on a date, make sure your company has an employee dating policy that would permit it.

- Take no for an answer.

- Know before you go. Develop an office relationship with your co-worker and get to know each other before you ask that person out.

- Fools rush in. If the whirlwind courtship goes sour, your workplace will be an extremely unpleasant place for you.

- Don't flirt on the job. It drives everyone else crazy.

- If you're dating someone who reports to you, expect to transfer that person to another supervisor.

- Be prepared to confirm with your employer the rumor (which will travel with lightning speed) that you are dating a co-worker.

Taking Liberties _____

You have a right to do what you want, with whom you want, when you're off the job. Employers don't always agree, and so they may seek to punish or even fire employees who violate what they consider a code of conduct even when the employees are not on the job. The theory here is that an employee always represents the company, even when he or she is off duty. Court cases have been filed involving employees fired for drinking, smoking, living together, motorcycling, and partaking in other dangerous activities. Usually, the employee wins.

Actually, when you think about all the downsides that can follow in the wake of an unsuccessful office romance—getting fired, getting demoted, getting sued for sexual harassment—you really have to ask yourself if it's worth the trouble. Of course, your author is a married man who works alone at home and has no co-workers, so what the heck do I know?

The concept of associational privacy rights, or freedom to do what you want when you're away from work, had its origins in a most surprising place—smokers' rights. The big tobacco companies sought to have states pass laws preventing employers from firing workers simply because they were smokers. The law in New York State that grew out of that smokers' rights movement says that individuals cannot be punished by employers for "recreational" activities. The question in New York cases in thus became whether dating or even sex is considered a "recreational" activity for the purposes of this statute. In other words, can an employee date, live with, or even have an affair with an individual, without any risk of being fired by a disapproving employer? In New York, the answer came down: Yes, procreation is recreation.

Across the country, similar laws are in place, protecting the rights of unmarried individuals to live together, to live together in gay or lesbian relationships, and even to have an extra-marital affair, without the interference of an employer. Judges often do not want to enforce the rights of individuals to carry on these kinds of relationships, not wanting to give them the judicial imprimatur. On the other hand, if a relationship or high-risk activity outside of work interferes with the work getting done, it's perfectly legitimate for an employer to fire an employee. If a spouse of an employee works for the competition, no firing or punishment is permissible unless there is evidence that the two will collude to share trade practices or harm the employer in some manner.

Stop Harassing Me!

Sexual harassment is defined as unlawful employment discrimination based on sex. The U.S. Supreme Court has recognized two different forms of sexual harassment. The first is called *quid pro quo* (Latin for "this for that") sexual harassment. This type of harassment involves a situation in which an employment opportunity is conditioned on unwelcome sexual advances, requests for sexual favors, or other verbal or physical sexual contact. In other words, if an employer (of either gender, straight or gay) intimates or openly states that a promotion, raise, new title, or better job assignment is conditioned upon sexual favors, then quid pro quo sexual harassment is said to have taken place.

Legal Dictionary

Sexual harassment—
Unwelcome sexual advances or the creation of an environment that is intimidating or hostile. Display of pornographic photos or telling sexually explicit jokes can create such an environment.

Taking Liberties

Employers are held strictly liable for sexual harassment practiced by supervisors or other employees, whether or not they knew it or should have known that it was happening.

The second form of sexual harassment is the existence of a "hostile environment" in the workplace. A hostile environment includes exposure to unwanted sexual advances, sexual photographs, physical contact, remarks, or otherwise creating an "intimidating, hostile, or offensive work environment." In this case, the unwanted sexual advances are not clearly tied to career advancement—they're just happening. Hostile environment sexual harassment requires a pattern of such acts. An isolated instance does not create such a pattern, unless that isolated incident is quite severe.

Sexual harassment became illegal through Title VII of the Civil Rights Act of 1964, initially in order to make sure that women had an equal chance for success in the workplace as did men. The law today applies whether the victim or the harasser is a woman or a man. Even if the victim and harasser are both of the same sex, it is still considered harassment if it is unwanted.

It may seem hard to believe, but there is actually a legal category called religious harassment, and it's against the law as well. Courts have held that it is not legitimate to require employees to attend religious services, regardless of the beliefs of the owners or bosses. It is not acceptable to attempt to "save" an employee who does not share the same religious beliefs or moral scruples as the employer. In one case, an employer was found guilty of religious harassment by telling an employee who was having a sexual relationship out of wedlock that "you're a sinner and going to hell." Courts have a very difficult time with these cases, because they balance the right to a harassment-free workplace against the rights of religious freedom and free speech of the religiously minded employers.

The Workplace in Six Acts

One of the most powerful and divisive issues over the past century has been the question of whether workers have the right to unionize and bargain collectively. The history of union organizing in the United States is filled with heroics and horror as businesses used violence and even murderous tactics to keep unions from entering their workplace. The story of the union effort in our society is extraordinarily fascinating and beyond the scope of this book. We want to focus on one issue—whether the individual has a civil liberty right to join a union.

In the United States today, unions are more prevalent in certain regions than they are in others. In the Northeast and Midwest, union power is strong and many workers in all fields from auto manufacturing to adjunct professors are members of unions. In other parts of the country, especially the South and the West, resistance to unions has traditionally been stronger.

Many of the states in regions with less of a union presence are called "right to work" states. In these states, it is harder for a union to become certified to represent workers at plants, factories, and offices. This resistance is a matter

Looking for Liberty

The International Ladies' Garment Workers' Union, one of the leading unions in America, was founded in the aftermath of the Triangle Shirtwaist Company fire. In less than 15 minutes, 146 women working as seamstresses in a New York City factory, were killed in a fire—because their employer kept the doors locked to keep them from leaving early.

of considerable debate and much bitterness even today. The question is whether people who do not belong to unions but get the benefits that unions collectively bargain for are "free riders"—they get union benefits without paying union dues. Others respond that such individuals are not "free riders" but that the workers in those states are actually captives to those states' policy of resisting unionization. The question is whether unions are a burden or a blessing. In those states, management will tell you that unions are not a good thing, while the workers in those states might say, bitterly, that "right to work" actually means management exploitation—and a right to work for less—or even a right to starve.

Beginning in the early 1960s, a series of laws were enacted based on the due process/equal protection doctrines found in the Fifth and Fourteen Amendments (see Chapter 2 for a review). The Equal Pay Act of 1963 declared that employers and unions cannot discriminate in terms of pay on the grounds of race or sex for the same job. Equal work requires equal pay. The Age Discrimination and Employment Act forbids age discrimination in the workplace against those over 40. The Rehabilitation Act and The Americans with Disabilities Act of 1990 protect handicapped individuals from discrimination at the hands of employers who employ 15 or more individuals.

Taking Liberties

It is illegal for employers to discriminate on the grounds of race, color, religion, sex, national origin, pregnancy, childbirth or related medical conditions, age, or disabilities.

As long as a person with a handicap can do the job with reasonable accommodations—a situation that does not cause an employer undue hardship—they cannot be discriminated against. Individuals who sue and win under the Americans with Disabilities Act are entitled to compensatory damages (what they lost as a result of being discriminated against), punitive damages, and legal fees. The Equal Opportunity Employment Commission interprets and enforces most of these rules.

The most important law against employment discrimination is the Civil Acts Right of 1964. This law mandates that there can be no discrimination on the grounds of any of the above-mentioned categories in businesses that conduct interstate commerce and have 15 employees or more. Why interstate commerce, you may ask? Because Congress does not have the right to legislate about matters that take place solely within one state or another. That's the way our federal system works. However, if an employer conducts business across state lines, the Constitution and a long string of U.S. Supreme Court cases make clear that Congress may enact rules for them.

There are three forms of discrimination that the Civil Rights Act of 1964 seeks to eliminate. The first is disparate treatment—denying a promotion, disciplining someone, or firing someone because of a person's race, color, or other protected class. The

second form of discrimination is called
disparate impact, meaning that an employer has
a neutral policy—one that isn't on its face
racially motivated or written in such a manner
as to prevent women or members of one religion or another from getting jobs or moving
ahead. But if that policy screens out a "disproportionate percentage of members of a protected class," and the employer cannot show
that there is a job-related reason for screening
those people out, it's considered disparate
impact discrimination, and it's illegal. The third
type of discrimination forbidden by the Civil
Rights Act of 1964 is harassment of any kind.

Statutes of Liberties
In 1993, at the beginning of President Bill Clinton's first term, he signed into law the Family and Medical Leave Act. Any business employing 50 or more individuals must allow them 12 weeks of unpaid leave for a birth, adoption, or the care of a serious health condition of a parent, spouse, or child.

Workplace Privacy

Employers today monitor the behavior of their employees in a variety of ways. They
listen in on phone conversations, read their employees' e-mail, and even employ surveillance cameras to monitor the behavior of workers and make sure that they are
behaving themselves on the job (e.g., not treating the supply room as their own private stationery store). Technology gives employers a huge boost when it comes to
monitoring the behavior of employees who use computers. Employers can use software showing what you are looking at on your computer when you are sitting at your
desk. They can also keep track of what's in your hard drive, and where you've been on
the web. (Downloading porn at the office—never a good idea.) If your job involves a
lot of typing, your employer can actually measure how many keystrokes per hour you
are entering. They can even tell how long you take away from your computer during
your breaks or idle time.

Why do employers do this? Why are they so nosy? The basic answer is that they have
to be in order to protect themselves. America, according to many experts, is experiencing an epidemic of sexual harassment. In addition, workplace violence is on the
rise, and homicide has become the leading cause of death for women at work. If an
individual becomes the victim either of sexual harassment or violence, the employer is
liable—whether or not they knew in advance that the perpetrator was likely to act in
such a manner. What the employer knows in advance doesn't matter. All that matters
is that the employer did not fire the person before his or her acts of sexual harassment
or workplace violence.

There's a rule of law that states that an employer can be sued if he or she hires—even retains—a person who commits wrongdoing. The rule is called *negligent retention*, and employers can be sued for retaining (a fancy way of saying "not firing") any individual who goes on to commit sexual harassment or violence in the workplace. Sexual harassment lawsuits today can result in verdicts in the tens of millions of dollars. The lawsuits that can arise from workplace violence can be equally prohibitive. Employers thus feel a greater compulsion than ever to know who is working for them, what they are doing, and even sometimes, what they do during off hours. The risks of not monitoring employees are simply too great. No employer, even a large corporation, can afford to lose eight-digit lawsuits for sexual harassment or workplace violence.

Legal Dictionary

Negligent retention— Failing to fire an employee who later commits a serious crime in the workplace.

Due to the prevalence of drugs in today's society, employers feel justified in monitoring the workplace bathrooms of those employees who drive trucks, operate heavy machinery, or do other things for which a clear mind is necessary. An employer who risks having a drunk or high employee in one of these positions is potentially liable for tens or even hundreds of millions of dollars in damages. Employers simply do not want to take the chance.

What legal justification do employers have for monitoring the behavior of their employees? It all comes back to the question of privacy. When you go to work, you have a reduced expectation of privacy, just as you have in your car or in school. You know that people are going to be observing you, with or without hidden cameras or computer technology. Since you have a lower expectation of privacy, employers have a higher right to practice modes of surveillance.

Employers will sometimes spell out in employee handbooks the fact that there is no such thing as privacy in this particular workplace. In other words, employers find ways to put workers on legal notice that they should not expect privacy, whether it be using their computers or phoning home to mom. Because of lawsuits involving sexual harassment and workplace violence, the stakes are much higher.

The courts recognize that employers have an obligation to their employees to provide workplaces that are free from sexual harassment and violence. Therefore, courts generally support employers when issues of workplace privacy violations come to trial. It's very hard for an employee to win a court case based on violation of employee privacy. First of all, employers can afford lawsuits much more easily than can individual employees. Employers have either in-house attorneys or attorneys on retainer who handle all of their legal needs. Most workers, on the other hand, are simply not in a financial position to hire a lawyer.

Even if they do hire a lawyer and go to the trouble of filing a case, courts usually find for employers. Most courts are unwilling to interfere with the employer-employee relationship unless the employer is doing something truly egregious, such as videotaping women employees in a changing room without a job-related reason. Although instances exist where employees prevail based on their right to privacy, these cases are few and far between.

You're Fired! ... Or Are You?

"Employment at will" means, in a broad sense, that the employer can terminate a worker, at any time, with or without a reason, and an employee can leave at any time, for no reason or for a particular reason. Today, Congress and the courts have placed substantial restrictions on the ability of an employer to fire a person without cause. In this section, we're going to explore the concept of *wrongful discharge*, the grounds for a lawsuit an employee may bring when he or she believes that a firing is unjust.

The American Civil Liberties Union notes that 80 million individuals are employed in the private sector in the United States. Only about 20 million of those people have work relationships governed by union collective bargaining agreements, which protect workers from unjust dismissal. The ACLU cites examples of a nursing home supervisor fired from her job after 10 years of service because she called in two hours late to say that her brother had died. Other individuals have been fired because they refused to work in unsafe or unsanitary conditions, falsify medical or billing records, or participate in the illegal dumping of toxic materials or even radioactive materials.

Legal Dictionary

Wrongful discharge lawsuit—The grounds of a lawsuit that an employee may bring when he or she believes that a firing is unjust.

Since the Bill of Rights only requires due process when the government (not the private sector) seeks to deprive an individual of life, liberty, or property (including a job), what sort of safeguards, if any, are in place for individuals in the private sector who believe they have been unjustly fired?

The right of employers to fire employees is limited in three basic areas. The first is where an employer has agreed, either explicitly or implicitly, to employment terms. If your employer has offered you a written contract guaranteeing that you will be employed for a fixed amount of time, or guaranteeing that you will not be fired without just cause, you cannot be fired. After all, both you and the employer signed the contract, and you are both bound by it. On the other hand, if the employer says during a job interview, "If you do a good job for us, your future is secure," You won't have quite as solid a case as a written employment contract, especially because the employer might deny he or she ever said this. Nevertheless, these words help to create a contract between you and the employer guaranteeing your right not to be fired without cause.

Employees in the private sector are said to work "at will," which means they may quit or an employer may fire them at any time, without cause. As our legal system has developed, and moved away from the master-servant relationship on which it was originally founded, limits on the ability of an employer to fire have evolved.

Today, there are two basic legal theories under which an individual may sue if he or she thinks that he or she has been wrongfully discharged. The first approach is called *contract theory*. In this case, an employee is able to show that the employee handbook specifies why people should be fired—and this employee did none of the things listed in that employee handbook. If that happens, it's considered a breach of the employment contract between the employee and the employer. Another aspect of contract theory is *promissory estoppel*, the principal that a promise made becomes binding if the person to whom the promise is made relies on that promise to his detriment. In the employment arena, promissory estoppel may come into play if an employer says "Quit your old job and come work for me"—but then they don't hire you. If you quit your job, you can sue that person for failing to make good on his promise.

Legal Dictionary _____

Contract theory—The concept in the law that a contract can be implied from circumstances. In this case, when an employer hires an employee, there is an implicit employment contract, even though the employer and employee don't actually sign such a document. The basis for that "contract" is often the employee handbook at that company.

Promissory estoppel—The rule that requires you to compensate someone who detrimentally relies on a promise you make and break. If Smith makes a promise to Jones ("Quit your job and I'll hire you"), Jones quits his job in reliance on that promise, and Smith then says, "I've changed my mind, you can't have the job," Jones can sue Smith on the grounds of promissory estoppel.

The other means of suing an employer for wrongful discharge is under tort theory. A tort is a civil wrong or harm that one person does to another that is not necessarily criminal in nature. For example, if person B smacks into the back of person A's car, person B has committed a tort and is therefore responsible for the damage even though no crime has been committed. (Unless, of course, person B was driving under the influence, driving negligently, speeding, or something along those lines.)

When does tort theory come into practice in wrongful discharge? Let's say that your boss tells you to violate a law regarding public safety or health and you refuse. If you are fired for that reason, you can sue for wrongful discharge under tort theory—your boss has done something wrong to you that is not necessarily a crime. An illustration: Mr. Burns tells Homer Simpson to dispose of some nuclear waste materials by throwing them out the window of his car on his way home from work. If Homer refuses and he's fired, he has an action against Mr. Burns in tort for wrongful discharge. Of course, as we all know, disposing of nuclear material by tossing it out of a car window is wrong, and probably violates a whole lot of people's civil liberties as well as a bunch of criminal statutes.

Employee handbooks often state the criteria for each position in the company. What you are expected to do as an employee in a particular department is often governed by terms in the employee handbook or manual. If you comply with the job requirements in the employee manual, you cannot be fired without just cause. There is an exception, however: The employer can place in the employee handbook or manual specific language stating that "nothing in this handbook is intended to form a contract of employment," or words to that effect.

Many employers today deliberately put language into their employee handbooks indicating that they can still fire employees at will, without just cause. If you are fired and you do not have a written employment contract, you may wish to study your employee handbook or manual before you call a lawyer. Your lawyer will definitely want to know whether there is a disclaimer in the employee handbook making clear that you can be terminated at any time.

Legal Dictionary

Public policy—A legal way of saying, "We, your government, think this is a good idea for society, so we are going to enact legislation to favor this trend."

There is also a *public policy* exception to at-will firing. The public policy exception to at-will firing means that there are certain situations where the government steps in to make sure that private employers do not violate public policies favoring the ideas the government believes beneficial. For example, the government thinks it is unfair for workers to be fired for filing a workers' compensation claim, for refusing to give perjured testimony (that is, lying on the witness stand in a court of law), or for serving on a jury.

Other individuals who have been wrongfully discharged and who were able to assert their legal rights under a public policy argument include an individual who complained about second-hand smoke in her office area, and an employee who was required to work with dangerous or malfunctioning equipment. According to the ACLU, employees who have been fired for these reasons were given redress—either their old job back or financial compensation—for having been fired for these reasons.

Congress and the states have passed many laws limiting an employer's ability to fire employees at will. These include the National Labor Relations Act, which governs employer-employee relationships where there are unions and collective bargaining. Title VII of the Civil Rights Act of 1964 prohibits discrimination against employees based on race, color, national origin, and religion. Older workers (those over 40) are protected against age discrimination by the Federal Age Discrimination in Employment Act. Employees cannot be terminated for filing an OSHA claim. OSHA stands for the Occupational Safety and Health Act, and it is intended to provide employees with safe, hazard-free, workplaces. Those with disabilities who can be reasonably accommodated cannot be discriminated against because of their disability, under the Americans with Disabilities Act. And the Family and Medical Leave Act offers employees unpaid time off, up to 12 weeks, to care for themselves or close family members who develop serious medical conditions, or after the birth or adoption of a child. If you seek to take time under the FMLA, you cannot be fired for doing so.

The ACLU rightly points out that millions of employees who do not belong to any of the protective groups we have just mentioned have zero protection against wrongful discharge. Even members of protected groups—individuals with disabilities, those over 40, and members of minority groups—are only protected from wrongful discharge if they are fired because of their disability, age, religion, race, or other protected status. If their firing has nothing to do with those statuses, they are completely unprotected. Perhaps the issue of civil liberties in the area of wrongful discharge can be summed up in terms of the Golden Rule: Whoever has the gold, rules. And that would be the boss.

The Least You Need to Know

- The private employee-employer relationship is based on the master-servant relationship.
- Public employees have different rights than employees in the private sector.
- Discrimination of any kind is illegal in the workplace.
- Limits on the ability of an employer to fire have evolved.

Families and the Law

In This Chapter

- ◆ Parent vs. parent
- ◆ Kids' rights to divorce
- ◆ The scandal of foster care
- ◆ Adopted children's rights

What happens when families fall apart? How does society adjudicate the rights of husbands and wives, parents and children? In this chapter, we'll examine the aspects of family law in which we find rights in conflict. We'll look at the question of divorce and child care and how women's rights are affected. We'll consider children's rights in terms of custody, the foster care system, and adoption. We'll also examine the concept of emancipation—the process by which a minor becomes an adult in the eyes of the law by marrying, entering the military, or some other means, and how emancipation affects the responsibilities of the parents.

Divorce: The Lawsuit Nobody Wins

Divorce has been a part of every Western legal code going back to the book of Deuteronomy. In this section, we'll consider how the rights of women are often denied because of the way the American legal system works.

The great motivator and author Zig Ziglar comments, with no small amount of irony, "A lot more gets negotiated in the divorce proceeding than at the marriage altar." In the state of California, to obtain a driver's license, you must answer correctly 31 out of 36 multiple-choice questions about rules of the road. In order to become married in California, you must answer only one question: Are you currently married to someone else?

It's entirely possible that today's society has a skewed concept of the nature of love and marriage. When we go to the movies, we frequently see an attractive man bumping into an attractive woman under unusual circumstances. They meet and, after a limited amount of contact, often much of it physical, they realize that they are "in love." Of course, if two people are in love, the only thing to do is to get married (or to register under a Vermont civil partnership, as the case may be—see Chapter 5). The movie concludes with the couple winding their way happily into the sunset, but we see little or nothing of the actual marriage relationship that ensues. This leaves most moviegoers with the mistaken conception that "love" means a combination of sexual infatuation and an overall warm feeling about the other person. Those feelings probably aren't enough to sustain a short-term relationship to say nothing of a long-term marriage, which involves not just love but trust, commitment to similar goals and values, patience, acceptance, and compromise, to name just a few of the requirements.

Taking Liberties

The concept that two people must be in love in order to get married is a fairly new one in human history. Generally, marriages were arranged by parents with the idea that love would grow as a result of the (initially unsought) relationship. Sometimes it did and sometimes it didn't, but our batting average, based on freedom of choice, isn't much better today!

This misconception about what goes into making a good marriage may be why divorce is so common these days. Unfortunately, divorce is an economic and social disaster for all participants—except for divorce lawyers.

Often, when two people who should never have been together come to the same conclusion, albeit slowly, that their friends and relatives reached much more speedily, the cry can be heard throughout the land, "at least they didn't have children." That's no joke. The effect of divorce on children has been documented by sociologists, psychologists, and economists, and all of them are universally gloomy about the prospects for the children of divorce as they move into their own adult lives.

Children of divorce find it harder to trust others. If they grew up in a situation without parental authority, often a feature of single-parent homes, they might find it harder to respect authority, whether it comes in the form of an employer's order or a

police officer's badge. It has also been proven that children of divorce suffer dispro-
portionately because they may be financially unable to complete their secondary education. Children of divorce who come from economically challenged homes are also
more likely to need social services such as wel-
fare than children from intact families.

In a perfect world, people would marry the
right person the first time around, have 2.3
children, and love their partners and their kids
forever. In such a perfect world, there would be
no need for this chapter. Unfortunately, we live
in the real world, where divorce—and the economic and psychological dislocation that follows—is all too common.

> **Statutes of Liberties**
>
> Women who are not paid their
> full child support awards—and
> this is estimated to be more than
> 80 percent of all divorced
> women—must go to court in
> order to force the ex-husband to
> pay.

According to statistics in the *Vermont Law Review*, Winter 1989, more than 70 percent
of children of divorce live either in poverty or near poverty. Virtually every child lives
more poorly after divorce than before. Support payments rarely are substantial
enough to cover the costs of raising a child. There are several problems with going to
court for this purpose. First, it's expensive, and women who are struggling to pay the
bills without adequate child support are seldom in a position to pay an attorney.
Second, even if a judge agrees with the ex-wife that she is entitled to the money that
the original divorce court decreed for her, it can be still very difficult to execute a
judgment against an ex-husband who may have vanished or is in jail. Going to court
also constitutes something of a pin of the roulette wheel for the divorced woman, as a
judge may actually use the occasion to reduce the amount that the ex-husband is obligated to pay. According to one authority, the entire divorce system seems created for
the benefit of nonpaying fathers.

Do Children Have Rights?

There are three often conflicting sets of rights that exist in a divorce situation involving children: the state's right to ensure the child is given the best possible chance to
succeed in life and each of the parents' rights to determine the best course for their
children. Common issues that arise include education, religion, residence, and custody. Clearly, these issues, which may have contributed to the demise of the marriage,
now complicate the divorce proceeding, as parents battle to assert their rights as it
relates to the child.

In Puritan times, the law regarded children as the chattel, or property, of their father.
As the centuries passed and things became somewhat more humane, children began

to be recognized as individuals in their own right. In the 1800s, the concept of children as property was withdrawn in favor of a notion of the state as "super parent," with the responsibility of stepping in when birth parents were unable or unwilling to do the right thing for the child.

> **Looking for Liberty**
>
> The American Civil Liberties Union is one of the best sources of information about children's rights, for adults ... and for kids. Their website, www.aclu.org, offers a wealth of information about civil liberties in language that kids can understand.

As we've discussed, children are not entitled to full constitutional rights, as are adults, but they are entitled to a great deal of protection under both the U.S. Constitution and the Bill of Rights. The history of children's rights over the last century, and especially over the last 20 years, has been a process of recognizing the fact that children are entitled to make decisions for themselves, even when those decisions are sometimes in conflict with the views of the parents or state.

The Privacy Rights of Children

The two major areas in which children have been found by the courts to have privacy rights are contraception and abortion. As we discussed in Chapter 5, the 1960s Supreme Court decision in *Griswold* made the bedroom a zone of privacy into which the government could not intrude. Later cases extended a right of privacy in sexual matters to older minors. For instance, a 15 year old does not have to have parental permission and need not notify a parent if he or she wishes to acquire contraceptives. Currently, no state or federal laws require minors to get parental consent in order to get contraception.

> **The Law of the Land**
>
> Gender was at the core of many laws until recent times. For example, just as the law presumed that mothers are better at parenting than fathers, the law also presumed that male heirs were better at handling estates than females. If an estate didn't specify who was to make decisions, the male heirs were automatically given that role!

Similarly, abortion, that hotly contested subject to which we devoted part of Chapter 5 of this book, is considered a privacy right in *Roe* v. *Wade*. Later Supreme Court decisions extended some abortion rights to minors. As the country has moved into a more conservative era, some of the freedoms that older minors had with regard to abortion are being chipped away, and some statutes requiring parental notification or 24-hour delays for minors that would not be required of adults, have been found constitutional. Nevertheless, older minors—children 15, 16, and 17—do have certain privacy rights in the extremely delicate areas of contraception and abortion.

I mention abortion and contraception as indicators of the fact that for decades courts have declared that children do have privacy rights, and that society does judge them capable of making certain decisions without the assistance of adults. That framework of allowing older minors important decision-making rights has been considered by some courts to be a precedent for the granting of rights to children when their parents are getting divorced.

Children and Divorce

In the past, courts looked to two tests or presumptions when making decisions about children, especially when it comes to custody after divorce. The first is the concept of "the best interests of the child." Normally, the people best able to make a decision about what would constitute the best interests of the child are the parents. When parents are unable to agree or incompetent to make such a decision, the question of what is in the best interest of the child has traditionally fallen to the states to decide. Family court traditionally appoints a lawyer to represent the interests of the child in any divorce or post-divorce hearing.

The second concept to which courts adhered for decades was the "tender years" hypothesis. This approach states that because a mother has a greater influence over a child in the first weeks, months, or years of life, the state should award custody of a very young child to the mother and allow her to make all the important decisions.

From a constitutional point of view, there is an even greater problem with the tender years presumption. The Fourteenth Amendment to the U.S. Constitution requires equal protection for all members of society. This requirement means that unless there is an extremely compelling reason, the state may not treat men and women differently in the courtroom. To presume that mothers know best in the early weeks or years of life is to deny equal protection to fathers, something courts are no longer willing to do. Today, more than half the states have passed statutes forbidding courts to employ the tender years hypothesis.

Taking Liberties

There are several problems with the tender years thesis. First, advocates of the approach are often unable to agree as to just what period really is at issue here. Some believe that the first few weeks of life make all the difference, while others extend the thinking to the kindergarten stage. There is no unanimity among tender years advocates.

If the courts are not going to presume that mothers know best, and if courts are now willing to say that children are entitled to a voice in their post-divorce lives—in effect, saying that the state is no longer the best arbiter—these questions are now raised:

 ◆ What rights should a child have in his parents' divorce proceeding?

 ◆ At what age should these rights come into play?

The primary issue involves custody. With increasing frequency, courts are allowing children to indicate to the court with which parent they wish to spend the rest of their childhoods. It's easy to make a case for allowing a child to express a desire. So often, children are used as pawns in bitter divorce proceedings, and parents sometimes seek custody rights not because they wish to spend time with their children, but in order to frustrate their ex-spouses and drag on the course of divorce proceedings. Therefore, it makes sense that a child would know where his or her best interests would lie. Or does it? Frequently, a child will choose the more lenient or "fun" parent. Deep down, children want a sense of order and discipline, but for many children, especially many adolescents and teenagers, that sense is buried way, way, *way* deep down and rarely evidences itself to others. In such instances, a child may not be in the best position to judge with which parent he or she is likely to find the best home.

> ### Statutes of Liberties
>
> The purpose of having laws is to provide a sense of certainty to people, so that they'll know in advance how to conduct themselves. The difficulty with divorce and children's rights is that every case is so different, and therefore it's almost impossible to make "bright line" or firm rules that govern large numbers of cases.

In addition to thinking they want to live with the more lenient parent, children also tend to want to live with the parent with whom they share particular religious views. The First Amendment makes clear that the government cannot "establish" religion, and some courts interpret this to mean that children in a divorce proceeding should not be subjected to religious instruction or practice that violates their norms or religious scruples.

Yet another issue involves race. Most courts display a great deal of sensitivity toward the issue of the race of the parents raising a child. When a marriage between two members of the same race ends in divorce, and one of the ex-spouses marries a person of another race, children's rights advocates suggest that a child should be free to indicate a preference for the racial composition of the home in which he or she will be raised. The trouble with this issue is that the Equal Protection clause of the Constitution means that the courts are on thin ice when they consider race in their decision to place a child after a divorce. To deny a parent the right to raise her child based on a subsequent marriage to a person of a different race has been found by an increasing number of courts to violate the Equal Protection clause of the U.S. Constitution.

Along those same lines, a parent's sexual behavior can also be a determining factor. It may be disturbing to a child if a parent is carrying on sexual relationships with more than one individual in a short period. Courts are beginning to consider whether exposure to such sexual practices may be damaging to the child. One practice the courts shy away from is establishing moral rules for people. Courts do not want to be the arbiters of the sex lives of Americans. Therefore, when the issue of a divorced parent's sexual practices arises, a court will only act on that issue if it is clear that serious damage is being done to the child. If one or both of the parents is homosexual, fear that this may affect the sexual preference of the child is not considered reasonable grounds to remove a child from such a home. This is an area the Supreme Court has yet to address.

The other complicated factor in this matter is recognizing the fact that children can have different levels of maturity regardless of their age. It therefore becomes difficult to establish hard-and-fast rules as to what age a child should be permitted to weigh in on any of the foregoing issues. Since divorce law varies from state to state, there are no federal guidelines on this issue. As with so many of the items we discuss in this book, the area of children's rights in divorce situations is evolving and we certainly have not yet heard the last word on the subject.

> ### Looking for Liberty
>
> What happens if one of the parents is gay or a lesbian? The debate continues in American society as to whether such a person should be granted custody, on the grounds that he or she might influence the sexuality of the child. The gay and lesbian rights organization GLAAD (www.glaad.org) is at the forefront of this debate.

Foster Children and the Law

The American foster care system is one of the most tragic secrets in our society, shocking because the system works so poorly. Indeed, until a private group commissioned a study in the late 1990s, it was actually unknown just how many children were in the foster care systems of many states. It is also shocking because children may find themselves in "foster care drift," moving from home to home without ever establishing true family bonds throughout their entire family childhood. Studies indicate that such children are far more likely to end up on welfare or behind bars.

The system is something of a secret because most individuals not involved with foster care have little reason to think about it. Unless they live next door to a group foster home or are seeking to adopt a child, most Americans never have contact with the foster care system. Thus, abuses, such as foster "parents" who fill their home with children to collect the maximum amount of money from the state, go unchecked.

Today, there is also the phenomenon of for-profit foster care home companies, which often situate foster children in states far from the families and friends.

Children enter foster care in several ways. Often parents voluntarily place their children in foster care because they recognize their inability, be it financial, physical, or emotional, to raise their children for the time being. Alternatively, courts often remove children from homes where there have been findings of abandonment, neglect, mental illness, or severe and repeated abuse.

Once a child finds her way into the foster care system, the nightmare truly begins. Theoretically, caseworkers are supposed to maintain caseloads of over 25 children each. In reality, strained budgets and a general sense of neglect mean that many big-city caseworkers may have 75 to 125 cases. It's all too easy for children to slip through the cracks, for their whereabouts to go unnoted, and for them to find even worse abuse and neglect in foster homes than that from which they were "rescued" in the first place.

Taking Liberties

The foster care laws specify that children who are designated as "special need" will bring in more money to the state foster care system than those who are not thus designated. As a result, states go out of their way to declare virtually anything a trigger for special needs designation—and those extra bucks. Some states declare that a child's race dictates that he or she is a special needs child. Some states actually say that a child's religion will have the same effect. According to one commentator, states have so stretched the meaning of the term "special needs" as to render it meaningless.

A foster child becomes legally ready for adoption upon termination of the birth parents' rights to direct their lives. In theory, foster care children are supposed to have their cases reviewed every 6 to 12 months. The termination process, however, can drag on for years. There is a societal presumption that parents who seek to adopt children are only interested in healthy white babies. However, there are countless families seeking to adopt children of any age and racial background, but their desires to adopt children and give them loving, stable homes are thwarted by a system that only collects money as long as the children are still in their clutches.

Taking Liberties

Advocates for children's rights are now seeking to create the right for children to pursue their own termination action.

Traditionally, caseworkers have the responsibility of pursuing termination actions against parents who are unable or unwilling to fulfill their parental responsibilities. With some caseworkers averaging five times the number of cases that they would be handling in an ideal world (one might argue that in an ideal world that there would be no need for foster care), it is all too easy for termination proceedings to be delayed for years—years that the children will never get back. As the great columnist Jimmy Breslin wrote, "Dies the child, dies the city." There may be as many as three-quarters of a million American children in foster care at any given time this year. The societal consequences of allowing them to languish in that system are unthinkable.

Adoption and Privacy Rights

One of the most painful decisions a parent may make is the decision to give up a child for adoption. This happens, of course, for a number of reasons—the child is born out of wedlock, the parent is too young, or for religious reasons. Delivering a baby to be put up for adoption and physically surrendering that child to the adoption process are without question brutally painful experiences for most women. One of the most pressing civil liberties issues involved weighs the right of the child to learn the identity of his birth parents against the privacy rights of those birth parents.

Very strong arguments can be made on both sides of this question. For the birth parents, courts frequently hold that a right of privacy exists and that court records once sealed with regard to adoptions should never be opened. It might be incredibly embarrassing to a woman who is now married, the mother of other children, and a member of a community to have her past unexpectedly confront her. Typically, when a child is adopted, a new birth certificate is created, substituting the names of the adopting parents for the names of the birth parents. Many individuals have allowed their children to be put up for adoption because state authorities promised that their privacy would never be violated and that the original birth certificates or hospital records would never be unsealed.

On the other hand, courts have long recognized that children placed into adoption have a right to know "who they are and whose they are." They need this information for emotional reasons, so that they can understand the religious, ethnic, and perhaps racial background of their birth parents. They also often need this information for medical reasons, so that they can provide their genetic and hereditary information to their doctors. For many adopted children, there exists a sense of loss and longing to

Looking for Liberty
Jean Paton is considered one of the leading individuals in the adoption rights movement. Her 1954 book, *The Adopted Break Silence*, was an important contribution in the field. She was the first adopted individual to question the rules regarding the sealing of adoption records.

know the circumstances into which they were brought into the world, a longing that lasts deep into adulthood.

This clash of rights creates a tough situation: To satisfy the desires of one group would mean to frustrate the desires of another. There is seemingly no middle ground of whether to unseal information surrounding adoptions or not. This area of the law has evolved a great deal and is still very much in flux.

Prior to the late 1940s, social workers in the adoption field recognized the importance of keeping birth and medical records for adopted children. It was only in the post-war period that the privacy of birth mothers—and fathers—became legally enshrined in law. By the 1970s, adopted children began to organize and challenge laws that sealed birth records. Today the law varies from state to state, and it would appear that the pendulum is swinging back toward the rights of adopted children. Similarly, some birth parents are seeking out their children to ease the sense of emotional heartache that the adoption process still engenders.

The Emancipated Child

The fourth and final topic we will examine in this chapter is the question of *emancipation*—the situation in which a parent is relieved of legal obligations relating to a child, and the child then assumes those obligations on his or her own behalf.

There is a very strong preference in society and in the law that parents be financially, legally, and morally responsible for their children. Under certain circumstances, a child, generally 15 or older, may seek a legal state of emancipation, which means that such obligations are no longer legally in effect. When a child is emancipated, the parent is no longer financially responsible for that child's food, clothing, shelter, education, and similar necessities of life. Events that trigger emancipation are when a minor marries (there are legal cases involving such marriages), joins the military, or voluntarily leaves a home in which there is physical or emotional abuse.

Legal Dictionary

Emancipation—The situation in which a parent is relieved of legal obligations relating to a child. The child is now responsible for paying his or her own way in life and also is responsible in terms of criminal and civil law.

The question of rights arises when either the parent does not believe that he or she is obligated to keep on paying or when the event that triggered the emancipation is legally nullified. Many times, young people want total freedom to make decisions as they see fit—and yet they want their parents to bankroll those decisions, however repugnant the parents may find them. Courts rule that children, even into their early 20s, receiving economic aid from their parents cannot have their cake and eat it too. In other words, if you want Dad's money, you have to accept Dad's authority. This may be harsh from the child's point of view, but the fact is that parents have (some) rights, too! The courts have held repeatedly that parents do not have to bankroll the lives of children who are living lives of which the parents disapprove.

The second case in which emancipation becomes a legal question is when the marriage of a young person is annulled, or that child leaves the military while still a minor. If a 16 year old marries another person his age or even younger, and then that marriage is subsequently annulled, what does that do to the state of emancipation? Is emancipation nullified under those circumstances? In other words, if your 16-year-old daughter has a marriage that doesn't last, and now she is 17, does the parent automatically have to start paying for food, clothing, shelter, and education for that child?

The Law of the Land

Can a child enter the military while lying about his or her age? There is no constitutional prohibition on such an action, and countless Americans have entered the military to serve their country despite the fact that they were not of legal age to do so.

Let's say a 17 year old goes into the military, triggering emancipation. Parents may be very pleased to learn that they are no longer responsible for going to court every time young Johnny gets into another bar fight. (What Johnny is doing in bars at age 17 is beyond the scope of this book.) Let's say that Johnny washes out of basic training, for getting into … you guessed it, another bar fight. Does this mean that his parents are once again on the hook for Johnny's financial—and legal—obligations? Can the parents be dragged into court every time Johnny breaks the law?

In both cases, the answer is a definite maybe. State laws vary on emancipation and ultimately it all comes down to a combination of state law and the manner in which the judge deciding the case feels like determining it. The bottom line: Just because your child issues an emancipation proclamation, don't be too quick to turn his or her bedroom into a den.

The Least You Need to Know

- Divorce affects all family members, both adults and children.

- The area of children's rights in divorce situations is still evolving.

- The foster care system works very poorly, depriving many children of happy childhoods and loving families.

- Parents do not have to bankroll the lives of children who are living lives of which the parents disapprove.

Chapter 20

Students' Rights

In This Chapter

- ◆ Freedom of the school press?
- ◆ Just saying no
- ◆ Teenage sex
- ◆ Parental warning: explicit lyrics

Remember Tommy Order? You met him in Chapter 1. He's Laurie Order's 15-year-old son, the one who just found out that his high school principal has forbidden the publication of his article in the school newspaper. In this chapter, we're going to take a closer look at Tommy Order and all his fellow teenagers, and discuss whether you have to be a certain age before the Constitution and all of its attendant rights regarding personal liberty take effect.

Specifically, we will examine the areas of free speech for teenagers, including school newspapers and "message" t-shirts, to see whether schools have a right to restrict students in ways that other institutions in American society do not. We'll also turn to the subjects of student privacy, discipline, and to what extent religion may be practiced in public schools.

Student Newspapers

Being a teenager is all about testing limits. In developmental psychology terms, the adolescent and post-adolescent periods are the time when young people stop taking their cues primarily from their parents and begin to listen to their peers. This development is a natural and healthy, if at times extremely painful, part of the process of maturation. By shifting "allegiance" from parents to a circle of friends, a teen begins to develop his or her own sense of autocracy and independence. There's nothing easy about being a teen, and there's nothing easy about being an adult charged with their emotional and intellectual growth.

The Law of the Land

It is unconstitutional for a public school to display the Ten Commandments in a hallway or classroom.

Compounding the traditional difficulties that educators and parents have always faced, the times we live in present extraordinary new challenges. The level of violence in schools, symbolized by the killings at the Littleton, Colorado high school and others, is unprecedented. While there have always been disciplinary problems in schools, it is hard to recall situations in previous decades where students would seek to resolve their problems with lethal force.

In such an environment, where students' actions can literally have deadly consequences, it is not surprising that school administrators would like to exert more control over students. Changing times and mores in adult society support this desire of school leaders to clamp down on the freedoms that students enjoyed in times that were, if not more peaceful, perhaps simply more naïve.

Tinkering With Freedom

The roots of free speech on high school campuses date back to the late 1960s, when Americans were deeply divided over the correctness of our involvement in the Vietnam War, already in full swing. Famously, the debate over whether Vietnam was a noble war or an unjust war crime spread to America's college and high school campuses. In Des Moines, Iowa, a group of middle and high school students was suspended for wearing black armbands protesting the Vietnam War. The students were not speaking out in class, disrupting, marching, or doing anything other than simply wearing the black armbands. The Des Moines school district found this practice objectionable and disruptive, and suspended the students, who claimed that the wearing of black armbands was constitutionally *protected free speech*. The case went all the way to the Supreme Court. Ironically, young people today have more personal freedom than ever before, and yet their legal rights have been curtailed compared with the rights of students even a few decades ago.

In the 1969 landmark decision *Tinker* v. *Des Moines School District*, the U.S. Supreme Court ruled that the students should not have been suspended because the wearing of black armbands was political speech protected by the U.S. Constitution. In other words, the Supreme Court was saying that just because you're young and in school doesn't mean you're not protected by the First Amendment. From 1969 on, for almost two decades, students enjoyed an unprecedented amount of freedom to express themselves on campus.

Legal Dictionary

Protected speech— Speech or conduct that the First Amendment guarantees shall not be interfered with by state action. "Speech" may also include acts like the wearing of armbands, making a peace sign, or other symbolic acts of communication.

Freedom Diminished

Times changed. By the 1980s, America had done a slow about-face from the freedoms and liberal trends of the '60s. The 1980s were a time when conservative ideas predominated. President Ronald Reagan was in the White House, and Americans seemed more preoccupied with financial matters than philosophical questions. At the same time that America was becoming more conservative, American society was becoming a more vulgar place. This is quite a paradox, of course, but the 1980s were a time when both Ronald Reagan and Howard Stern were ascendant.

In the middle part of the decade, a New Jersey high school student named Matthew Fraser gave a nominating speech for a friend at a student government assembly at his high school. The speech was replete with sexual innuendo, and Fraser was suspended. He took his case to the Supreme Court, which decided, in the 1986 case of *Beth El* v. *Fraser*, that vulgar, offensive, or lewd speech and sexually explicit language was in fact not protected by the First Amendment. The Supreme Court seems to be declaring that there had to be a balance between the students' First Amendment rights to freedom of expression and the educators' need to maintain order and decorum on high school campuses. In short, the rollback of the freedom that *Tinker* v. *Des Moines* promised only 17 years earlier had begun.

Two years later, a new landmark U.S. Supreme Court decision was announced, further limiting the free speech rights of high school students. Hazelwood, Missouri, a city of 27,000 residents, is located in the northwest section of St. Louis County, just north of the airport.

During the 1982 to 1983 school year at Hazelwood East High, three Hazelwood East students, staff members of the school newspaper *Spectrum*, charged that school officials violated their First Amendment rights by deleting two pages of articles from the May 13, 1983 issue. The articles focused on two issues: unmarried, pregnant students at the high school, and high school students who are children of divorced parents. In the latter article, one of the students openly criticized his parent by name. The students contended that when the faculty and administration of Hazelwood East High School withdrew those articles from the newspaper, the students' First Amendment rights were violated. The U.S. Supreme Court, by a five to three margin, disagreed.

In the 1988 decision *Hazelwood School District* v. *Kuhlmeier*, the U.S. Supreme Court held that students do have First Amendment rights, but teachers and administrators have an even greater right to limit students' right of free expression if doing so is "reasonably related to a valid educational policy." The Court held that writing about unmarried, pregnant students and children of divorced parents posed three problems for the school. First, the articles violated the privacy of the individuals who were the subjects of the article, notwithstanding the fact that some of them were interviewed by the article writers in preparation for the stories. Second, the Court was concerned that these articles could trigger legal liability for the schools that students or their parents might sue because of the way they were portrayed in the articles. Finally, the Court wrote that a discussion of sexual matters, such as appeared in these articles, was inappropriate for a high school newspaper.

You don't have to be a constitutional scholar to wonder how the U.S. Supreme Court squared its decision in this case with its landmark *Tinker* v. *Des Moines* decision, which gave students broad rights to freedom of expression. The Supreme Court reasoned that wearing black armbands was simply a choice that students made, something that took place on school grounds. The Hazelwood student newspaper could be viewed as the "voice of the school," meaning that it could reasonably appear that the school itself was either condoning the points of view the students were expressing, or that the students were expressing the point of view of the school with regard to the issues of unmarried, pregnant students and children of divorced families.

Justice William J. Brennan, writing for the minority, disagreed strenuously with the decision in *Hazelwood*, calling it "thought control." And a lawyer representing a journalists' organization offered this sardonic comment: "We want [students] to learn about the First Amendment, but just don't want them to exercise it until they graduate." In short, by 1988, the Supreme Court had further curtailed the First Amendment rights they had bestowed on students with the *Tinker* decision.

Today, school boards across the country rely on *Hazelwood* to exert control over the content of high school newspapers. Therefore it wouldn't be a surprise if Tommy Order's article on bomb-making resources on the Internet fell prey to censorship at the hands of his principal or faculty advisor. Is there anything Tommy can do about it? He could try to take the case to the U.S. Supreme Court, but good luck to him: The Court has not spoken directly on this issue in 14 years, and does not appear especially troubled by the fact that students' rights are limited in this manner. In fact, writes Clay Weisenberger, in the *Journal of Law of Education*'s January 2000 issue, "the exceptions [to *Tinker*] may prove to swallow the rule."

This Is Your T-Shirt on Drugs

Another aspect of free speech for teenagers, especially these days, is the question of "message t-shirts," clothing that seek to communicate advertising, humor, or a political point of view. The courts across the United States are divided as to whether school officials can limit the messages that students can display on their bodies. Clay Weisenberger, in the aforementioned article on student free speech, lists some of the message t-shirts that have been litigated, and he points out that there really is no consistent rule for administrators, teachers, students, or parents to follow.

For example, in 1992, in *McIntire* v. *Bethel Independent School District No. 3*, the Oklahoma court prohibited the school from suspending students for wearing the Bacardi rum advertisement t-shirt that says "The best of the night's adventures are reserved for those with nothing planned," because the school failed to provide evidence that the t-shirts disrupted classes. On the other hand, in the 1992 decision *Broussard* v. *School Bd. of Norfolk*, a court in Virginia said that wearing a t-shirt reading "drugs suck" in a middle school, where the students are 11 to 15 years old, was not permissible, because of the sexual connotations of the word "suck" and the relative youth of the students.

Looking for Liberty
"If Virtue and Knowledge are diffused among the people, they will never be enslaved. This will be their great Security."
—Samuel Adams, 1779

If you want, you can play along at home. What would you do if you were the Supreme Court of Massachusetts and the case came before you in which a student was suspended for wearing the following two shirts to school: (1) "See Dick drink. See Dick Drive. See Dick Die. Don't be a Dick." (2) "Coed Naked Band: Do it To the Rhythm." If you answered that the Massachusetts Supreme Court would have upheld those suspensions, you're right. Go to the head of the class. (See the 1996 case of *Pyle* v. *South Hadley School Committee*.)

Another fascinating case—the 1992 decision *Chandler* v. *McMinnville School District*, 978 F.2d 524 (9th Cir. 1992)—involved a school district in which a teachers' strike was going on. Substitute teachers, who were not part of the union, had been brought in to instruct the students, some of whom were punished for wearing buttons that said "scab" on them. Applying the *Tinker* rule the court decided that students have free speech as long as it's not disruptive. The court overturned the suspension of the students because classes had not been disrupted by the presence of the buttons.

Until the Supreme Court speaks about a given issue, the lower courts are essentially left to themselves to figure out how best to handle a situation. The Supreme Court has not yet taken the trouble to speak about the question of message shirts on campus, so administrators and teachers have a great deal of power in determining what is acceptable and what is not. The key tests appear to be whether the message in question is disruptive or vulgar, whether the activity is school-sponsored or private, and if the age of the students is younger or older. The younger the student, the less likely it is that the student will have the right to wear the t-shirt of his or her choice.

Looking for Liberty
"If liberty means anything at all, it means the right to tell people what they do not want to hear." —George Orwell

Drug Testing

In an era of rampant teenage drug abuse and experimentation, parents, teachers, and school administrators want to do everything they can to limit or eliminate the use of drugs on and off the high school campus. Schools have begun to institute guidelines that include required drug testing for any student involved in an extracurricular activity.

This testing policy came before the U.S. Supreme Court in 1995, when a teenager sued after being denied the right to play football when he refused to take a drug test. By a six to three majority, the U.S. Supreme Court upheld random drug testing for high school student athletes. The Court relied on the fact that student athletes who go to practice or play games while drunk or high may exhibit impaired judgment and subject themselves and others to injuries. The Supreme Court said that since high school athletes shower and undress as a group, they have a lower expectation of privacy, and therefore random drug tests would be far less intrusive than in the lives of, say, kids on the math team. The Supreme Court further noted that high school athletes are generally considered opinion leaders, so if it's possible to limit the use of drug taking by student athletes, that sort of message might filter down to the other students who follow their lead.

In a subsequent case, *Trinidad School District No. 1* v. *Lopez*, the Colorado Supreme Court sought to determine whether members of a high school marching band would be required to undergo drug testing before taking part in band practices. The Court determined that band members should not be subject to random drug testing for the following reasons:

1. The worst thing that could happen is that they play the wrong note. In other words, there was no risk of injury from band members who play while impaired.

2. Since band members do not shower together (at least not at school), they do not have the lower expectation of privacy that high school athletes have.

In June 2002, in *Board of Education of Independent School District No. 92 of Potta-watomie County, et al* v. *Earl*, the United States Supreme Court held that it was entirely legitimate for public schools to require random drug testing of all students who take part in extracurricular activities, not just athletes. Two students from Tecumseh, Oklahoma argued that their privacy rights were violated and that they had been subject to an unreasonable search and seizure prohibited by the Fourth Amendment. The Court disagreed, citing the nationwide epidemic of drug use and evidence of increased drug use in schools in that district. The Court said that the policy was a "reasonable means of furthering the school district's important interest in preventing and deterring drug use among its schoolchildren." In other words, if you want to play in the band, be a cheerleader, or even compete on the chess team, be prepared to undergo random drug testing if your school chooses to implement such a policy.

The Key to Your Locker

As discussed, the Fourth Amendment to the Constitution prohibits unreasonable searches and seizures. We've also seen that minors are entitled to protection by the U.S. Constitution and the Bill of Rights, although they are frequently afforded lower amounts of protection. We have also seen that certain circumstances lead to lower expectations of privacy. For example, a person who is under arrest or in jail has a much lower expectation of privacy than a person who is moving freely in society does.

Similarly, the school campus is an institutional setting where students have a reduced expectation of privacy and, therefore, have less privacy. For many of us who grew up in a relatively more bucolic age, it's rather shocking to think that educators would have to draw up policies for weapons searches. Welcome to twenty-first-century America. School administrators are entitled to draw up search policies so that students and teachers alike understand what the rules are. What are those rules?

Taking Liberties

"You can cage the singer but not the song."

—Harry Belafonte

The key is reasonableness. School administrators and teachers do not need a warrant in order to search a student or a student's property, nor do they need "probable cause" that a violation of a law has occurred. School officials only need to have "reasonable suspicion" that if they were to search a certain student, they would find evidence that he or she has violated the law or is about to do so.

"Reasonable suspicion" doesn't mean that a teacher can search a student just because the teacher doesn't like the way the kid is dressed on a given day. Instead, there has to be some sort of credible information that the student might be involved in a drug or weapons-related crime. The more specific the evidence against the student, the more likely it is that a court will uphold the search and allow the results of that search to be used against the student. The American Civil Liberties Union offers as examples of legitimate "reasonable suspicion" in these cases:

♦ A search of a student's purse, after a teacher saw her smoking in the restroom.

♦ A search of student's pockets, after a credible source phones in a tip that this student was either using or selling drugs.

Reasonable suspicion does not mean freedom to search the student by any means the school official chooses. The search has to be reasonably related to the suspicion of the school official. The ACLU offers a continuum of student searches. Searching a jacket or book bag requires, perhaps, the lowest level of suspicion. A higher level of suspicion would trigger a pat-down, perhaps for a weapon or other contraband. Only the highest level of suspicion could possibly justify a strip search, which is the greatest violation of a student's expectation of privacy. In many states, strip searches are prohibited by statute.

The ACLU adds that just because the teacher doing the search finds the item she was seeking—the cigarettes, or the drugs—does not mean the teacher has to stop searching the student. Indeed, finding one item of contraband on a student would give the school official permission to broaden the search.

What about a student's locker? While it's true that students have a high expectation of privacy when it comes to their lockers, many courts have held that students have no privacy rights in this domain. It is best for school administrators to inform students that a locker is not private property and is still subject to searches by school administrators. The more clearly students have been told that they should not expect a high degree of privacy anywhere on campus, the more likely it is that a court would uphold a search of a locker, desk drawer, clothing, etc.

Schools are also entitled to search a student's car parked on school grounds where "reasonable suspicion" exists. In fact, the privilege of bringing a student vehicle on to school premises is often conditioned on consent by the student driver to allow search of the vehicle when there is reasonable suspicion that the search will yield evidence of contraband.

The Right to Remain Silent

Students do not have to answer the questions of school officials anymore than individuals have to answer questions of police officers. The ACLU advises that if a teacher suspects a student of having committed a crime, "Don't explain, don't lie, and don't confess, because anything you say can be used against you." The ACLU suggests that students instead ask to see their parents or a lawyer.

In the event that a student is caught with drugs, guns, or other contraband, or violating some other aspect of school law or policy, the constitutional right of due process kicks in. In the schoolyard setting, due process means that a student has a right to a hearing in order to tell his or her side of the story. In the event that the student is found guilty of the infraction, due process means that the punishment must fit the crime. If a student is to be suspended for more than 10 days, that student can call in a lawyer. Students do not have the right to appeal minor punishments, such as detention or cleaning the blackboards. According to the ACLU, corporal (physical) punishment has been banned in 21 states. In states where physical punishment is permitted, the penalty must be in proportion to the offense that the student has committed.

Statutes of Liberties

The federal government did not play a role in local school issues for many years, as the Constitution leaves such issues to the states. Two things caused a change: First, some states failed to guarantee rights to members of minority groups. Second, issues having to do with schools poll well with prospective voters.

Equality in Education

The ACLU provides an excellent source of information about students' rights on its website, www.aclu.org. The ACLU points out that all students are entitled to equal educational opportunity, regardless of their socioeconomic background, race, religion, or where they live. Students may not be discriminated against based on pregnancy, HIV status, disability, or sexual orientation. Students cannot be treated differently in public schools based on their sex, i.e., no more shop classes for boys and home economics for girls. Girls cannot be expelled or barred from extracurricular activities or graduation ceremonies—let alone the classroom—if they are pregnant.

The ACLU also points out that "tracking" the placing of students in college preparatory classes versus vocational training classes is often a function of race and class. In other words, school administrators often consciously or unconsciously believe that minority children from poor homes are less intelligent than white, middle-class kids, and such minority children are often shunted into lower-track classes. The lower the track, the ACLU comments, "the less you're expected to learn—and the less you're taught." Individuals and their families who feel that they are being driven into lower tracks despite the fact that they can handle higher standards should fight hard to be put into the better classes, and the ACLU stands ready to assist such students and their families in that battle.

Legal Dictionary

Injunction—The process by which a court steps in and either demands the immediate cessation of a particular practice, or requires that one do a specified act, in order to protect another's rights.

Religion in Public Schools

Yet another civil liberties debate that will not go away, the question of school prayer seems to reassert itself with every school year. The questions generally center on whether prayer times or certain religious holidays (namely, Christmas and Hanukah) are permitted to be observed in public schools.

The general constitutional rules (at least, until the Supreme Court makes a different decision) are these: School-sanctioned prayer is not permissible. Bible study groups may take place, as long as they are after school and not organized by teachers. In addition, they can only take place if groups of other religions are given permission to start their own study groups, should they so choose. Bibles cannot be distributed during the school day. Graduation prayers similarly are unconstitutional because they would make children who do not pray uncomfortable. This is true regardless of who is leading the prayer, and whether the prayer is of one religion or is nondenominational.

The ACLU suggests that students with religious interests organize a separate gradua-tion event such as a "baccalaureate"—something held off school grounds, and not sponsored by a school. As for holiday celebrations, courts have held that general sym-bols like Christmas trees or Hanukah menorahs are practically secular in nature now, and are not overtly religious or offensive to nonreligious individuals. Therefore, such elements are permissible on school grounds during the holiday season. On the other hand, nativity scenes or other declarations of faith and belief are not permissible on school property.

> **The Law of the Land**
>
> School prayer is not permissi-ble in public schools in the United States, due to the constitu-tional prohibition of the mingling of church and state.

An Ohio mother sued her son's school district for 1.5 million dollars after the school made clear to her seventh-grade son that he could not write a letter to Jesus as part of a school assign-ment.

According to FoxNews.com for August 5, 2002, the young man, Phil Vaccaro, had been given an assignment to write a friendly letter to someone who dramatically changed his life. The school claims that it did not permit him to write the letter because it would be "difficult to get a written reply from Jesus." The mother was out-raged, and said that the teacher, "told him he could not write that letter because Jesus wasn't a real person—that he didn't exist. How dare they throw their atheistic values upon my child?" Phillip's mother, Peggy Koehler, removed her son from the school after the incident.

The case sheds light on the difficulty that school administrators and teachers face as they seek to uphold laws relating to religion and the classroom. This is truly an area in which there are no easy answers.

The Least You Need to Know

- The rights students won in the landmark *Tinker* case have slowly eroded away.

- There really is no consistent rule to follow when it comes to students' First Amendment rights.

- The Fourth Amendment does not completely apply to students either, with ran-dom drug testing now permissible.

- You have a right to pray whenever you want to, as long as you don't disrupt classroom instruction or other educational activities—or try to force others to pray along with you.

Part 5

Statutes of Liberties: The Laws That Affect Your Life

In this section, we'll examine some of the most important laws that affect your civil liberties. Affirmative action regulates the means by which government determines who gets jobs and admission to schools. The Freedom of Information Act allows you to unearth some (but not all) of the secrets government keeps. The Internal Revenue Code governs every penny you earn. And RICO—the Racketeer Influence and Control Act—was a law originally intended to attack organized crime; instead, it's become a weapon used to chill free speech. We'll look at each of these laws in detail—how they were created and how they can be abused. We'll conclude with a peek into the future of civil liberties, especially in this post-September 11 environment.

Chapter 21

Affirmative Action

In This Chapter

- ◆ Gray areas of admissions
- ◆ Past precedents and current opinions
- ◆ The old boys' network
- ◆ Grrr power?

The great English writer George Orwell once commented that an Englishman explains everything about himself the moment he opens his mouth—his accents and manner of speaking reveals where he comes from, the socioeconomic level of his family, his educational attainment, what he does for work, and how he lives. In the United States, a far more egalitarian society, your socioeconomic standing in life is based not so much on where you grew up, but where you went to school.

The right to education is one of the most important aspects of American culture, and the denial of that right is one of the most severe limitations on an individual's future that he or she could face. In this chapter, we are going to consider some of the civil liberties issues that surround the subject of affirmative action in education and the workplace.

One of the themes about civil liberties law that you might have picked up by now is that no rule is cast in stone. Times change and attitudes change.

What seem like immutable principles of law may dissolve, sometimes incrementally and sometimes in a heartbeat. The subject of affirmative action, which only a few short years ago seemed to be a firmly entrenched principle in American education and throughout the rest of American society, is under fire, on campuses, in communities, and in the courts.

A Place in the Sun?

Perhaps the most insidious U.S. Supreme Court decision of all time (definitely in the top 10) was *Plessy* v. *Ferguson*, an 1896 decision upholding the concept of "separate but equal." In other words, the U.S. Supreme Court held that it was entirely legitimate for states to segregate African Americans and whites as long as they provided equal facilities for both racial groups.

As anyone with the slightest background in American history realizes, "separate but equal" really meant "separate but separate." African Americans had no access to the kind of quality education that whites enjoyed throughout the first half of the twentieth century. The U.S. Supreme Court eventually overruled *Plessy* in its famous 1954 case of *Brown* v. *Topeka Board of Education*. Thurgood Marshall, later a member of the U.S. Supreme Court, argued the case on behalf of the NAACP. The Supreme Court in *Brown* took note of sociological studies that indicated that African American students were not given the same quality of educational opportunities that their white peers enjoyed. "Separate but equal" was now discredited—at least in the eyes of the law. It took years of struggle and displays of courage by individual African Americans, sometimes backed by National Guard troops, before African Americans could enter the educational institutions that formerly had been reserved for whites.

Taking Liberties

The question of affirmative action weighs a sense of responsibility about inequities of the past against the needs of all members of society today.

During the civil rights era of the 1960s, a new approach to thinking about race evolved: affirmative action. The idea behind affirmative action was that the government could not wait passively for states, cities, and individuals to reverse decades of racist practices. Instead, affirmative action meant that government and private institutions alike would have to examine their admission practices (for schools) or hiring practices (for businesses) and lend a helping hand to individuals who would not have been admitted or hired on the basis of standardized tests. It became mandatory to consider the economic and social backgrounds of minority applicants for colleges and universities, and for jobs. Since they did not have the same access to educational opportunity as did white applicants, they could not be judged fairly on the same scale.

Therefore, it became legitimate to provide preferences in educational admission or in hiring members of minority groups.

For example, if an African American student and a white student scored the same on a standardized test, affirmative action meant that the African American student would have an edge in terms of college admission. Minority students would receive special scrutiny to determine their likelihood of succeeding in an institution of higher education, a factor that was not fairly represented by their transcript or standardized test scores.

Supporters of affirmative action point to a number of important reasons for affording minorities special consideration. First, affirmative action can be considered a form of restitution for generations of slavery. Second, affirmative action helps to destroy the "old boy network"—the social ties among privileged families that provide America with its traditional leadership caste. By introducing a diverse student body to institutions of higher learning from which America's leaders are traditionally drawn, the old caste system would begin to melt away and a broader pool of individuals could aspire to leadership in American society.

The third reason advanced in favor of affirmative action is the concept of creating a cadre of minority group leaders. African Americans have traditionally referred to their leaders as the "Talented 10," that percentage of African Americans who had somehow managed to gain quality education and rise to positions of authority and prominence in the African American community. By opening up more places in top educational institutions to minority members, the pool of individuals who might become leaders of their minority groups would thus be increased.

A fourth reason for providing affirmative action was what economic theorists call "market failure." In other words, if you think of the world of education as a marketplace, where buyers are potential students and sellers are the institutions of higher learning, the "market" had thus far delivered only white students, with very few exceptions, over the years. If you look at the totality of the American population, African Americans and other minorities have traditionally been under-represented in institutions of higher learning, thus indicating that the "market" for education had failed to reach all of its potential consumers. The fifth, and in many ways most attractive, reason for affirmative action is the concept of diversity—the idea that colleges and universities, like any institutions, benefit when they have a diverse group of individuals on their campuses. It should be noted that when affirmative action first came into existence as part of the 1964 Civil Rights Act, the law was not meant to create racial quotas. During the Johnson administration of the mid-1960s, the federal government began to require that federal contractors take steps to ensure they had adequate numbers of minority members among their workforce prior to receiving government contracts. While these requirements were not meted out in terms of firm numerical quotas, the concept of reserving places for individuals from minority groups soon became the policy at educational institutions and employers across the land.

Pushback ... and Bakke

Whenever there is powerful social change, there is often pushback or resistance. Such was the case with affirmative action. Older readers may recall the stone throwing at demonstrations in the Boston area and other cities to protect affirmative action and bussing in public schools. The debate over affirmative action took place not just in the street but also in the courtroom and halls of Congress.

Opponents of affirmative action attacked each of the above rationales for affirmative action. For example, they stated that it was not possible to provide true restitution for slavery. Since virtually every ethnic or religious group had been discriminated against at one point or other in history, if society sought to provide restitution for one group, there could be no end to the matter, as all groups would thus qualify for restitution. As for the critical issue of diversity, opponents claimed that it was actually racist to assume that having African Americans would make a campus more diverse than if the school admitted, say, fundamentalist Christians, Moslems from abroad, atheists, democrats, and republicans in the place of African American students. Above all, opponents of affirmative action felt that individual whites who had better test scores or qualifications for jobs, and who were themselves blameless in America's history of racism, unfairly bore the brunt of social policy.

> ### The Law of the Land
>
> "No state shall make or enforce any law which shall abridge the privileges or immunities of citizens of the United States; nor shall any state deprive any person of life, liberty, or property, without due process of law; nor deny to any person within its jurisdiction the equal protection of the laws."
>
> —Fourteenth Amendment

These were the positions in the affirmative action debate in 1978, when the U.S. Supreme Court decided the case of *Bakke* v. *University of California Board of Regents.* In *Bakke*, a white applicant to medical school sued when he was passed over twice in successive years for admission, and African Americans who had received lower test scores and grades had been admitted in his place. A divided Supreme Court held that diversity on campuses was so important that colleges and universities could practice affirmative action and admit minority students with poor records in the place of white students with better academic records.

Again, times change. In the quarter century since the *Bakke* decision, American society grew more conservative, and court challenges to *Bakke* began in earnest. A Texas case, *Hopwood* v. *Texas*, struck down an affirmative action program at the University of Texas Law School, apparently either ignoring or distinguishing the U.S. Supreme Court decision in *Bakke*. To "distinguish" a case, in courtroom terms, is to decide that the case isn't relevant to the proceedings at hand.

Before we get into the facts of the Hopwood case, it is worth noting that a basic principle of American constitutional law is this: When the U.S. Supreme Court speaks, what it says is the law of the land. Its decisions bind all courts, and lower courts throughout the country do not have the right to overturn its decisions. Therefore, it was extremely striking when, in 1996, the U.S. Court of Appeals in Texas, a court one rung below the U.S. Supreme Court, ignored a Supreme Court decision.

Taking Liberties _____

It's also worthy of note that Texas was the home of an early discrimination case. An African American man named Heman Sweatt sued the University of Texas Law School, seeking admission. This was in an era when African Americans were expressly prohibited from attending the University of Texas School of Law. Initially, Sweatt's court case was rejected, under the principle then reigning of "separate but equal." In fact, the Texas Court of Civil Appeals, which heard the case, actually ordered the State of Texas to create a separate law school for African Americans rather than admit Sweatt to University of Texas School of Law. Texas complied, creating the School of Law of the Texas State University for Negroes. The only problem was that this school had neither permanent faculty nor library staff, and was not accredited. So, Sweatt returned to court four years after his first case, and this time he was ordered admitted to the University of Texas School of Law, which had previously been open only to whites.

In the 1996 Hopwood case, four white students had applied for admission to the University of Texas Law School in 1992. They were rejected even though their applications were stronger than those of African American students who were, essentially, admitted in their place. At the University of Texas School of Law, as at many law schools, the application decision is based almost entirely on a combination of the student's college GPA and his or her Law School Admission Test (LSAT) scores.

The U.S. Court of Appeals hearing the Hopwood case determined that these four white individuals had been unfairly discriminated against and that they were not obligated to personally atone on behalf of white America for the wrongs that had been done to African Americans over the centuries. The University of Texas School of Law

> ### Looking for Liberty
>
> "Whenever the issue of compensatory treatment for the Negro is raised, some of our friends recoil in horror. The Negro should be granted equality, they agree, but he should ask nothing more. On the surface, this appears reasonable, but it is not realistic."
>
> —Dr. Martin Luther King Jr., writing in 1964, *Why We Can't Wait*

appealed this case to the U.S. Supreme Court, which chose not to hear it. The legal term for such a denial of a hearing by the U.S. Supreme Court is called *denial of certiorari*. When the U.S. Supreme Court "denies cert," or chooses not to hear a particular case, it does not have to give any reasons, and generally does not. The fact that the U.S. Supreme Court chose not to hear the case raised troubling questions for supporters of affirmative action nationwide. Did this mean that the U.S. Supreme Court was not "standing up" for the principles it had enunciated in *Bakke*? Was the Supreme Court, so to speak, backing off from *Bakke*? Was affirmative action still a viable concept in the law, or had its time passed?

Upheld by U.S. Sup Ct. June 2003

In a 2001 case, a federal appellate court upheld the right of the University of Michigan Law School to consider race as a factor when reviewing applications for admission. The federal appeals court said that the law school was within its rights to give special consideration to African American, Hispanic, and other applicants. The University of Michigan Law School's policy states, "Collectively, we seek a mix of students with varying backgrounds and experiences who will respect and learn from each other."

Obviously, this decision, which hinges on the diversity justification for affirmation action, is in direct conflict with the opposite conclusion reached in the University of Texas School of Law case. All eyes are turned to the U.S. Supreme Court to see whether it will reconsider the issue, and if so, how it will rule.

Intriguingly, the chairman of the House Judiciary Committee actually wrote to the chief judge of the court of appeals who decided that case, seeking related information and court documents. The congressman, F. James Sensenbrenner Jr., a Republican from the state of Wisconsin, wrote to the court describing his concerns that the means by which the decision was reached had been rigged. Federal appellate court rules provide specific ways in which the judges making any given decision are to be chosen; Congressman Sensenbrenner feared that the court had subverted its own rules in order to pick judges who would make the ruling that the court made.

The action of Congressman Sensenbrenner shocked many legal authorities, as the judicial branch is not traditionally subject to this manner of oversight from Congress. Of course, the decision stood, despite the congressional investigation.

We said at the beginning of this chapter that civil liberties issues and decisions are not cast in stone, and that things change over time. Are we in a period when the pendulum is swinging against affirmative action? Or was the *Hopwood* decision a mere incongruity? Only time will tell. While the decision was not the death knell for affirmative action, as it is only binding on a handful of states in the South, it certainly sends a strong message that affirmative action may indeed be on the way out.

> **Statutes of Liberties**
>
> The 1965 Voting Rights Act was passed by Congress and signed into law by President Lyndon B. Johnson in order to make it possible for millions of African Americans to be able to register to vote, a right denied them for centuries.

Affirmative Action at Work

Since the 1960s, legislators and courts have sought to fashion remedies for job discrimination. For decades, it was virtually impossible for African Americans or members of other minorities to gain entry to such fields as police work, fire departments, and trade unions. Some unions were entirely white until the advent of affirmative action. In some cases, the only way to become a member of a union was to be the relative of another member. In some police departments, it would be common for brothers, sons, and nephews to follow relatives onto the police force. Although there might not have been an announced policy of hiring only from a pool of relatives, neighbors, and friends, there existed a de facto policy of not hiring minorities. This is one of the prime reasons for the creation of affirmative action laws in the first place.

During the 1980s, the U.S. Supreme Court upheld a variety of workplace affirmative action plans involving police departments, fire departments, and trade unions such as sheet metal workers. In all of these cases, plaintiffs had proven that it was virtually impossible for a member of a minority group to enter into a particular union or civil service position. The court in the city or town where the discrimination was

Legal Dictionary

Denial of certiorari— Term meaning that the U.S. Supreme Court has decided not to hear a given case.

taking place would then create an affirmative action program that would give preferences to members of minority groups or women who had been discriminated against in the past. As always with affirmative action, the goal was not to reward individual African Americans or other minorities, or to punish individual whites. Rather, the idea was to level the playing field and create some sort of redress for decades of discrimination.

By the 1990s, however, public opinion—and legal decisions—began to shift. You could say there was something of a backlash against affirmative action programs. American society began to sympathize with the more qualified white individuals denied jobs than members of the minority groups who had experienced decades and even centuries of oppression. That shift in public opinion began to find its way into legal decisions. Although not required to pay attention to public sentiment, the Supreme Court generally reflects the mores of the time in which it makes decisions.

By the late 1990s, the Court was deciding cases such as *Taxman* v. *Board of Education of Piscataway, New Jersey*. In this case, the school district had the opportunity to retain one of two equally qualified teachers, one white and one African American. The Board of Edu-cation chose the African American teacher because it wanted to send a message that it was aware of racial discrimination in American society. The Supreme Court upheld the challenge of the white teacher, declaring that such an action by a school board was unconstitutional. Legal commentators saw the *Taxman* case as the beginning of a shift away from the firm pro-affirmative action stance the Supreme Court had taken only a decade earlier.

The Court did not explicitly overrule *Bakke*, but the decision certainly appears to take some of the power away from the *Bakke* decision. When the Supreme Court whittles away at an important decision like this, without explicitly overruling it, it often leads to confusion in the lower courts.

Looking for Liberty

Thurgood Marshall, later a U.S. Supreme Court Justice, successfully argued before the Court in the case of *Brown v. Board of Education*, which outlawed discrimination in schools and overturned the 1896 "separate but equal" principle of the U.S. Supreme Court case *Plessy v. Ferguson*.

At the same time the *Taxman* decision was coming down, the voters of California passed Proposition 209, the California Civil Rights Initiative. This proposition amended the state constitution to prohibit all race-conscious decision making in state contracting, education, and employment. In other words, under Prop 209, the state of California could not practice any affirmative action. The people of California were essentially reflecting the same point of view as the Supreme Court, which feared that America was sliding into "a regime of racial and ethnic rights and entitlements."

By the late 1990s, the official Supreme Court standard for affirmative action cases was called *strict scrutiny*. This phrase meant that affirmative action programs had to be "narrowly tailored" (not amorphous or overbroad) to promote a compelling state interest. Was it still a compelling state interest to reverse the effects of decades of hostility and discrimination to minorities in the workplace? Apparently not. As we saw in the education arena, the Supreme Court let stand the Texas court's ruling in the *Hopwood* decision. Legal commentators viewed *Taxman*, the Texas case, and Prop 209 as a signal that Americans were turning away from affirmative action as a means of redressing inequality in the workplace.

Gender Discrimination

Women have also suffered from enormous inequalities in the workplace. Women generally make less money at the same kinds of work than do men. According to many commentators, females bump up against the "glass ceiling," the unspoken rule that women can generally not rise to the highest levels of success and power in the business world. Women have been shut out of many career fields for decades, and are only able to make their way in small numbers into areas such as police departments, fire departments, or trade unions—the same groups that frequently discriminated against minorities.

Legal Dictionary

Intermediate scrutiny—A level of analysis that the courts use to determine if a law that appears to favor one group over another is constitutional. The lowest level of scrutiny involves a "rational relationship." In those cases, there must be some sort of rational relationship between the law and the objective that law seeks to bring about. The next level of analysis is called "intermediate scrutiny." Used most frequently when examining gender cases, it focuses on whether or not the government has an "important" objective in enforcing the law.

Women took these struggles to the U.S. Supreme Court, only to find that the Court was less moved by their plight than by that of minorities who had suffered discrimination in the workplace. The Supreme Court has made clear that it feels much more of a responsibility to protect minorities than it does to protect women. When an affirmative action program is created to benefit women instead of African Americans or other minorities, the Supreme Court, by its own admission, is far less likely to be sympathetic. It does seem odd that the U.S. Supreme Court would feel so comfortable in picking and choosing which groups should be entitled to a higher level of protection from employment discrimination and which groups should not.

Women have made major advances in securing legal rights even in the more conservative era of the last 15 years. With the help of the ACLU, Shannon Faulkner sued the military institute The Citadel and won the right to attend that previously all-male school, despite a prolonged and concerted effort to oppose the presence of women there. And a 1998 decision, *Ellerth* v. *Burlington Industries*, advanced the rights of women to sue for sexual harassment in the workplace even in the absence of financial or job-related injuries.

Yet the Court continues to prolong gender discrimination and limit women's rights, especially in comparison to the stands it takes on racial discrimination. In the 1998 case, *Gebser* v. *Lago Vista Independent School District*, the Court created a standard regarding the responsibility of schools for the sexual harassment conduct of individual teachers that many experts believe is impossible to meet. In other words, schools can only rarely be held responsible if a teacher sexually harasses a student. And in the 1999 case of *Nguyen* v. *INS*, the Court held that it is legitimate for out-of-wedlock children born overseas to become American citizens more easily if the mother is American than if the father is American.

The Least You Need to Know

Brown over Plessy ◆ It wasn't until 1954 that the idea of "separate but equal" was finally overturned.

◆ Affirmative action stems from a desire to redress our country's blemished history of discrimination.

◆ The Supreme Court generally reflects the mores of the time in which it makes decisions.

◆ The Supreme Court still has a long way to go to establish equal legal rights for women.

Chapter 22

Freedom of Information Act

In This Chapter

- Secrets of the U.S. government
- Your own privacy
- Filing a request
- Limitations of FOIA

Remember how exciting it was when you were a little kid and you knew something that nobody else did? There's no question about it—secrets are fun. Secrets make us feel powerful, because we all like to know things that other people don't know. If you used to watch Frankenstein or Dracula movies, there was always that spine-tingling thrill that came when you knew that the monster was hiding behind the door, but the person on the screen had absolutely no idea. Yes, secrets give us a sense of power and excitement. The problem comes when the government's ability to keep and use secret information about citizens rises to the level of a violation of our civil liberties.

Uncle Sam's Got a Secret!

When it comes to secrets, your government is no different from you or me. The government likes to keep secrets, too. A lot of secrets. In fact, in the course of every minute of every working day, the U.S. government classifies as secret a total of … well, that figure's secret, but you can be sure that the government creates a huge amount of secret files every day of the year.

Some reasons for this are obvious. For national security purposes, it simply would not do to announce troop movements, weapons deployment, or planned military actions. Similarly, the government relies upon foreign operatives to provide us with timely information about political events around the world. If the identities of these individuals became known, they would be in mortal danger and few others would be likely to step up and take their places. For the same reason, identities of Central Intelligence Agency operatives, members of the defense intelligence community, and the code makers and code breakers at the National Security Agency require the utmost secrecy in which to do their work.

The government, of course, does a lot more than wage wars and protect the citizenry, as important a function as that is (especially in today's post-September 11 environment). The government also provides a wide range of services to the public, from health information and social security payments to welfare and immigration status. If you are receiving any sort of assistance from the government, it's unlikely you would want the government to reveal that information to anyone else.

> ### Statutes of Liberties
>
> One of the most powerful weapons that the U.S. government possessed wasn't guns or bombs. It was the personal files of FBI chief J. Edgar Hoover. He maintained files on everyone of importance in and out of the government, and never hesitated to use—or threaten to use—those files to make sure he got his way.

> ### Looking for Liberty
>
> How detailed were FBI files on famous people? See for yourself at http://foia.fbi.gov/brecht.htm. Here you'll find more than 350 pages of formerly classified information on the poet and author Bertold Brecht, who was investigated due to concern over ties he may have maintained with the Soviet government and other communists.

The government also maintains the health records of both individuals and communities. The idea is to catch health problems quickly, before they turn into public health crises. For this reason, the government maintains records, constantly updated, on illness and death in the United States. Any person with AIDS or other life-threatening or communicable illness is likely to be quite insistent that the government keep such information private. That's not hard to understand, either.

In the business world, the government also maintains an enormous amount of information. Take the area of patents and trademarks. Everybody thinks it's a good idea to encourage inventors to come up with new products and processes that make our lives easier and richer. Because of this, we offer protection to individuals and businesses that come up with new ideas, whether it's for a new drug or a safer automobile tire. The government therefore maintains patent records of each of the new products that inventors seek to protect. Some of the information is publicly available, but a great deal of it is safeguarded to protect the business interests of the inventors. So you can make a strong case for the idea that the government has to protect trade secrets and other key business information that it weighs when granting patents or trademarks, or otherwise regulating our nation's business community.

Another area in which virtually everyone would agree that privacy is necessary is the world of taxes. Federal, state, and local governments collect taxes, and in so doing learn all about the personal lives of citizens, families, and businesses. When you file your tax form, you are informing the government of a lot more than just how much money you make. You are telling the government how you made the money, what kind of real property (houses, apartment buildings, cars, boats) you own, how much you spend on medical care, how much you give to charity, and an enormous amount of other personal information. If a family has one or more members who are blind, for example, that information is filed as a part of one's tax return because individuals receive additional exemptions for blindness and other disabilities.

> **Taking Liberties**
>
> Most of us don't think about the fact that we expect the government to keep our tax returns private. It never even crosses our minds that the government would possibly publicize that information. We have a huge expectation of privacy when it comes to our tax records, and to any other personal records that the government maintains.

"We Never Make Mistakes"

There is not much room for argument that the items we have discussed above are all worthy of secrecy, and that the government has a responsibility to keep this information away from prying eyes, whether it be a neighbor down the block or an enemy bent on destroying the American way of life. There are many other areas in which the government is expected to keep secrets; this is just a representative sampling. There are, however, many occasions in which the government wants to keep secrets for reasons that are not entirely justifiable.

Let's say, for example, that the FBI is found to be maintaining secret files on individuals it distrusts—labor leaders, civil rights leaders, entertainers, gays, or other individuals who have never been accused of committing crimes. This is exactly what the FBI did for decades. The FBI has so much information on public figures, members of congress, and even those in the White House that its power usually went unchallenged. Should the government be keeping secret files on people? Should those people be denied access to those files, if they were to discover that they were the subject of such investigations?

Moreover, what if the government itself commits wrongdoings, and then seeks to cover them up? For example, there was the crackdown on alleged communists in the 1950s, which destroyed the reputations of thousands of innocent individuals. Or take the Watergate break-in of June 1972, after which the executive branch of the federal government spent a vast amount of resources to keep its actions secret. Then there was Oliver North, who was leading covert, renegade actions that violated U.S. law. Should the government have a right to draw a curtain around the actions of an Ollie North, if it would consider the release of such information embarrassing?

Legal Dictionary

Agency—For the Freedom of Information Act, "agency" only means an arm of the federal government. Private businesses and states are not subject to the act.

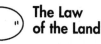

The Law of the Land

The founders of the Constitution didn't exactly practice "government in the sunshine" in the late nineteenth century, but they would probably be shocked by the degree to which today's government creates—and keeps—secrets in a wide variety of areas.

What about significant events in recent American history, such as the assassinations of President John F. Kennedy or Senator Robert F. Kennedy? Investigators have intimated connections between the government and the Mafia. Certainly much information about the Kennedy assassinations has never come to light, and is still secreted away in government storerooms. Indeed, the entire file surrounding the JFK assassination does not have to be made public until the year 2017—and only if the then president believes that such a release of information will not be detrimental to national security. (Ten bucks says Oliver Stone already has his FOIA request typed up.) Does that seem right?

There have been many other situations in the last 50 years that have brought a huge amount of embarrassment to the U.S. government. The shooting down of Gary Powers' U-2 spy plane over the Soviet Union in the 1950s. The Bay of Pigs fiasco and the Cuban Missile Crisis during the Kennedy Administration, when America was at the brink of nuclear war with the Soviet Union. America's involvement in Vietnam. The failed Iranian hostage mission in 1980. The 1985 bombing of the Marine barracks in Beirut that left more than 250 Marines dead. America's involvement in the war in Kosovo in the 1990s. The relationship between the Clinton Administration and donors from mainland China. The list goes on and on.

The Freedom of Information Act

How much information should be kept secret and how much should be revealed to the public? How do you determine what would be a violation of national security if it were released? Who is to make those decisions? How can there be adequate oversight of such a process if the government itself is both the keeper of the secrets and the entity that decides whether such secrets should be revealed?

These are not easy questions, to say the least. In the 1960s, the U.S. Congress passed a law, the Freedom of Information Act, which for the first time gave the average citizen, the news media, and businesses the right to peek behind the curtain of government secrecy and learn exactly what secrets were being kept ... and why.

The Freedom of Information Act essentially allows individuals to write to certain <u>federal</u> agencies and request from them specific information that the agency maintains. According to the American Civil Liberties Union, individuals have sought agency records on the following sorts of issues:

♦ Health and safety reports from the Food and Drug Administration on silicone breast implants

♦ Information on deported Haitian refugees from the Immigration and Naturalization Service

♦ Statistics on consumer boycotts from the Department of Commerce

♦ Names and addresses of military service members who participated in nuclear weapons testing from the Atomic Energy Commission

♦ FBI and CIA records on the assassination of President Kennedy

Does the Freedom of Information Act (which we will hereinafter refer to as "FOIA") guarantee you access to *any* information that the government has? Not at all. First, there are specific limits to which government agencies can be the subject of FOIA requests. For example, when Congress passed the FOIA, one of the agencies it exempted from the law was ... Congress!

Second, if a person's request for information is not specific enough or not directed to the right office or arm of the government, it is likely to be turned down. Third, government agencies

> **Statutes of Liberties**
>
> According to the ACLU, other topics that individuals have learned about through the Freedom of Information Act include information about public health, environmental hazards, consumer product safety, government spending, labor relations, business decisions, taxes, history, foreign policy, national defense, and the economy.

are sometimes slow to respond to FOIA requests, and information does not always get you to citizens as quickly as they might hope. If an agency does not wish to reveal information, there are many ways it can delay or deny a request. Bureaucrats know how to bury things!

Which agencies of the federal government are covered by FOIA?

- ◆ Defense Department
- ◆ Office of Management and Budget
- ◆ National Security Council
- ◆ FBI
- ◆ Nuclear Regulatory Commission
- ◆ Federal Communications Commission
- ◆ Federal Trade Commission
- ◆ Environmental Protection Agency

State records are not affected by the FOIA, but every state has its own freedom of information laws. In this chapter, we will be focusing solely on access to federal records and secrets.

Their Lips Are Sealed

The FOIA exempts certain organizations such as certain federal entities from its requirements because there are some secrets that the government needs to keep. In addition to Congress, FOIA does not apply to the federal courts or the staff of the executive office, such as the White House chief of staff, the White House counsel (the president's lawyer), or anyone else whose job it is to assist the president. The FOIA also does not apply to private businesses, schools, or private organizations.

In addition to specific agencies or offices exempt from FOIA, there is a broad range of information that is also protected from release. In other words, there are provisions within FOIA protecting information that would compromise national security. This includes some weapons information, scientific research, anything that might compromise international security, or CIA records. The release of other information is forbidden due to other laws. This includes personal tax information, the structure of the CIA, business trade secrets, or information the release of which would place in danger the life of the informant. You also cannot obtain with FOIA medical records, personnel files, or anything else that would violate an individual's personal privacy. FOIA furthermore does not provide access to law enforcement investigation material or banks.

Possession and Control Requirement

The FOIA has a requirement that the documents you wish to see be in the "possession and control" of the relevant federal agency. Possession means that the agency actually already owns this document.

Agencies are not required to do research and create new documents for FOIA requestors. Instead, you can only request documents that currently exist and are in the agency's files. The "control" rule means that the agency does not have to contact other agencies to request the document from them, and it has to be in their lawful control. For example, just because an individual stores personal papers at a federal agency does not mean that those papers can be reached under the Freedom of Information Act. Those papers may be "residing" at that agency, but they are not under the agency's control.

According to the FOIA, "any person" can make a Freedom of Information Act request, including U.S. citizens, corporations, universities, state and local governments, members of Congress, and even foreign nationals and permanent resident aliens.

Taking Liberties

Want an easy way to file your own FOIA request? Just follow the excellent template provided by The Reporters Committee for Freedom of the Press at their website, www.rcfp.org/foi_lett.html, and you'll be on your way!

Looking for Liberty

The American Civil Liberties Union calls some of the post-September 11 surveillance and secrecy techniques of the federal government "an end run around the Constitution."

Here's how to make a Freedom of Information Act request. You write to the Freedom of Information Act office at the agency you believe to contain the records you need. (Don't write to an individual at that agency; individuals change jobs or quit, so you are better off writing to the FOIA officer at that agency.) This means that you need to decide which agency is likely to have the records. You can find a list of all government agencies and their FOIA office address at www.law.house.gov/cfraddr.htm.

An easy way to determine which federal agency is the right place to turn is through the Federal Information Center (FIC). The FIC has telephone numbers throughout the country and is charged with the responsibility of helping you find the right agency, the right office, and the right address.

In your letter, be as specific as you can about the records you wish to see. The government is not under an obligation to go on "fishing expeditions" for FOIA requestors. If a request is not specific, the agency to which you have submitted it can either reject the request or send it back to you as overbroad, and ask you to cut it down to a manageable size. The way you phrase your request has everything to do with how successfully—and how quickly—it will be handled. You can find resources online, such as the American Civil Liberties Union's website (www.aclu.org/library/foia.html) to help as you draft your FOIA request. Alternatively, you might seek out a lawyer to draft it for you, depending on the importance of your request.

Keep in mind also that if there is extensive research or photocopying to be done, guess who is going to pay for it! We'll give you three guesses, and the first two cannot be "the federal government." It's you, baby. In addition, if your request is for very sensitive material, the responding agency has the right to "redact" or edit those documents so that they can be released without violating privacy laws, natural security interests, or any other such rules. In that case, you may end up paying a great deal of money to have photocopied pages that are either completely or almost entirely blank.

How Fast Is FOIA?

In theory, the agency has 10 business days from the time it receives your request to process your FOIA letter. Depending on the complexity of your request, the response time may take them longer. Keep in mind that "responding" simply means telling you how long it is going to take (and how much money it's going to cost) to perform your entire FOIA search. Some government agencies are faster than others, while some simply do not want individuals to have an easy time getting at government records and so will do everything in their power to restrict your ability to learn their secrets. Some authors have reported that agencies will drag their feet on requests, will deny that they have the information if you do not name the very specific file in which it is contained, charge prohibitive photocopying costs, provide limited seating for individuals who wish to inspect records on-site, and other tricks. For example, if you are interested in the records surrounding the assassination of Robert F. Kennedy Jr., you would actually have to request records pertaining to the "assault" on RFK. Kennedy survived for

Legal Dictionary

Ex post facto clause—
The part of Article I Section 9 of the U.S. Constitution forbidding changing the punishment of a given crime after that crime has been committed. FOIA requests sometimes turn up evidence of wrongdoing that might not have been criminal at the time the acts were committed; this clause prevents such acts from being punished now.

about a day after he was shot, and therefore the FBI files were opened up as assault files instead of assassination files. So, if you asked for information pertaining to the assassination of Robert F. Kennedy Jr., you would get little or nothing.

How do you learn to phrase a Freedom of Information Act request in such a way that it will get you the results you want? You may want to hire an expert in FOIA requests, specifically someone with a background for the particular agency you are wishing to contact. The government does not give up its secrets lightly. For sensitive information surrounding assassinations or anything else that may be potentially embarrassing to the government, you are going to have to work very hard in order to have a successful Freedom of Information Act request.

Is There a File on Me?

Maybe. If you ever worked for the federal government, or if you have ever received benefits such as social security from the federal government, there is a good chance that a government file does in fact exist on you. You may use the Freedom of In-formation Act in order to gain access to that file. If you are going to request information about yourself, try to provide as much information as you can so that the government can locate that file, including your full name, date and place of birth, social security number, previous names or nicknames by which you have been known, and previous addresses.

Taking Liberties

Thanks to an FOIA request, NASA actually had to admit it was considering mind-reading techniques to be used at airports to identify potential hijackers!

The Privacy Act is a federal law passed in 1974 that offers another way to find out what information the government may keep about you. Under the privacy act, U.S. citizens and permanent resident aliens have three specific rights: (1) access to any records the government may keep about you; (2) the right to correct any mistakes you find in those files; and (3) the right to sue agencies of the federal government if they refuse to correct your record or if they refuse you access to it.

What's the difference between the FOIA and the Privacy Act? Well, for starters, the Privacy Act only allows you access to your own records. It denies access to your personal records to anyone other than yourself. Under the Privacy Act, you can be charged for photocopying your record but not for search costs. You will be charged for most search costs pertaining to FOIA requests, whether they are about you or about anyone or anything else. If you are interested in finding out what the government knows about you, the ACLU recommends that you make requests for agency records under both FOIA and the Privacy Act, since the specific rules for each law can be different.

After you have filed your Freedom of Information Act request, there are five likely scenarios.

1. The government responds quickly and provides you with all the information you request. Hey, it could happen. Just don't count on it. More likely ...

2. The agency asks for more time. The agency might say that your request has been received, is being processed, and that a search for those records has begun. The agency might also let you know that they are calculating the fees for your request or that they are currently inundated with requests and therefore would like a little more time.

3. The agency might say your description was inadequate. The agency might therefore ask for more specific information about the files you seek. The ACLU suggests that you rewrite your request or even try to make an appointment with the official processing your request to get more help. Remember, government officials are people, too! (We discovered this through our own Freedom of Information Act request.)

4. The agency might say the information you requested does not exist. If you think or know that this is not true, work with the agency, which might be short staffed or under-funded. Try to help them by providing information as to why you believe the information does exist and is in their possession and control. Don't go nuclear just yet.

5. The agency may say that the information you request is exempt from disclosure. As we have seen, there are many reasons why government agencies have the right to resist FOIA requests. The information sought may violate national security, the privacy of a taxpayer, or the privacy of a recipient of social security, or it may be the trade secret of a business. If it is true that some part of the information you seek is protected by government regulation, this does not provide the agency with an instant reason to deny your entire request. The agency still has an obligation to provide you with that part of the requested information that can legitimately be shared with the public.

Proprietary info is owned by someone

Feeling Unsatisfied?

If you believe that the government agency from which you are requesting information is *stonewalling*, obfuscating, or even outright lying (Oh my gosh! The government lying!), you still have rights. You can bring an appeal to a higher level of authority within the agency. According to the ACLU, such appeals are often successful because higher-level officials are often less reticent about revealing information (that is, they are not going to fire themselves). You are entitled to a final ruling on your appeal within 20 working days, according to FOIA.

If that appeal does not work, you may ask your congressperson or senator to put pressure on the agency to provide the information. The federal government, like so much of life, operates on a huge "favor bank." Agencies do not like to disappoint congress people and senators, who, after all, provide funding for those agencies. There is a very good chance that by leaning on your congressperson or senator to lean on the agency, you will get the results you seek.

Legal Dictionary

Stonewalling—A term made popular during the Watergate investigation of the Nixon Administration in the early 1970s; it means "refusing to comply through footdragging or other bureaucratic techniques."

Taking Liberties

The U.S. State Department is also governed by the FOIA. You can visit their online reading room at http://foia.state.gov/.

If this approach is unavailing, you can go to court and file a lawsuit. The problem with going to court is that it can take a long time and be very expensive. You may need the information right now—not a year from now. Theoretically, a judge can order a federal agency to pay for your legal costs if you prevail. But what if you lose? Then you are stuck paying for the lawyer, and there's nothing much worse than paying for a lawyer who lost your case. Even if you win, the judge is not obligated to make the agency pay your legal costs. That's not exactly how the government works.

The ACLU lists a wide variety of private organizations that will help you with your Freedom of Information Act request and/or lawsuit. The ACLU reminds individuals that while the documents you seek may be important to you, the organizations you wish to enroll on your behalf to find that information are generally understaffed, under-funded, and over-committed. So there is no guarantee that you will get the help you need from them. It's worth a try, nonetheless, and you can find the list of those organizations at that aforementioned ACLU website, www.aclu.org/library/foia.html.

Do you always need FOIA? Not if you have a computer. If you have access to the web, a huge amount of government information is already available. It may take some digging, but you can find an enormous amount of information that the government has either made public of its own volition or due to someone's Freedom of

Information Act request. The best starting place is the Department of Justice's website, www.usdoj.gov, which provides a fair amount of FOIA information. You can find CIA declassified documents at its Freedom of Information website, www.foia.ucia.gov/records.asp. You can find a lot of fascinating FBI information at its Freedom of Information Act website, foia.fbi.gov/ foiaindex.htm. (Remember that you do not use www. to access this FBI website.)

Taking Liberties

Actually, your FBI is all over the map, with field offices throughout the United States. While this is beneficial from the point of view of investigative work, it makes things hard on Freedom of Information Act requestors. It means that you must query not just the FBI's central office in Washington but also every FBI field office that might possibly contain the information you seek. (Nobody said this was going to be easy!)

You can find fascinating code-breaking and code-making information at www.nsa.gov and you can learn about the assassination of President Kennedy at the National Archives and Records Administration, www.nara.gov/research/jfk/index.html. According to Internet expert Kim Komando, you can find at this Kennedy website an index to more than four million pages of information about the assassination. As we said earlier, it won't be until 2017 before everything to do with the Kennedy assassination is made public, but reading those four million pages of documents will certainly occupy you until that time.

How much your FOIA request will cost to process depends in part on who you are. If you are a business, you will be charged fees for searching for records, processing the records, and photocopying them. If you are a school or a noncommercial scientific institution, or if you are a member of the news media, you will be charged only for photocopying after the first hundred pages. If you are an individual citizen and not a member of any of those groups just mentioned, you will be charged for records, searches, and photocopying. The good news is that you do not pay for the first two hours of search time, or the first hundred pages of photocopying.

The Department of Justice, for example, currently charges 10 cents per page for photocopying. The Justice Department will actually give you a break; if your FOIA request involves photocopying that costs less than 14 dollars, you won't be charged at all. (Presumably, it would cost the Justice Department more money to bill you so they don't even bother with small amounts.) Agencies currently charge 10 to 30 dollars an hour depending on their own budget and the complexity of the issues involved in your research. The fee will be waived on occasion if you can show that the information that you seek to be made public will assist the entire public in understanding some aspect of the government. If you are making a request about yourself, it is unlikely that you will receive a fee waiver, because revealing information about the average person generally has no effect on the sum of knowledge about the government that we all share.

Limits to FOIA

While FOIA has provided thousands and thousands of researchers, reporters, investigators, private individuals, businesses, and scientists with access to vital government information that otherwise would never have been made public, it certainly has its limits. The limit we have discussed already comes into play when the agency in question does not want to reveal the secrets you are requesting. In this last section of this chapter, we are going to look at another limit on the Freedom of Information Act: What happens when the government turns over part of its work to a private company?

For many years now, the federal government has sought to "privatize," or turnover to private businesses, some of the functions it has traditionally performed. For example, today many prisons and jails are run by private companies, allowing the government to get out of the prison business. While this saves the government a great deal of effort and money, there are certain constitutional issues that come into play.

> ### Looking for Liberty
>
> "A people who mean to be their own governors, must arm themselves with the power knowledge gives."
>
> —James Madison

For example, does a private company have to provide the same constitutional rights to prisoners as does the federal or state government? How are those rights to be monitored? For our purposes, does a privately-run prison have to provide the same sort of FOIA documents that a government-run prison would have to provide? Take the case of food stamps. In many parts of the county today, food stamps are provided not directly by the federal government but by private government contractors. Can private providers of food stamps be required to provide the same level of information that a government agency would have to provide under FOIA?

In both cases, the answer is no. There is little way of finding out if, for example, a company running a prison is providing the full panoply of prisoners' rights (discussed in detail in Chapter 15) to its inmates. Similarly, when not-for-profit companies or for-profit businesses take over government responsibilities in the area of social services or food stamps, those organizations are not obligated by FOIA to provide information to interested parties. Some legal commentators have suggested extending

FOIA to such private enterprises working at the behest of the federal government. But for the time being, FOIA does not extend that far.

In short, FOIA and the Privacy Act are excellent, if imperfect, ways of creating the concept of government-in-the-sunshine. The only potential downside for individuals who seek information under FOIA is that if the government has not already created a file on you, once you make a FOIA request, you can pretty much be sure that there will be one now! Nonetheless, the rights provided by FOIA are practically unique in the history of the world and are unmatched by any other society on the globe today. You've got questions; the government has to provide the answers.

The Least You Need to Know

- ◆ The rights provided by FOIA are practically unique in the history of the world and are unmatched by any other society today.

- ◆ Certain government secrets are yours for the peeking—if you know where, who, and how to look.

- ◆ The documents you wish to see must be in both the "possession and control" of the relevant federal agency.

- ◆ Information on JFK's assassination is scheduled to be made public in the year 2017.

Chapter 23

Taxing Matters:
Internal Revenue Service

In This Chapter

- ◆ Byzantine bylaws for taxes
- ◆ The privilege of paying taxes
- ◆ Haves vs. Have-nots
- ◆ Due process is overdue

Our federal tax system harms civil liberties much more than many people realize. Not only is the code excessively complex and difficult to understand, the IRS often abuses the rights of citizens when it enforces the code. Tax matters play themselves out in a legal arena quite different than those that address civil or criminal matters. In many respects, our tax system is unfair and denies you constitutional rights you've come to expect. In fact, the IRS would have you believe that the Bill of Rights doesn't apply to them at all.

With so much power in the hands of the IRS, it's important to know how to not become a victim. New laws were recently enacted to address the flagrant abuses of the IRS. We will discuss how those laws affect you and how you can avoid a tax-auditing nightmare.

"Ignorance of the Law Is No Excuse"

How many times have you heard this one? It is the responsibility of every citizen to know the nation's laws and comply with them. The old maxim applies to the tax code just as equally as it applies to anything else. However, the complexity of the code and the constant amendments to our tax laws make compliance, for many taxpayers, unusually difficult.

> **The Law of the Land**
>
> In the 1926 case of *Bowers v. Kerbaugh-Empire*, the Supreme Court noted that a statute that is "so vague that men of common intelligence must necessarily guess at its meaning and differ as to its application, violates that first essential of due process of law." Sure sounds like they're talking about the tax code!

The federal tax rules and regulations span over 45,000 pages and offer over 700 different forms (be sure to choose the right ones!). To add insult to injury, many rules frequently change. For instance, pension tax laws have changed substantially nearly every year since the early 1980s, leaving employers baffled over how to comply. And did you know there were over 440 amendments to the tax rules in the 2001 tax cut law alone?

When the tax system consists of more than 45,000 pages of law and regulation, compliance is no easy matter. Most taxpayers make every reasonable effort to appropriately comply with the law. However, their efforts are often defeated because they do not understand what the law requires. Oddly, a tax professional may prove to be no help either. The tax laws are now so complex that even many tax professionals are often ignorant of all the nuances of the code.

Each year from 1987 to 1991, *Money* magazine conducted a study of the competence of various tax professionals. Editors of the magazine created a hypothetical family financial profile and presented those facts to 50 different tax professionals in the private sector. The instructions were simple: Compute the tax liability of the hypothetical family based upon the facts provided and any applicable tax laws. Guess what? In every survey ever sent out, 50 different tax professionals came up with 50 different answers. Even more astounding is the fact that not one tax professional came up with the right answer!

> **Taking Liberties**
>
> In 1993, the IRS overcharged taxpayers five billion dollars in penalty assessments.

Don't think the IRS knows the answers either. According to the report of the General Accounting Office (GAO), nearly half of all IRS audits are erroneous, and about 40 percent of the penalty revenues collected each year were wrongfully assessed. Additionally, the GAO report reveals that each year the IRS telephone taxpayer assistance hotline provides approximately 8.5 million Americans with the wrong answers to basic questions about the tax laws.

Is the Tax System "Voluntary"?

Hardly. If it were, few people would pay taxes. The income tax currently supplies more than half of the federal government's revenue. How will the government support itself without an income tax? In the early part of our nation's history, the federal government relied solely on tariffs and excise taxes, but this revenue wasn't enough to support the activities of a growing and more powerful government. This shortfall led Congress to ratify of the Sixteenth Amendment to the Constitution, which empowered Congress to levy an income tax. The government needs these taxes to pay for the costs of goods and services that we can't provide well on our own—things like the military, postal system, highways, etc.

The Law of the Land

"Congress shall have power to lay and collect taxes on incomes, from whatever source derived, without apportionment among several states, and without regard to any census or enumeration."

—Sixteenth Amendment, U.S. Constitution.

It's wrong to think that Uncle Sam can open his pocketbook and allow you to keep yours closed, but this doesn't stop thousands of scam artists around the country from claiming that the payment of income taxes actually is voluntary. Those claims are false! The requirement to pay a personal income tax is set forth in section 1 of the Internal Revenue Code. To support their claim, tax protestors point to the Form 1040 instruction booklet, which refers to the filing of a tax return as voluntary. It reads: "You are among the millions of Americans who comply with the tax law voluntarily."

> What do they really mean by "voluntarily"? That only means that an IRS agent won't show up at your door on April 15 and decide what you owe. The word voluntary refers to our system of permitting taxpayers to assess their own tax liability and file the appropriate returns, rather than have the IRS determine the tax for them. Paying your taxes, however, is not voluntary, and we've got some case law to prove it. For instance, the 1989 case *United States* v. *Schiff* puts it this bluntly: "The payment of income taxes is not voluntary." In other words: A taxpayer's legal obligation to comply with tax laws is as voluntary as a driver's legal obligation to stop at a red light. Although in both cases enforcement depends on the 'voluntary' actions of individuals, compliance with the law is not optional and all violators are on notice that noncompliance will be punished.

—*Department of Correction* v. *Duncan Keizer*, et al., OATH No. 1481-98 (N.Y. Nov. 30, 1998).

To ensure compliance with the voluntary part, IRS computers examine your financial information. Employers and financial institutions also report your income. So if you didn't file, or did file but underreported your income, the computer will catch it, and you can expect the IRS to "voluntarily" get in touch with *you*. Failure to file your return and pay taxes owed could subject you to fines and imprisonment. In short, if you voluntarily fail to file your tax return, you may also be volunteering for an orange jump suit with free room and board at Uncle Sam's penitentiary.

> **Statutes of Liberties**
>
> Good news for Form 1040 filers: Your compliance is strictly voluntary! Bad news: Failure to comply may result in fines and imprisonment.

Is the Tax System Fair?

That depends on whom you ask (and how much in taxes that person you ask is paying). In many ways, our tax system is unfair. Taxpayers within the same salary bracket are treated unequally by the many exemptions, credits, and deductions provided in the tax code. For example, homeowners receive preferential treatment in our tax system by way of itemized deductions for mortgage interest and property taxes. Renters could easily pay thousands more per year because of these intricacies. Also, there are more than 50 tax provisions that provide differing benefits depending on whether you're married, divorced, or single. In essence, the tax code is used by Congress to encourage or discourage a particular lifestyle.

> **Looking for Liberty**
>
> Chief Justice John Marshall once said, "The power to tax involves the power to destroy."

Additionally, our due process rights are ignored in many respects by the federal income tax regime. The IRS is granted broad authority to obtain private confidential records without court intervention or supervision. Without a warrant, the IRS can obtain your personal records from banks, credit agencies, and other financial institutions. In fact, the IRS regularly conducts Fourth Amendment-style searches and seizures, without the necessity of a warrant or probable cause.

During 2001, for example, the IRS arbitrarily decided to target taxpayers who use credit cards issued overseas, demanding that credit card companies reveal confidential records. The IRS had no reason to suspect illegal activity on the part of any such taxpayers, nor was there actual proof that these cardholders were tax evaders. But this didn't stop the IRS from conducting a fishing expedition into the private financial affairs of American citizens. The IRS received millions of private financial records from MasterCard and American Express that involve cardholder accounts in 30 countries. The broad authority to obtain private records without court supervision has been aptly referred to by the Supreme Court as the "power of inquisition."

Guilty Until Proven Innocent

Generally, in our legal system of justice, you are presumed innocent until proven guilty. This rule applies whether you're being sued in a civil matter or charged by the state in a criminal case; the plaintiff or prosecutor carries the burden of proving that you are at fault. However, there is an exception to the general rule: the IRS.

In the vast majority of cases, the IRS does not have to prove that the taxpayer is guilty. Rather, it is the taxpayer who must prove that the IRS has made an error. So, if you receive a notice of deficiency from the IRS, chances are, unless you can afford to bring them to court, you're stuck paying the taxes. That's the oddity of it: A taxpayer must bring the IRS to court to prove the IRS is wrong. It's like being the victim of a car accident and having the at-fault driver receive unfettered discretion to wipe out your bank accounts, seize your assets, and snatch your paycheck to pay for injuries and damages unless, and until, you drag him into court and persuade a judge that you're the innocent party.

> **Statutes of Liberties**
>
> If the IRS sends you a "Notice of Deficiency," you have 90 days from the date on that notice to file a petition with the tax court. If you miss the 90-day cutoff, you are required to pay the tax. Although, you may sue for a refund, your option to sue before payment is gone.

Although you have the option to sue the IRS to prove your innocence, your court options aren't too impressive either. Your choices are to litigate in either the U.S. Tax Court, U.S. District Court, or U.S. Court of Federal Claims. If you select the U.S. Tax Court, you lose the right to a jury trial. Since the tax court is an administrative court, not an Article III court, no jury trial is required. To obtain a jury trial, you must file suit in a U.S. District Court. But before that can happen, all taxes, penalties, and interest that the IRS claims you owe must be paid in full. The last option—the U.S. Court of Federal Claims—is the least favored of the three: You must pay the taxes in full, *and* you have no right to a jury trial.

The burden of litigation, especially the time and expense, often overwhelm the average taxpayer. To relieve the expense burden, you may be awarded costs and attorney's fees if you prevail and the court finds that the IRS's position was not substantially justified.

Without Judge or Jury

As you can see, the "guilty until proven innocent" concept is quite clear. The collection methods available to the IRS are equally unfair. Not only can the IRS automatically stamp the word "guilty" on your forehead, they can collect their money in the smoothest and swiftest way possible.

Let's illustrate this by example. Your neighbor Bob complained for years about your barking dog in the backyard. He finally sues you for nuisance and the judge sides in Bob's favor, awarding him damages in the amount of 1,000 dollars. You were found guilty and are now liable for the dollar amount of this judgment. Now let's assume you refuse to pay Bob. Bob must go through a burdensome route to collect on his judgment, including filing additional paperwork with the court and paying a filing fee to pursue either wage garnishment, bank levy, or property liens. Not so for the IRS! The taxman doesn't need court intervention for collection.

Legal Dictionary

Tax lien—A legal claim to charges that are due to the IRS. A lien allows your property to be attached and sold if necessary to satisfy the delinquent tax.

If a tax bill goes unpaid, the matter is referred to collection personnel for action. A *tax lien* may be promptly filed against you if the IRS feels it needs to protect its interest. A tax lien may be filed in any county in which you own real estate. The IRS has the option to foreclose upon the property or wait until you sell it, in which case the IRS will collect any money that results from that sale. A tax lien may also be placed on personal property, such as autos, boats, or campers.

The IRS may also serve a legal notice to your bank, demanding that they surrender any assets in your accounts, including cash, stocks, bonds, and retirement savings. In some cases, one or more of your accounts may qualify for an exemption from this levy. Otherwise, the bank will remit the full balance in your account to the IRS, up to the amount requested in the notice of levy. Thus, any checks submitted to your account for collection thereafter may bounce.

Taking Liberties

"The art of taxation consists in so plucking the goose as to obtain the largest possible amount of feathers with the smallest possible amount of hissing."

—Jean-Baptiste Colbert, the Seventeenth-century financier of Louis XIV

In addition, the IRS may garnish your wages. The wage garnishment is the most powerful tool used to collect back taxes owed. Once a wage garnishment is filed, the employer is required to remit to the IRS a large percentage of each paycheck. This can be very embarrassing since the employer is now aware of your tax problems. Another downside is that, in most instances, it leaves you with insufficient income to pay your bills.

The individual under the gun from the IRS has one good option: to attempt to reach an offer in compromise. An offer in compromise is an effective way to resolve a tax debt and stop the collection activities described above. An *offer in compromise* is a contract between you and the IRS that allows you to pay a reduced amount in full settlement of the tax debt. However, the IRS will only agree to an offer in compromise if there is doubt as to the actual tax liability or if you are financially unable to pay the full amount of the debt. A current statement of your financial affairs signed under penalty of perjury must be furnished before a compromise agreement will be considered. You can be assured that the IRS will verify your financial information by reviewing prior years' tax returns, and by reviewing bank, courthouse, and state motor vehicle records.

The program benefits the IRS by providing more revenue than it would otherwise receive and by encouraging future compliance by taxpayers. Be aware that if you default on the terms of the compromise agreement, the original tax liability can be revived, which sets you back to square one.

Legal Dictionary

Offer in compromise—
An agreement to pay an amount that is less than the full tax liability due.

New Protections

In 1998, Congress passed the Internal Revenue Service Restructuring and Reform Act. This new law extends taxpayer rights by shifting the burden of proof to the IRS if certain conditions are met.

Under the new laws, the IRS must now prove its point on any factual issue, provided that the taxpayer, among other things, (1) introduces credible evidence, (2) complies with substantiation requirements, (3) maintains adequate records, and (4) cooperates with the IRS. Thus far, reports show that the new laws have made few changes within the IRS. Before the burden of proof shifts, someone must determine whether you've fully "cooperated" or "complied." Who do you think will make that decision? (I'll give you a clue: It's not *you*.)

Although the new laws provide little strength in reversing the "guilty until proven innocent" standard, there are a number of protective measures in the statute that restrict the IRS's previously unrestricted right of collection. Of particular note:

Statutes of Liberties

The IRS must now comply with the Fair Debt Collection Practices Act. The FDCPA regulates the activities of debt collectors. In general, the IRS cannot harass, oppress, or abuse any person in connection with the collection of taxes.

- The IRS must provide 30 days notice before levying a taxpayer's property.

- Your principal residence cannot be levied without court approval.

◆ The IRS cannot seize your residence to satisfy a liability of 5,000 dollars or less.

◆ The IRS is subject to the Fair Debt Collection Practices Act.

In an effort to make the IRS more taxpayer-friendly, they also reduced the agency's ability to go after affluent tax cheats. Our kinder, friendlier IRS now picks on the working poor. At the behest of Congress, the IRS has diverted its army of enforcement agents from chasing down wealthy tax cheats to catching lower-income tax evaders.

Odds have improved significantly for those in the upper-income brackets. Among taxpayers with incomes above 100,000 dollars, the chances of being audited after 1998 are slim to none. In fact, the General Accounting Office reports that audits for the affluent group dropped more than 30 percent after the 1998 reforms, but taxpayers grossing less than 100,000 dollars are 25 percent more likely to be audited. In fact, over half of all 2001 audits targeted people claiming the earned income tax credit, a benefit claimed by low-income taxpayers. This is an oddity considering the affluent group is more likely to have income that is easier to hide. Our most affluent Americans cheat the tax system out of billions of dollars each year. In the last decade, three of America's top 10 wealthiest persons reneged on their tax liabilities.

Taking Liberties

Following the 1998 Reform Act, the IRS reduced its full-time staff by more than 30 percent. Auditing the wealthy often takes a long time, and usually requires use of a corpus of lawyers, accountants, and consultants. The opposite scenario exists for the poor, who cannot afford to pay for top-notch legal representation.

Since a quarter of our congressional members are themselves millionaires, some will argue that they are biased to enforcing the code against their fellow compadres. Remember how hard President George H. W. Bush worked to get approval for the estate tax repeal, a tax generally collected from only the wealthiest two percent of the population? Public confidence is undermined in a tax system where not all citizens pay their fair share for government services; where the wealthy are the only one's who won't get caught and punished.

The IRS admits there is a problem and has requested Congress to give the IRS more resources to enforce the law equally for the rich and the poor. These are areas that our elected politicians must work to resolve. If they don't, next time around, you can exercise your right not to check their name on the ballot form.

How Can You Avoid an IRS Audit?

In the end, every tax matter boils down to this one question. No letter from the government is more unappreciated than the one that starts: "Dear taxpayer, Your return has been selected for examination. You have 10 days to …"

It hardly helps to acknowledge that audits are necessary to give the tax system its credibility (after all, a tax system's effectiveness is undermined if there were no ability to enforce and collect). So just how can you avoid an audit? To start, honesty and accuracy is of utmost importance. If you have two kids, but claim 12 dependents, you're really asking for it. If you added incorrectly or claimed a larger deduction than the law allows, the IRS computer will catch it. However, sometimes honesty and accuracy is not enough. For this reason, it is important to know how the process works in order to understand how to avoid an audit.

> **Statutes of Liberties**
>
> Federal law places a timeline on the IRS's ability to audit your returns. Generally, the limitations period is three years from the date you filed your return. If, however, you failed to report more than 25 percent of your income on the tax return, the limitation period extends to six years. If you filed a fraudulent return, or failed to file a return at all, no limitation period applies.

Most tax returns are selected for audit by a computer-generated program that uses a mathematical formula to compare your deductions to other similarly situated taxpayers. The formula considers income, deductions, family size, and profession to select returns that have a high probability of being inaccurate. For instance, a family of six living in Bel Air would rarely have an income of 35,000 dollars or less; and a taxpayer with a 40,000 dollars salary would rarely have 25,000 dollars in charitable contributions. If anything looks unusual, you may want to include receipts with your return to ward off an audit.

The IRS pays particular attention to returns filed by taxpayers in specific professions. For instance, if your salary consists of mostly tip-income, you will be a prime target for an audit. It may be useful to keep a daily journal of your tips to ward off any future claim of underreporting. Also, being self-employed will increase your chances of being audited. The IRS is aware of the myriad of improper business deductions claimed by self-employed taxpayers, so be prepared to prove your expenditures as deductible expenses.

Even if you don't practice in one of these targeted professions and you have followed all the appropriate precautions, you can still be selected for an audit by random. The IRS computer selects a small number of returns for audit on a random basis—a process often called the "audit lottery." This is one lottery you don't want to win. However, if you're honest and accurate in your reporting, and maintain good records to prove your financial information, then you should fair fine with the IRS.

The Least You Need to Know

- ◆ If you fail to file a tax return and pay taxes owed you may be fined and/or imprisoned.

- ◆ To overturn a final decision of the IRS, you must file suit in the U.S. Tax Court, U.S. District Court, or U.S. Court of Federal Claims.

- ◆ If you are financially unable to pay a tax assessment, you may be able to lessen the burden with an "offer in compromise."

- ◆ Honesty, accuracy, and maintaining good records are the keys to avoiding an IRS auditing nightmare.

Chapter 24

Shh! ... Here Comes RICO

In This Chapter

◆ The Mafia connection

◆ Winning at RICO

◆ Predicate crimes

◆ RICO on ice

One of the most powerful tools in the arsenal of the criminal justice system for destroying the power of organized crime is a statute known as the Racketeer Influenced and Corrupt Organizations Act. If you take the first initials of this law, you get the acronym RICO.

Most people who are not lawyers will tell you that RICO is an Italian first name. How it ended up the name of a law meant to destroy the economic power of organized crime is a very good question. At a minimum, it demonstrates a very high degree of insensitivity on the part of the U.S. Congress toward Italian Americans, who deeply resent being tarred with the "Mafia" brush. But this chapter is not about the presumed violation of the civil liberties of Italians that occurred when a popular Italian surname became the code name for an anti-Mafia law.

Instead, this chapter tells the story of how a law that set out to break up racket and put racketeers behind bars has actually become a tool for chilling free political speech protected by the First Amendment. One of my doctor friends says, "That anything you take enough of that can help you, can also hurt you." There is little doubt that RICO, while a successful tool in the hands of prosecutors to defeat organized crime, has turned into a true civil liberties nightmare.

Follow the Money

Organized crime is not easy to contain. The law of secrecy that surrounds it means that it is very difficult for prosecutors to get information about who is conducting organized crime activities. Organized crime leaders are generally insulated from the day-to-day illegal business practices of their lieutenants. So the question becomes, how do you diminish the power of individuals who are extremely difficult to prosecute? The answer is that you create a new crime. Traditionally, crimes are things that you do—extortion, murder, loan sharking, running a prostitution ring. The RICO law came up with a brand new idea—the idea of a crime being something that you *are*. RICO punishes the status of an individual as a *racketeer*, or someone engaged in illegal or unsavory business practices.

Legal Dictionary

Racketeer—Someone engaged in illegal or unsavory business practices.

Let's say an individual commits one act of loan sharking and then five years later is convicted of running an illegal casino. Normally, these crimes would have to be prosecuted separately. Under RICO, however, the prosecution could allege that the defendant is engaged in a "pattern" of illegal racketeering acts. Each of the individual acts is called "predicate" crimes. By stringing together these predicate crimes into a recognizable pattern of criminal behavior, special criminal penalties—both jail time and fines—could be imposed. Thus, it would be possible to attack the leaders of organized crime, by charging them with the maintenance of a criminal organization.

Organized crime members sometimes force their way into legitimate businesses as (highly unwanted) partners. This enables the organized crime members to launder money and eventually purchase outright the business through intimidation. The goal for prosecutors is to attack this process of taking dirty criminal money and putting it into legitimate businesses. RICO permits prosecutors to "follow the money" and seize assets—businesses, houses, whatever—that belong to organized crime members convicted of conducting ongoing criminal patterns of behavior.

As you can imagine, prosecutors loved RICO from the start. Organized crime figures were well, less than joyous about it. Many organized crime figures went to jail and forfeited large amounts of money through the RICO process. But Congress wanted to go a step further, to protect the innocent business owners whose lives had been turned upside down.

Congress created a second type of RICO statute, called civil RICO, to go alongside its big brother, criminal RICO. Only the state—i.e., a prosecutor, a district attorney—could bring charges under criminal RICO, seeking jail time and fines for alleged organized crime figures. Under civil RICO, any businessperson whose business had been negatively affected by organized crime members could go to court and file a civil suit to regain what had been illegally taken away. In fact, RICO offered "triple damages," meaning that for every dollar you could prove you lost due to organized crime, the courts would award you three dollars. Because of this tremendous financial incentive for plaintiffs (and their attorneys), civil RICO became a very popular tool for business people to recoup their losses.

Taking Liberties

Not surprisingly, Italian Americans were less than pleased with RICO's nickname and the anti-Italian overtones, but the name of the law has never been changed.

Civil RICO is a lawyer's dream. First, they do not need to convince a prosecutor to bring an indictment. You or I could stroll down to the courthouse this afternoon and file RICO charges against anyone we thought was conducting a pattern of criminal behavior. Normally, there is a concept in American law called prosecutorial discretion, which means that there is a boatload of crimes out there in the world, and prosecutors simply are not required to go after every single crime committed. They must use their discretion and go after those cases where they think they have the highest likelihood of winning. Fortunately, civil RICO does not involve prosecutors, so if you want to sue, no one is stopping you.

The next pleasant aspect of civil RICO, from the plaintiff's point of view, is the evidentiary standard. As we all know from TV shows about lawyers, a criminal case results in a guilty verdict only when the prosecutor has proved its case "beyond a reasonable doubt." On a percentage basis, this means that there is, perhaps, a 95 to 98 percent chance that the prosecution is right and that the defendant is guilty of the crime with which he or she has been charged. Since it's not possible to prove things absolutely, at least most of the time, that standard of 95 to 98 percent is the law of the land.

In civil cases, RICO or otherwise, the standard is much lower. The standard is "a preponderance of the evidence." We discussed this issue in Chapter 15 when we were talking about the O. J. Simpson verdicts. Simpson won the criminal trial but lost his civil case. That's because the evidence against him was somewhere between "beyond a

Criminal

reasonable doubt"—that, say, 90 percent standard—and the "preponderance of the evidence" standard of the civil cases, which pretty much means 51 percent. In other words, if you can prove that it is 51 percent more likely than not that things happened the way you say they happened, then you win in civil trial. Civil RICO has that lower, 51 percent preponderance of the evidence standard and the lower the standard of evidence that you have to produce, the more likely it is that you are going to win your case.

What do you have to do to be a target of civil RICO? There are four basic types of unlawful conduct that are considered predicate offenses for civil RICO. That is to say, if a person is found to have committed some combination of these four acts in a 10-year period, he will lose a civil RICO trial.

Here are the four types of conduct:

♦ Use or invest income derived from a pattern of racketeering to acquire an interest in an enterprise.

♦ Acquire or maintain an interest in any enterprise through a pattern of racketeering activity.

♦ Conduct or participate in the affairs of an enterprise through a pattern of racketeering activity.

♦ Conspire to violate any of the foregoing provisions.

Statutes of Liberties

If this law is confusing to you, you're not alone. The use of civil RICO is so complex that lawyers take multi-day seminars just to get a handle on its use.

Conspiracy simply means that you make a plan with someone else to commit a crime; for many crimes, conspiracy, or the act of planning a crime, is in itself a separate crime.

What does all that legalese mean? It means that an individual or business that makes money from illegal activities and then takes that money and runs a business using that money may be prosecuted under civil RICO.

And what does this have to do with civil liberties, you may ask? Well, try this on for size. Let's say that the "enterprise" that we are discussing is an antiabortion group that seeks to shut down abortion clinics. Let's further say that this antiabortion group uses the U.S. mail to solicit funds from donors around the country to support it in its quest. This antiabortion organization performs some acts that are entirely legal—picketing, leafleting, providing information—but mixes in some tactics that are either illegal or borderline illegal, such as harassing young women about to enter abortion clinics, stealing fetuses from clinics, bombing the center, or threatening the lives of doctors or other individuals who work to perform abortions. The antiabortionists may make hundreds or even thousands of telephone calls a day to abortion clinics, thus tying up their phone lines and keeping it impossible for real clients to get through on the phone. They might also telephone abortion clinics and claim to be women in need of counseling and then schedule blocks of time for appointments. Of course, they never show up for these appointments, thus denying those slots to women who actually need abortion counseling or services.

As we said, some of those acts are legal and are protected speech under the First Amendment. Others of those acts are either illegal or simply wrong. Now let's say that a pro-choice group—one that favors the availability of abortions—decides to use civil RICO to shut down the antiabortion groups. The civil liberties question is, can they?

One of the predicate crimes for a RICO finding is mail fraud. If an organization is using the U.S. mail to solicit donations, but then is turning around and using some of that money on illegal activities, there is a good possibility that a court would determine that mail fraud has taken place. Remember, the RICO rules state that a defendant must commit two or more predicate acts in order to be found guilty under the RICO statute. If an organization is found to have committed mail fraud twice, it could well be liable under civil RICO. Additionally, it may be guilty of the underlying criminal offenses as well.

> ### Looking for Liberty
>
> The National Organization for Women won million-dollar lawsuits using civil RICO against antiabortion protesters. Animal rights activists have expressed concern that civil RICO could be used against them as well.

This is not a theoretical issue. There have been at least three cases where pro-choice individuals and groups have brought civil RICO claims against antiabortion groups and their leaders. In one such case, *Northeast Women's Center, Inc. v. McMonhgle*, the judge found the antiabortion group's activities, which included extortion, theft, and mail fraud, to have violated RICO standards. This case ended in a judgment of over 60,000 dollars entered against the antiabortion protestors, who were now considered racketeers and violators of the RICO statute.

A second case, *Feminist Women's Health Center v. Roberts*, followed the logic in *McMonhgle* and found that a second antiabortion group had committed enough predicate crimes to merit a civil RICO violation. Finally, the *Town of West Hartford v. Operation Rescue*, another leading civil RICO case involving a challenge to antiabortion groups, lost for technical reasons. Nonetheless, there is a pattern here. If you do not like antiabortion protestors, then civil RICO sounds like a fantastic idea. If, on the other hand, you are a proponent of the First Amendment, perhaps civil RICO ought to give you chills.

Chilling Effect

The legislative history of the criminal and civil RICO statutes indicates clearly that the sole purpose of RICO is to redress economic injury that occurs to businesses infiltrated by the Mob. Neither the U.S. Senate or the House of Representatives, when they were initially drawing up the RICO statutes, ever envisioned that RICO could become a tool in the hands of political groups that wanted to find ways to silence their opposition. While most people would consider the burning down of abortion clinics, attacks on doctors, or the harassment of women seeking abortions to be reprehensible, the question is whether civil RICO is an appropriate vehicle for attacking such behavior.

The Law of the Land

More than 1,000 RICO cases are filed each year, but the Supreme Court has not yet ruled over its constitutionality.

It's not only antiabortion groups that are feeling the heat from civil RICO. Some cigarette manufacturers have been attacked with claims. Cigarette manufacturers may not be any more popular than abortion providers, but the whole point of the American legal system is to protect points of view that are not part of the mainstream.

Keep in mind that anyone can sue anyone else under civil RICO. As soon as Smith sues Jones under civil RICO, the news media can announce that Jones is "an alleged racketeer," a label nobody wants attached to their reputation. And even if the case is subsequently thrown out of court, it would be virtually impossible to undo the damage to one's good name. Ray Donovan, the secretary of labor in the Reagan administration who had been wrongly accused—in court and in the media—of committing crimes, asked, when his ordeal was over, "What office do I go to to get my reputation back?" There is no such office. If a person's reputation is damaged by a civil RICO suit and the claim that he or she is a racketeer, there is practically no way in the American court system to undo the damage.

The news media, as we all know, feeds on scandal. When someone is accused of racketeering, the incident makes headlines. When someone is found to be not guilty of such charges, or if such charges are dropped, it's unlikely that tidbit of information will show up on the front page or on the evening news. News like that is shunted to the side if it appears anywhere in the media at all. This is especially true in the modern era, in which many Americans receive their news not from newspapers or even television, but from the web. There, you are given a single page of headlines—six or eight stories, if that many. It is extremely rare for the dropping of a lawsuit to make its way onto the front page of a CNN.com or FOXnews.com.

When a law exists and can be used to limit the amount of freedom of speech that Americans enjoy, that law is said to have a *chilling effect* on freedom of speech. Courts take very seriously the question of chilling effects and usually act quickly to undo the damage caused by a law that "chills" free speech. You can make a very strong case that civil RICO does have a chilling effect on free speech, simply because it is an extremely powerful tool that can destroy reputations—without any checks or balances. Also, the courts seem not to mind that civil RICO has strayed far beyond its initial purpose, which was to redress solely *economic* crimes. Instead, today, civil RICO is used as a tool for attacking unpopular positions or institutions.

Legal Dictionary

Chilling effect—A change in behavior brought about by the passing of a law or a court's decision.

Ironically, one of the crimes that serves as a predicate for criminal or civil RICO is extortion, which is defined as taking something from another person by coercion or intimidation. How ironic it is that RICO initially sought to punish individuals—members of organized crime—who coerce or intimidate others into giving up valuable things, such as their businesses. Now, some of the organizations using civil RICO have a powerful tool that allows them to coerce or intimidate groups into giving up some of their own free speech rights.

Is civil RICO, thus used, a violation of the civil liberties of individuals whose opinions and ideas may not be in the mainstream? It sure looks that way. At some point in the future Congress may work to repair the damaged caused by this unintended use of civil RICO to further social causes, but for now, civil RICO in this sphere is bad medicine.

The Least You Need to Know

- RICO was originally created to allow arrests of organized crime members.

- To win a RICO case as a plaintiff, you need only prove a preponderance of the evidence.

- Committing a combination of two predicate crimes in a 10-year period can sink a civil RICO defendant.

- Some organizations use civil RICO to intimidate groups into giving up some of their own free speech rights.

The Future of Civil Liberties

In This Chapter

- ◆ To sum it all up
- ◆ Protecting our rights
- ◆ What you can do
- ◆ A wise man once said …

Where do we go from here?

We've seen throughout this book that the civil liberties, the civil rights, and the freedoms that you enjoy as an American are constantly in flux. In some ways, you have far more rights than did your forefathers a century ago. In other ways, you face challenges to your privacy that your great-grandparents could never even have imagined.

It's Really Up to You

If you are a member of a minority group, you have seen events tilt in your favor over the past 40 years—and you may have seen them begin to slip the other way. If you are an individual committed to a particular point of view, you might find your ideas under siege. You might discover that other individuals or groups are using new weapons such as civil RICO to silence you.

If you are a middle school or high school student, I should first commend you for having read this far! You are growing up in a world far more dangerous, complex, and bewildering than that which your parents or grandparents faced. You have to handle challenges and make decisions with regard to drugs, sex, and a whole host of issues that were never considerations in past times. There may be metal detectors at the doors of your school, drug-sniffing dogs, or other intrusions into your privacy. You may have to undergo random drug testing merely to play a team sport or perhaps for no particular reason at all.

> **The Law of the Land**
>
> "[S]ecure the blessings of liberty to ourselves and our posterity ..."
> —Preamble, U.S. Constitution

> **Taking Liberties**
>
> The delicate balance needed is the question of how to protect the individual's freedoms, which we cherish so deeply as part of the American heritage, while at the same time protecting our nation from those who would cause harm to it.

All of us live in an era where privacy is under siege. In a time of national emergency, such as our own post-September 11 world, there is a natural swing of the pendulum toward restricting personal freedoms in the name of protecting society. Today, this need for more careful scrutiny of individuals as they board planes, use the Internet, or simply live their lives comes against a general societal trend to give the government more power and to restrict further the rights of individuals.

You have a role to play. I hope that reading this book has been an eye-opening experience for you. It certainly has been one for me! Before I began work on this book, I had no idea just how deeply our personal freedoms are threatened by the new technologies that have come into play in the last 10 years. For example, only five years ago, people thought that giving your credit card number out over the Internet was no different from handing it to a waiter at a restaurant. The difference between handing your credit card to a waiter and putting those numbers over the Internet, it turns out, is immense. Not just one set of potentially prying eyes, but countless snoopers can and do have access to your private data, every time you send it out over the Internet.

Ubiquity of computers means that it has never been easier for businesses, credit bureaus, insurance companies, and health-care providers to keep files on each of us. At the same time, it has never been easier for those same institutions to make mistakes and record incorrect information in our files, or release those files to individuals or organizations that should never have had access to them. Privacy, it turns out, is much more fragile than any of us might have expected, and the Internet is far less secure than any of us might have dreamt the first time we went online.

On the job, we have seen how employers can monitor the work lives (and perhaps the private lives as well) of their employees, via cameras and software programs that monitor Internet use, keyboard strokes, or even time away from the computer. We have seen that the policy of affirmative action, which began to *redress* the wrongs done to African Americans and other minorities over the centuries, has begun to erode in the light of changing public opinion. On the road, we have seen that police have broad powers to stop and search cars without the use of warrants, and often because of racial profiling.

Legal Dictionary

Redress—Legal remedies to make up for previously caused harm. From the old French word for "rearranging."

In schools, we've seen that students have a diminished right of privacy second only to that of prison inmates. While students cannot be physically searched without a very high expectation that they have committed a crime, they nevertheless have virtually no privacy. Drug tests can be demanded, lockers can be investigated, and even purses and pockets can be searched under certain conditions. In many states, corporal punishment is still permissible in public schools.

In our homes, while the Fourth Amendment still requires warrants for most searches, we still have a lesser degree of privacy than we might realize. Technology gives law enforcement officers tools to monitor the heat coming from our houses to make sure that we are not turning our homes into meth labs. (Yes, they need a warrant to use those tools, but it's just one more way in which our privacy is threatened.)

Individuals who are not members of the law enforcement community have access to technology that picks up signals from baby monitors so they can see what doors are open, facilitating break-ins. Our cell phone communication can be monitored and our Internet habits studied by others without our knowledge or permission. These are additional violations of our privacy if not strictly speaking civil liberties issues.

Lurking in our shadows, it would seem, is the government, seeking to regulate our lives; marketers, seeking to sell us goods and services; identity thieves, seeking access to our personal data; and a medical establishment that maintains files on millions of us. If civil liberties and privacy mean anything to us, we must each be responsible for safeguarding them. We cannot count on the government to do the job for us; the government has far too much invested in intruding on our privacy. We cannot count on business to protect our privacy, because business cannot sell and resell our names, addresses, and consumer preferences quickly enough. We cannot count on the courts, because as the country turns more conservative, the courts reflect that turn, in decisions ranging from affirmative action to school prayer to the use of civil RICO in noneconomic crimes. In short, the only possible guarantor of your civil liberties … is you.

A National ID Card?

One of the ideas floated around Washington every few years is the concept of a national ID card. This would tie together in one convenient place all the information about us—social security information, drivers license information, potentially even IRS data. Once the government starts tying together all the various databanks that contain information on us, there would be no end in sight.

The idea of the national ID card came to the fore once again after the September 11, 2001, attacks. Supporters claimed that such a measure was necessary in order to monitor the movements of individuals who sought to cause harm to the country. The problem, of course, is that it would still remain possible—and even easy—for individuals to subvert that system and create false identities for themselves. Many of the September 11 hijackers were able to receive Virginia driver licenses based upon fraudulent notarized documents that they had created. The very people we would wish to capture with such national ID cards would slip through the net, while the activities of the nearly 300 million Americans alive today would be easier than ever for the government, business, health-care system, and criminals to monitor. Is that what we want?

> **Looking for Liberty**
>
> EPIC, the Electronic Privacy Information Center, is a clearing-house of information about limiting governmental intrusion on individual privacy. You can visit them at www.epic.org.

We are the greatest country in the world. The fact that millions of people each year risk their fortunes and their lives to join us confirms that fact. There has never been a society in human history that offers the level of freedoms to its citizens as does the United States. Only in America, as the expression goes, would the American Civil Liberties Union go to court four separate times on behalf of Nazis to allow them the opportunity to enjoy the same free speech rights that the rest of us take for granted. Only in America could so many of the great advances in civil liberties and civil rights first have taken place.

> **Statutes of Liberties**
>
> The U.S.A. Patriot Act, passed in the aftermath of the September 11, 2001, attacks, gave the FBI a wide assortment of surveillance tools it had long been seeking. With an enemy as amorphous as terrorists, though, when can we know, if ever, that the danger has passed?

It's easy to forget, of course, that the only reason we *needed* advances in civil liberties and civil rights is because so many Americans were denied them for so long. Women have been permitted to vote for less than a century. African Americans have been guaranteed the right to equal employment, equal educational opportunities, equal housing, and even the right to vote for less than 40 years. We have to be very careful patting ourselves on the back lest we sprain our arm muscles. We have to guard against spending so much time congratulating ourselves that we overlook the fact that freedom and privacy have been deeply eroded over the last 10 or 15 years, with neither government nor the private sector willing to stand up and say that this is wrong.

In short, if your civil liberties mean anything to you—and I hope that after having read this book, you see the extraordinary value in each of the freedoms we enjoy—it truly is up to you to work to protect them. Become involved with groups that support civil liberties. Get involved in the political process. Stay informed—it's all too easy to ignore the news, especially since it is so often bleak and sensationalized. Keep abreast of what is going on in Washington. Let your representatives in Congress and the State House know how you feel about issues of privacy and other civil liberties matters. If you are in school, at whatever grade level, work to educate your fellow students about their rights. Learn about the record of the police in your community and find out what you can do to make sure that laws are enforced fairly.

The alternative to taking action to protect our freedoms is to watch them continue to seep away, sometimes slowly, sometimes with blinding speed. After the 2000 election, none of us can claim that our vote doesn't matter. The individual you send to the White House picks replacements for departing Supreme Court justices ... and also hundreds of judges in federal courts across the country. Your vote will determine the legacy that our era will leave to the next generation. Be involved.

The Law of the Land

"The privilege of the writ of habeas corpus shall not be suspended, unless when in cases of rebellion or invasion the public safety may require it."

— U.S. Constitution, Article I, Section 9.

Does the Sept. 11 attack constitute "invasion" that triggers limiting of constitutional legal protections? The Justice Department apparently decided the answer was yes, holding many suspected terrorists without access to attorneys.

Civil liberties are like the muscular system in the body of the human being. It really is a case of "use them or lose them." The civil liberties we do not seek to protect and enhance will atrophy—we have seen this happen time and again in this book. If America is to remain great—and by great, I mean free—it truly is up to every single one of us.

When Benjamin Franklin emerged from deliberations over the Declaration of Independence in 1776, the citizens of Philadelphia asked him, "What have you given us?"

His reply: "A republic, if you can keep it."

Now that responsibility falls to us.

The Least You Need to Know

- We've come a long way, baby, but we still have a ways to go.
- America enjoys more civil liberties than most other nations.
- Our civil liberties are what make America the great country it is today.
- Everyone is responsible for helping to maintain our civil liberties.

Words to Stay Free By

abate—The legal term for ceasing an action.

aggravating factors—Reasons for increasing punishment in a criminal case, such as torturing or sexually abusing a victim.

ancient lights—The nineteenth-century doctrine, long since discarded, forbidding the construction of buildings that blocked neighbors' light.

battery—Harmful or offensive intentional contact.

bigamy—The state of being married to more than one person.

blanket waivers—General consent forms that permit doctors or other health care providers to release information to insurance companies, government agencies, and others.

blockbusting—An illegal real estate practice of preying on the racially motivated fears of homeowners to induce them to list and sell their houses.

bright line rules—Clear, unambiguous guidelines in the law.

checks and balances—The system of dividing power among the judiciary, the legislative, and the executive branches, to keep any one branch of government from becoming too powerful.

chilling effect—Anything that unconstitutionally restricts freedom of speech.

civil liberties—The specific rights, such as freedom of speech, press, religion, and due process of law, that individuals enjoy under the American system of government.

civil rights—The government's responsibility to take positive actions to make sure that citizens have equal rights and equal opportunity under the law.

civil union—A newly recognized legal relationship between same-sex couples that grants them many of the legal rights that married couples enjoy.

comity—The rule that states accept each others' legal decisions, especially those concerning marriage and divorce.

commercial speech—The legal term for advertising.

common law—The body of English law that the founders of this nation brought with them; a source of legal rules that are neither judge-made nor passed by state legislatures or Congress.

consanguinity—The distance along the family tree that is required for a couple to get married.

constructive permission—The assumption that someone has given permission to someone else; generally based on that first person's actions or failure to act.

Consumer Reporting Agency (CRA)—A bureau that gathers and sells financial information about individuals who apply for jobs, insurance, charge accounts, personal loans, or anything else where someone is extending credit or trust. The three CRAs are Equifax, Experian (formerly TRW), and Trans Union.

contract theory—In labor law, the idea that a contract can be implied from the act of hiring someone to work for you.

Court of Appeals—The tier of federal courts just below the U.S. Supreme Court.

curtilage—A legal term for the areas on a property surrounding a home, such as the driveway or toolshed.

distinguish—To find that a particular legal precedent (a previously decided case) does not apply in a given situation.

double jeopardy—A violation of the constitutional freedom from being tried or punished twice for the same crime.

emancipation—The situation in which a parent is relieved of legal and financial obligations relating to a child and the child now assumes those responsibilities.

eminent domain—The right of the government to take private property for its own uses, providing they give fair compensation to the owner of the property.

Equal Protection Clause—The right of all Americans to fair treatment under the law; part of the Fifth Amendment to the U.S. Constitution.

Federal Communications Commission (FCC)—The government agency entrusted with regulating the airwaves for radio, TV, cell phones, etc.

Federal Trade Commission (FTC)—The federal agency responsible for consumer protection and a competitive marketplace.

flame—To send e-mail, often personal, rude and highly critical, to another.

forfeiture—The means by which the government can take away property in civil or criminal actions.

full faith and credit—Language from the Constitution indicating that states must respect each others' decisions.

good will—The reputation and patronage a business has in a community.

hate speech—Speech that insults the ethnicity or racial background of individuals.

identity theft—A crime in which an individual steals your personal data in order to get credit cards, Social Security benefits, or a host of other things in your name.

injunctive relief—A ruling that forces a person to cease a nuisance behavior or other actions.

just compensation—The responsibility of the government to pay fair prices for property taken through condemnation or eminent domain actions.

libel—A publication of false facts that damages reputation.

magistrate shopping—The practice of choosing a court in which to bring a case based on the likelihood that a particular judge will see things your way.

Magna Carta—The document signed by England's King John in 1215, limiting the power of the King and granting power to landowners and the church.

"Make My Day" statutes—State laws that make permissible the defense of one's home with deadly force.

Miranda rights—The rights that police must inform arrested individuals to ensure that their statements or confessions are not coerced.

mitigating factors—Reasons to lessen punishment in a given criminal case.

narrow-casting—Advertising or programming directed at a small segment of the market.

natural rights—The theory that individuals enter society with certain rights and that no government can take away those rights.

negligent retention—Hiring, or not firing, an individual likely to commit crimes in the workplace.

nuisance—Something that interferes with the right of an individual to enjoy his or her property.

offer in compromise—An agreement to pay an amount that is less than the full tax liability due.

plaintiff—The individual or entity that initiates a law suit.

polygamy—The state of having multiple marriage partners at the same time.

privilege—An obligation to maintain a confidence and a right to expect that the confidence will be maintained that arises between people in certain relationships. Types of privilege include those between client-attorney, spousal, doctor-patient, and priest-penitent.

probable cause—A situation where an impartial judge or magistrate would issue a warrant to search a person, car, or home.

product placement—The placement of a product in a television show or movie for advertising purposes.

promissory estoppel—The legal principle that makes a person legally responsible for the promises he or she makes, as in the case of an employer who induces a worker to quit her job with a promise to hire her. Should that employer not fulfill the promise of employment, the worker who quit her previous job could sue that employer for damages.

prosecutorial discretion—The power prosecutors have to choose which cases to bring to court and to determine which do not merit prosecution.

public figure—In libel law, an individual with a diminished expectation of privacy.

public policy—A legal way of saying, "We, your government, think this is a good idea for society, so we are going to enact legislation to favor this trend."

racial profiling—The police practice of pulling drivers over based on their race, national origin, or ethnicity.

racketeer—Someone engaged in illegal or unsavory business practices.

redlining—The illegal banking practice of choosing not to lend money for property in minority or inner city neighborhoods.

sodomy—The term "sodomy" comes from the biblical story of the cities of the plain, Sodom and Gomorrah. According to biblical commentators, the men of the city of Sodom practiced homosexuality, and for that behavior, the city was destroyed. The term has since acquired a broader connotation, including anal intercourse, bestiality, and oral sex.

Star Chamber—The name of a British court disbanded in 1641, today a derisive term meaning any court operating secretly and without limits on its power.

Stare decisis— A Latin term meaning "things that have already been decided"; the rule that courts are bound by prior judicial decisions in similar cases.

statute—A law.

strict scrutiny—A means by which courts analyze laws; most importantly today in the context of laws that give minority groups special rights.

Superfund—A fund created by the government to pay for the worst waste disposal and hazardous-substance sites endangering either human health or the environment.

tax lien—A legal claim to charges that are due to the IRS. A lien allows your property to be attached and sold if necessary to satisfy the delinquent tax.

tort—A civil wrong; an illegal (but not necessarily criminal) act committed by an individual or business.

wage garnishment—A legal notice sent to your employer that instructs the employer to remit to the IRS a certain sum of money from your paycheck.

warrant—An authorization or justification for a particular action; a judicial writ authorizing an officer to make a search, seizure, or arrest.

work product—The research and thinking process that a lawyer goes through when working on a case.

wrongful discharge—The lawsuit an employee may bring when he or she believes that a firing is unjust.

The Bill of Rights

The Bill of Rights is the mother lode of American civil liberties. Much of what we have discussed and much of what protects us in our daily lives derives from these brief paragraphs. Senator Sam Ervin of North Carolina, chairman of the Watergate Committee of the Senate that led to the end of the Nixon Administration, said that he carried with him everywhere the U.S. Constitution and the Bill of Rights. We could do worse.

The following text is a transcription of the first 10 amendments to the Constitution in their original form. These amendments were ratified December 15, 1791, and form what is known as the "Bill of Rights." Source: www.archives.gov.

Amendment I

Congress shall make no law respecting an establishment of religion, or prohibiting the free exercise thereof; or abridging the freedom of speech, or of the press; or the right of the people peaceably to assemble, and to petition the Government for a redress of grievances.

Amendment II

A well regulated Militia, being necessary to the security of a free State, the right of the people to keep and bear Arms, shall not be infringed.

Amendment III

No Soldier shall, in time of peace be quartered in any house, without the consent of the Owner, nor in time of war, but in a manner to be prescribed by law.

Amendment IV

The right of the people to be secure in their persons, houses, papers, and effects, against unreasonable searches and seizures, shall not be violated, and no Warrants shall issue, but upon probable cause, supported by Oath or affirmation, and particularly describing the place to be searched, and the persons or things to be seized.

Amendment V

No person shall be held to answer for a capital, or otherwise infamous crime, unless on a presentment or indictment of a Grand Jury, except in cases arising in the land or naval forces, or in the Militia, when in actual service in time of War or public danger; nor shall any person be subject for the same offence to be twice put in jeopardy of life or limb; nor shall be compelled in any criminal case to be a witness against himself, nor be deprived of life, liberty, or property, without due process of law; nor shall private property be taken for public use, without just compensation.

Amendment VI

In all criminal prosecutions, the accused shall enjoy the right to a speedy and public trial, by an impartial jury of the State and district wherein the crime shall have been committed, which district shall have been previously ascertained by law, and to be informed of the nature and cause of the accusation; to be confronted with the witnesses against him; to have compulsory process for obtaining witnesses in his favor, and to have the Assistance of Counsel for his defence.

Amendment VII

In suits at common law, where the value in controversy shall exceed twenty dollars, the right of trial by jury shall be preserved, and no fact tried by a jury, shall be otherwise reexamined in any Court of the United States, than according to the rules of the common law.

Amendment VIII

Excessive bail shall not be required, nor excessive fines imposed, nor cruel and unusual punishments inflicted.

Amendment IX

The enumeration in the Constitution, of certain rights, shall not be construed to deny or disparage others retained by the people.

Amendment X

The powers not delegated to the United States by the Constitution, nor prohibited by it to the States, are reserved to the States respectively, or to the people.

Appendix C

Further Reading

Now let us praise outstanding authors, writers, compilers, and legal experts. These are the books, law review articles, magazine articles, essays, and other sources from which this book was prepared. My thanks to all of these writers and I acknowledge gratefully the hard work they did in creating their works.

Abrams, Idelle. *Random Drug Testing in the Employment Context.* In The Public Interest 8 (1988): 20-28.

Adamitis, Elizabeth M. *Appearance Matters: A Proposal to Prohibit Appearance Discrimination in Employment.* Washington Law Review 75 (2000): 195-223.

Adams, Arlin M., and Charles J. Emmerich. *A Heritage of Religious Liberty.* University of Pennsylvania Law Review 137 (1989): 1559-1671.

Beauchamp, Robert Brooks. *'Shed Thou No Blood': The Forcible Removal of Blood Samples from Drunk Driving Suspects.* Southern California Law Review 60 (1987): 1115-1141.

Berman, Jeffrey A. *Constitutional Realism: Legislative Bans on Tobacco Advertisements and the First Amendment.* 1986 University of Illinois Law Review (1987): 1193-1231.

Bierman, Jr., Donald L. *Employment Discrimination Against Overweight Individuals: Should Obesity be a Protected Classification?* Santa Clara Law Review 30 (1990): 951-976.

Black, Kimberli R. *Personality Screening in Employment.* American Business Law Journal 32 (1994): 69-124.

Borten, Laurence Drew. *Sex, Procreation, and the State Interest in Marriage.* Columbia Law Review 102 (2002): 1089-1128.

Brown, Brant K. *Scrutinizing Juvenile Curfews: Constitutional Standards and the Fundamental Rights of Juveniles and Parents.* Vanderbilt Law Review 53 (2000): 653-683.

Burnette, Brandy M. *Investigatory Newsgathering: Promoting the Public Interest or Invading Privacy Rights?* Cumberland Law Review 31 (2001): 769-801.

Buss, William. *School Newspapers, Public Forum, and the First Amendment.* Iowa Law Review 74 (1989): 505-543.

Cacioppo, Nancy. *Fearing Loss of Liberties.* Journal News 13 Mar. 2002: B1.

Califa, Antonio J. *RICO Threatens Civil Liberties.* Vanderbilt Law Review 43 (1990): 805-850.

Cantrell, Charles L. *Search Warrants: a View of the Process.* Oklahoma City University Law Review 14 (1989): 1-96.

Carrieri, Joseph R. *The Caseworker's Handbook: The Foster Child's Journey Through the Foster Care System.* Practicing Law Institute: Litigation and Administrative Practice Course Handbook Series 151 (1991): 179-280.

Castle, Dana F. *Early Emancipation Statutes: Should they Protect Parents as Well as Children?* Family Law Quarterly 20 (1986): 343-372.

Caswell, Kathleen. *Opening the Door to the Past: Recognizing the Privacy Rights of Adoptees and Birthparents in California's Sealed Adoption Records While Facilitating the Quest for Personal Origin and Belonging.* Golden Gate University Law Review 32 (2002): 271-310.

Corr, Kevin. *A Law Enforcement Primer on Vehicle Searches.* Loyola University of Chicago Law Journal 30 (1998): 1-25.

Dagrella, Jerry R. *Wealthy Americans Planning to Renounce Their Citizenship to Save on Taxes Have a New Problem to Consider: This Time Congress Means Business.* The Transnational Lawyer 13 (2000): 363-390.

Dean, Jennifer L. *Employer Regulation of Employee Personal Relationships.* Boston University Law Review 76 (1996): 1051-1073.

Dinolfo, Elise. *The First Amendment: Free Speech or Ticket to Abuse?* Seton Hall Constitutional Law Journal 4 (1994): 621-660.

Dolgin, Janet L. *Religious Symbols and the Establishment of a National 'Religion'.* Mercer Law Review 39 (1988): 495-516.

Dworkin, Terry Morehead. *It's My Life—Leave Me Alone: Off-the-Job Employee Associational Privacy Rights.* American Business Journal 35 (1997): 47-97.

Eskridge, Jr., William N. *Comparative Law and the Same-Sex Marriage Debate: A Step-by-Step Approach Toward State Recognition.* McGeorge Law Review 31 (2000): 641-672.

Faust, Heather. *Challenging the Paternity of Children Born During Wedlock: An Analysis of Pennsylvania Law Regarding the Effects of the Doctrines of Presumption of Legitimacy and Paternity by Estoppel on the Admissibility of Blood Tests to Determine Paternity.* Dickinson Law Review 100 (1996): 963-990.

Feiser, Craig D. *Privatization and the Freedom of Information Act: An Analysis of Public Access to Private Entities Under Federal Law.* Federal Communications Law Journal 52 (1999): 21-62.

Feldman, Jared A. and Richard J. Katz. *Genetic Testing & Discrimination in Employment: Recommending a Uniform Statutory Approach.* Hofstra Labor and Employment Law Journal 19 (2002): 389-428.

Foggan, Laura A., Brian Nuterangelo, and Jennifer Chung. *Employment Law Exposures.* American Law Institute—American Bar Associations Continuing Legal Education SE64 ALI-ABA 789 (Jan. 13, 2000): 789-810.

Gardner, Chadwick N. *Don't Come Cryin' to Daddy! Emancipation of Minors: When is a Parent 'Free at Last' From the Obligation of Child Support?* University of Louisville Journal of Family Law 33 (1995): 927-948.

General Accounting Office. *Monitoring the Accuracy and Administration of IRS's 1989 Test Call Survey.* GAO/GGD-90- 37 (January 1990): 3.

General Accounting Office. *Collecting Delinquent Taxes and Communicating with Taxpayers.* GAO/T-GGD-94-50, November 9, 1993, p. 6.

General Accounting Office. *IRS's Service Centers Need to Improve Handling of Taxpayer Correspondence.* GAO/GGD-88- 101, July 1988, p. 14.

Gidari, Albert. *A Service Provider Perspective on the USA PATRIOT Act.* E-Commerce Law Report 4.2 (2001): 9.

Gonzalez, Eduardo W. *"Get That Camera Out of My Face!" An Examination of the Viability of Suing "Tabloid Television" for Invasion of Privacy.* University of Miami Law Review 51 (1997): 935-953.

Gornbein, Henry S., and Jorin G. Rubin. *Listening In: Is Accessing Others' E-Mail or Recording their Telephone Conversations Legal during a Divorce or Custody Proceeding?* Michigan Bar Journal 81 (2002): 18-21.

Gruber, Jeremy E. *Re: Electronic Monitoring in the Workplace: Common Law and Federal Statutory Protection.* Practising Law Institute—Litigation and Administrative Practice Course Handbook Series 651 (2001): 351-379.

Hamden, Michael S. *An Overview of the Law Governing the Rights of Prisoner, Facts and Findings. 27 (2000): 15.*

Harman, Robert. *The People's Right to Bear Arms—What the Second Amendment Protects: An Analysis of the Current Debate Regarding What the Second Amendment Really Protects.* Whittier Law Review, 18 (1997): 411-444.

Harvard Law Review Association. *Rights Associated with Divorce and Child Custody Relationships.* Harvard Law Review 93 (1980): 1308-1350.

Hawkins, Karen L. *Collection Procedures and Defenses.* American Law Institute—American Bar Association Course of Study SG063 ALI-ABA 571 (2002): 571-620.

Janik, Art. *New PATRIOT Act will Infringe Upon Civil Rights of Americans.* U-Wire 31 Oct. 2001.

Jernigan, Adero S. *Driving While Black: Racial Profiling in America.* Law and Psychology Review 24 (2000): 127-138.

Jeruchimowitz, Howard K. *Tobacco Advertisements and Commercial Speech Balancing: A Potential Cancer to Truthful, Nonmisleading Advertisements of Lawful Products.* Cornell Law Review 82 (1997): 432-478.

Johnson, Kenneth E. *The Constitutionality of Drug Paraphernalia Laws.* Columbia Law Review 81 (1981): 581-611.

Joyner, Dawson L. *How to Deal With (And Survive) IRS Income Tax Audits.* The Colorado Lawyer 27 (Dec. 1998): 65-70.

Jurevic, Amy M. *When Technology and Health Care Collide: Issues with Electronic Medical Records and Electronic Mail.* UMKC Law Review 66 (1998): 809-836.

Kennedy, Edward M. *Senator Kennedy's Statement on 'Billionaires' Tax Loophole.* Tax Notes International 11 (1995): 152.

Kramer, Edward G. and Robert Maynard Hutchins. *Title VIII Fair Housing Litigation Comes of Age.* ATLA Annual Convention Reference Materials—Civil Rights Section 1 (July 2001): 333.

Kramer, Lynn Chuang. *Private Eyes are Watching You: Consumer Online Privacy Protection—Lessons from Home and Abroad.* Texas International Law Journal 37 (2002): 387-419.

Lamberg, Lynne. *Confidentiality and Privacy of Electronic Medical Records.* Journal of the American Medical Association 285.24 (17 June 2001).

Lee, William E. *Lonely Pamphleteers, Little People, and the Supreme Court: The Doctrine of Time, Place, and Manner Regulations of Expression.* George Washington Law Review 54 (1986): 757-811.

Lincenberg, Gary S., and Benjamin N. Gluck. *A Patriotic Critic of the PATRIOT Act.* Los Angeles Lawyer Feb. 2002: 52.

Love, Sheryl H. *Allowing New Technology to Erode Constitutional Protections: A Fourth Amendment Challenge to Non-Consensual DNA Testing of Prisoners.* Villanova Law Review 38 (1993): 1617-1660.

Luccaro, Daniel, Jason Mishelow, Brendan N. Snodgrass, and Jihee G. Suh. *Racketeer Influenced and Corrupt Organizations.* American Criminal Law Review 38 (2001): 1211-1275.

Madison, Allen D. *An Analysis of the IRS's Voluntary Disclosure Policy.* Tax Lawyer 54 (2001): 729-752.

Mangold, Susan Vivian. *Protection, Privatization, and Profit in the Foster Care System.* Ohio State Journal 60 (1999): 1295-1326.

Manley, Michael R. Ward *v.* Rock *Against Racism: How Time, Place and Manner Further Restrict the Public Forum.* Fordham Entertainment, Media and Intellectual Property Law Forum 1 (1991): 151.

Matyszewski, Mary Agnes. *Who Can Look at Your Medical Records?* Whittier Law Review 23 (2002): 713-717.

McQuillen, Michael G. *Prah v. Maretti: Solar Rights and Private Nuisance Law.* John Marshall Law Review 16 (1983): 435-455.

Mechanic, Gene. *Legal Challenges to Drug Testing in Public Employment.* LERC Monograph Series 7 (1988): 24-51.

Minton, Natalie A. *Equitable Estoppel Precludes Husband in Divorce Proceeding From Refuting Paternity to Avoid Child-Support Payments—Pietros v. Pietros.* Suffolk University Law Review 29 (1995): 625-630.

Money, March 1992, p. 90

Money, April 1993, p. 96.

Morganroth, Fred. *When is a Daddy not a Daddy?—The Doctrine of Equitable Estoppel in Paternity Cases.* Michigan Bar Journal 75 (1996): 646-648.

Morris, Lisa S. *Photo Radar: Friend or Foe?* UMKC Law Review 61 (1993): 805-826.

Nagle, John Copeland. *Moral Nuisances.* Emory Law Journal 50 (2001): 265-322.

Naumchik, Steven Tafoya. *Stop! Photographic Enforcement of Red Lights.* McGeorge Law Review 30(1999): 833-853.

Norton, Deirdre E. *Why Criminalize Children? Looking Beyond the Express Policies Driving Juvenile Curfew Legislation.* NYU Journal of Legislation and Public Policy 4 (2000): 175-203.

Oliphant, Richard Shawn. *Prohibiting Casinos from Advertising: the Irrational Application of 18 U.S.C. § 1304.* Arizona Law Review 38(1996): 1373-1404.

Osofsky, Jocelyn J. *Baker v. State: Is America Moving Towards Allowing Same-Sex Marriages?* Journal of Law and Family Studies 3 (2001): 79.

Peabody, Bruce G. *In the Wake of September 11: Civil Liberties and Terrorism.* Social Education 66.2 (1 Mar. 2002): 90.

Perry, Michael J. *Freedom of Religion in the United States: Fin De Siecle Sketches.* Indiana Law Journal 75 (2000): 295-332.

Perry, Steven. *Hidden Cameras, New Technology, and the Law.* Communications Lawyer 14 (1996): 1-22.

Pieper, Troy G. P*laying With Fire: The Proposed Flag Burning Amendment and the Perennial Attack on Freedom of Speech.* Saint John's Journal of Legal Commentary 11 (1996): 843-866.

Plesser, Ronald L., James J. Halpert, and Emilio W. Cividanes. *USA PATRIOT Act for Internet and Communications Companies.* Computer and Internet Lawyer 19.3 (2002): 1-9.

Podesta, John. *USA PATRIOT Act.* Human Rights 29 (2002): 3-7.

Poker, Mark Stephen. *Reaching a Deep Pocket Under the Racketeer Influenced and Corrupt Organizations Act.* Marquette Law Review 72 (1989): 511-537.

Pollitt, Daniel H. *The Flag Burning Controversy: A Chronology.* North Carolina Law Review 70 (1992): 553-614.

Reiss, Claudine R. *The Fear of Opening Pandora's Box: The Need to Restore Birth Parents' Privacy Rights in the Adoption Process.* Southwestern University Law Review 28 (1998): 133-156.

Richman, Amanda. *Restoring the Balance: Employer Liability and Employee Privacy.* Iowa Law Review 86 (2001): 1337-1361.

Robinson, Stacy. *Remedying Our Foster Care System: Recognizing Children's Voices.* Family Law Quarterly 27 (1993): 395-415.

Rollo, Anthony. *The New Litigation Thing: Consumer Privacy.* Plactising Law Institute—Corporate Law and Practice Course Handbook Series 1301 (2000): 9.

Rosenbluth, Jean. *Abortion as Murder: Why Should Women Get Off? Using Scare Tactics to Preserve Choice.* Southern California Law Review 66 (1993): 1237-1271.

Rothenberg, Lance E. *Re-thinking Privacy: Peeping Toms, Video Voyeurs, and the Failure of Criminal Law to Recognize a Reasonable Expectation of Privacy in the Public Space.* 49 (2000): 1127-1165.

Rubin, Edward L. *Nazis, Skokie, and the First Amendment as Virtue.* California Law Review 74 (1986): 233-260.

Russo, Charles J. and David L. Gregory. *Legal and Ethical Issues Surrounding Drug Testing in Schools.* Law Review of Michigan State University Detroit College of Law (Fall 1999): 611-644.

Ryan, Jennifer Jolly. *A Real Estate Professionals and Attorney's Guide to the Fair Housing Law's Recent Inclusion of Familiar Status as a Protected Class.* Creighton Law Review 28 (1995): 1143-1175.

Santiago, Michael R. *Chapter 99: Preventing Employment Discrimination Based on One's Genetic Characteristics.* McGeorge Law Review 30 (1999): 703-712.

Schuck, Peter H. *Affirmative Action: Past, Present, and Future.* Yale Law and Policy Review 20 (2002): 1-96.

Seufert, Scott C. *Going Dutch?: A Comparison of the Vermont Civil Union Law to the Same-Sex Marriage Law of the Netherlands.* Dickinson Journal of International Law 19 (2001): 449-473.

Seyferth, Paul D. *An Overview of the Employee Polygraph Protection Act.* Journal of the Missouri Bar 57 (2001): 226-231.

Shephard, Lois. *Looking Forward with the Right of Privacy.* University of Kansas Law Review 49 (2001): 251-320.

Shriver, Christina M. *State Approaches to Criminalizing the Exposure of HIV: Problems in Statutory Construction, Constitutionality and Implications.* Northern Illinois University Law Review 21 (2001): 319-353.

Shuford, Reginald T. *Any Way You Slice It: Why Racial Profiling Is Wrong.* Saint Louis University Public Law Review 18 (1999): 371-380.

Silverman, Lewis A. *Vermont Civil Unions, Full Faith and Credit, and Marital Status.* Kentucky Law Journal 89 (2001): 1075-1107.

Smiley, Jennifer E. *Rethinking the "Special Needs" Doctrine: Suspicionless Drug Testing of High School Students and the Narrowing of Fourth Amendment Protections.* Northwestern University Law Review 95 (2001): 811-841.

Stimson, Judith N. *When Can Telephone Conversations Legally Be Protected?* Fair Share 16.7 (1996): 8.

Swingle, H. Morley, and Kevin M. Zoellner. *Criminalizing Invasion of Privacy: Taking a Big Stick to Peeping Toms.* Journal of the Missouri Bar 52 (1996): 345-347.

Tarr, Andrew W. J. *Picture It: Red Light Cameras Abide by the Law of the Land.* North Carolina Law Review 80 (2002): 1879-1896.

Turcotte, John A. *When You Should Have Known: Rethinking Constructive Knowledge in Tort Liability For Sexual Transmission of HIV.* Maine Law Review 52 (2000): 261-300.

Vivaz, Dora Sybella. *Balancing Children's Rights into the Divorce Decision.* Vermont Law Review 13 (1989): 531-587.

Wauben and Wauben. *Let's Compromise: A Look at the IRS's Offer in Compromise Program.* The Colorado Lawyer 27 (May 1998): 73.

Weinstein, Brent. *The State's Constitutional Power to Regulate Abortion.* Journal of Contemporary Legal Issues 11 (2000): 461- 466.

Weisenberger, Clay. *Constitution or Conformity: When the Shirt Hits the Fan in Public Schools.* Journal of Law and Education 29 (2000): 51-61.

Wong, Caroline M. *Chemical Castration: Oregon's Innovative Approach to Sex Offender Rehabilitation, or Unconstitutional Punishment?* Oregon Law Review 80 (2001): 267-299.

Woodbury, Stephen E. *Aesthetic Nuisance: The Time Has Come to Recognize It.* Natural Resources Journal 27 (1987): 877-886.

Wright, Victor V. *Hopwood v. Texas: The Fifth Circuit Engages in Suspect Compelling Interest Analysis in Striking Down an Affirmative Action Admissions Program.* Houston Law Review 34 (1997): 871-907.

Young, Mark G. *What Big Eyes and Ears You Have!: A New Regime for Covert Governmental Surveillance.* Fordham Law Review 70 (2001): 1017-1109.

Liberty's Websites

We've covered a large amount of topics in a relatively small space. If you'd like to dig a little deeper, here are some of the websites that were most helpful in the preparation of this book. Our thanks to the creators, compilers, and webmasters of these outstanding sources of information.

Chapter 2

American Civil Liberties Union, *The Bill of Rights: A Brief History*, (ACLU Briefing Paper #9)—www.aclu.org/library/pbp9.html

A Brief History of the Bill of Rights and the First Amendment—www.freedomforum.org/packages/first/curricula/educationforfreedom/BriefHistory.htm.

The Civil Liberties Corner—www.onelaw.com/civlib/.

The Magna Carta of 1215—www.historylearningsite.co.uk/magnacarta.htm

The Magna Carta (1215)—www.thevrwc.org/historical/magnacarta.html

The Timetable of World Legal History—www.duhaime.org/hist.htm

Chapter 3

Standler, Ronald B. *Privacy Law in the USA*, (1997)—www.rbs2.com/privacy.htm.

Chapter 5

Abortion Statistics—www.abortiontv.com/AbortionStatistics.htm or www.abortionfacts.com/statistics/statistics.asp

Hertz, Frederick. *Vermont's New Civil Union Law*—www.samesexlaw.com/html/legal_alerts/alerts_2000_04.html

The Law on Assisted Suicide—www.pbs.org/wgbh/pages/frontline/kevorkian/law/

The Legalization of Abortion—www.lifecorner.org/legalization.html

No Constitutional Right to Assisted Suicide—www.humanlife.org/euth_supl/html/3-1.html

State Marriage Recognition Laws—www.actwin.com/eatonothio/gay/marriage.html

State Sodomy Laws—www.actwin.com/eatonohio/gay/sodomy.html

State Statutes Affecting Polygamy—www.geocities.com/polytidbits/statutes.htm

States that Ban Homosexual Adoption—www.actwin.com/eatonohio/gay/adoption.html

Where Do You Stand on Abortion?—www.abortion.com/abortion.html

Chapter 6

Beeson, Ann. *Privacy in Cyberspace: Is Your E-mail Safe From the Boss, the SysOp, the Hackers, and the Cops?*—www.aclu.org/issues/cyber/priv/privpap.html

Being Traced Over the Internet—privacy.net/Traced/

Gardner, R. L. *Protecting Your Privacy on the Internet*—lpd.lakelandgov.net/comm.info/internet_privacy.html

The IP Address: Your Internet Identity—consumer.net/IPpaper.asp

Privacy—www.novicecomputing.com/PRIVACY.HTM

A Privacy Analysis of your Internet Connection—How it Works—privacy.net/analyze/analyzehow.asp

Privacy and Information Security—www.russkelly.com/privacy.html

Privacy Rights Clearinghouse. *Privacy in Cyberspace: Rules of the Road for the Information Superhighway*—www.privacyrights.org/fs/fs18-cyb.htm

Privacy Rights Clearinghouse. *Children in Cyberspace: A Privacy Resource Guide for Parents*—www.privacyrights.org/fs/fs21-children.htm

Chapter 8

ACLU Urges Congress to Reconsider Destructive Drug War Strategy. ACLU Press Release (June 16, 1999)—www.aclu.org/news/1999/n061699a.html

Chapter 9

How Private is My Medical Information?—www.privacyrights.org/fs/fs8-med.htm

Lamberg, Lynne. *Confidentiality and Privacy of Electronic Medical Records.* Journal of the American Medical Association, vol. 285, No. 24 (June 27, 2001)—jama.ama-assn.org/issues/v285n24/ffull/jmn0627-1.html

Chapter 10

Fair Credit Reporting—www.ftc.gov/bcp/conline/pubs/credit/fcra.htm

From Cradle to Grave: Government Records and Your Privacy—www.privacyrights.org/fs/fs11-pub.htm

How Private is my Credit Report?—www.privacyrights.org/fs/fs6-crdt.htm

Identity Theft—www.consumer.gov/idtheft/

Privacy Rights Clearinghouse, *Privacy Survival Guide: How to Take Control of Your Personal Information*—www.privacyrights.org/fs/fs1-surv.htm

Chapter 11

Himmelsbach, Leo. *What Happens If I shoot a Burglar?*—www.totse.com/en/politics/right_to_keep_and_bear_arms/shotburg.html

Hobart, Peter. *Self Defense Law and the Martial Artist*—www.ittendojo.org/articles/general-4.htm

The Right to Own a Gun, The Court TV Cradle-to-Grave Legal Survival Guide (1999)—www.courttv.com/legalcafe/home/guns/gun_background.html

Some Problems With Warrants—www.forensic-evidence.com/site/Police/Pol_Warrants.html

Your Right to Self-Defense—www.uslaw.com/library/article/mzselfdefense.html?area_id=9

Chapter 13

Drunk Driving Laws by State—www.home-healthtesting.com/duilevels.htm

Traffic Stops: Police Powers Under the Fourth Amendment—Application of the Fourth Amendment—www.cass.net/~w-dogs/ltraf.htm

Privacy Rights Clearinghouse. *From Cradle to Grave: Government Records and Your Privacy*—www.privacyrights.org/fs/fs11-pub.htm

Chapter 15

Hamden, Michael S. *An Overview of the Law Governing the Rights of Prisoner, Facts and Findings.* vol. 27, p. 15 (2000)—www.ncpls.org/code/nala2.htm

Prisoners' Rights. ACLU Position Paper, (1999)—www.aclu.org/library/PrisonerRights.pdf

Prisoners' Rights—www.1-800-attorney.com/li/legal_topics.cfm?I_Display=2&LN_ID=65

Chapter 16

Environmental Protection Agency. *The Birth of Superfund*—www.epa.gov/oerrpage/superfund/action/old-20years/20years/ch2pg6.htm

Environmental Protection Agency. *Buying and Selling Property*—www.epa.gov/oerrpage/superfund/tools/today/prop4.htm

Environmental Protection Agency. *Coastlines*, (August 1999)—www.epa.gov/owow/mestuaries/coastlines/aug99/local.html

Environmental Protection Agency. *Property Values*—www.epa.gov/oerrpage/superfund/tools/today/prop3.htm

The Executive Office for Asset Forfeiture—www.eoaf.treas.gov/forfeiture.asp

Goodman, Stanley. *Eminent Domain: What Every Property Owner Should Know, Law You Can Use* (Ohio State Bar Association)—www.ohiobar.org/conres/lawyoucanuse/article.asp?ID=144

Institute for Local Self Government. *Historical Background of Regulatory Takings*—www.ilsg.org/doc.asp?intParentID=1839

Institute for Local Self Government. *Takings in Plain English*—www.ilsg.org/doc.asp?intParentID=271

National Fair Housing Advocate Online, Federal Fair Housing Law FAQ—
www.fairhousing.com/101/federal_laws.htm

Larson, Aaron. *Criminal Forfeiture.* (May 2000)—www.expertlaw.com/library/
pubarticles/Criminal/Forfeiture.html

Oliver, Vose, Sandifer, Murphy & Lee. *Just Compensation*—www.eminentdomainlaw.
net/compensation.html

Oliver, Vose, Sandifer, Murphy & Lee. *The Power of Eminent Domain*—
www.eminentdomainlaw.net/power.html

Chapter 18

American Civil Liberties Union. *Introduction to Wrongful Discharge*—
www.aclu.org/issues/worker/legkit6.html#current

Employee Lawsuits: *Limited Rights of Employee Privacy*—www.uslaw.com/
library/article/carel9PrivacyRights.html?area_id=43

Illegal Interview Questions—www.collegeview.com/career/interviewing/
durring/illegal_questions.html

Meckler, Bulger & Tilson. *Wrongful Discharge*—www.mbtlaw.com/pubs/
articles/wrongdis.html

Privacy Rights Clearinghouse. *Employee Monitoring: Is There Privacy in the
Workplace?*—www.privacyrights.org/fs/fs7-work.htm

Vikesland, Gary. *For Employer and Employee: Sex Without Sexual Harassment*—
www.employer-employee.com/dating.html

Chapter 19

Becker, Mark. *Mennonite Resistance to Draft Registration,* (1985)—www.yachana.org/
research/writings/draft/

Conna Craig & Derek Herbert. *The State of the Children: An Examination of
Government-Run Foster Care.* (1997)—www.ncpa.org/~ncpa/studies/s210/s210.html

Chapter 20

American Civil Liberties Union. *Ask Sybil Liberty: About Your Right to Privacy*—
www.aclu.org/students/slprivacy.html.

American Civil Liberties Union. *Ask Sybil Liberty: About Your Right to Religious Freedom*—www.aclu.org/students/slrelig.html.

American Civil Liberties Union. *Ask Sybil Liberty: Keeping Your School Records Private*—www.aclu.org/students/slrecord.html

American Civil Liberties Union. *Ask Sybil Liberty: Your Right to Equality in Education*—www.aclu.org/students/slequal.html.

American Civil Liberties Union. *Ask Sybil Liberty: Your Right to Fair Treatment*—www.aclu.org/students/slfair.html.

U.S. Department of Education. *Searches for Weapons and Drugs*—www.ed.gov/offices/OESE/SDFS/actguid/searches.html.

Chapter 22

American Civil Liberties Union. *Using the Freedom of Information Act: A Step-by-Step Guide*—www.aclu.org/library/foia.html

Department of Justice Freedom of Information Act Reference Guide (August 2000)—www.usdoj.gov/foia/referenceguidemay99.htm

Electronic Privacy Information Center. *Your Rights to Federal Records: Questions and Answers on the Freedom of Information Act and the Privacy Act* (1992)—www.epic.org/open_gov/rights.html

Komando, Kim. *Government Secrets on the Web*. (2002)—www.usatoday.com/life/cyber/ccarch/2002/04/22/komando.htm

Chapter 23

The Economist, Paris Briefing, September, 2002, online edition—www.economist.com/

Internal Revenue Service. *The Truth About Frivolous Tax Arguments*—www.irs.gov/pub/irs-utl/friv_tax.pdf

Taxes? Stop Throwing Your Money Away!—www.voluntarytaxes.com/

Chapter 25

Gregory T. Nojeim. *A National ID Card, National ID Systems and Their Impact on Civil Liberties*. (1998)—www.aclu.org/congress/t091798a.html

Index

M